Money

A
Mirror Image
of the
Economy

Green Monetary Theory for Sustainable Development
Revised 2nd Edition
Continual update, concept expansion, version 1.8, 2010

J.W. Smith

The Institute for Economic Democracy Press

We believe all ideas should have maximum exposure. Thus for any properly cited individual quotation up to 500 words no permission is necessary.

By expanding upon parts of this manuscript, or nesting your work within the framework of this in-depth study, you can present a clearer picture while producing a book in six months as opposed to six to ten years. Permission will be granted (ied@ied.info) to those qualified.

The authors, the Institute for Economic Democracy, and their officers and supporters, specifically retain full rights to this and other published research so that others may use it, correct it, expand upon it, and produce an ever-more powerful and workable plan for world development and elimination of poverty. At only the cost of alerting others to this unique research, universities and serious progressive groups within the developing world will be granted the right to expand upon this work, translate, and publish. Please request the latest manuscript.

Published by: the Institute for Economic Democracy Press
235 Dabney Lane, Pamplin, VA 23905
888.533.1020 - www.ied.info - ied@ied.info

In Cooperation with the Institute on World Problems
worldproblems.net and Earth Rights Institute - earthrights.net

Library of Congress Cataloging-in-Publication Data

Smith, J. W., 1930-
Money : a mirror image of the economy / J.W. Smith. -- 2nd ed.
    p. cm.
Includes bibliographical references and index.
ISBN-13: 978-1-933567-12-9 (pbk : alk. paper)
ISBN-13: 978-1-933567-13-6 (hbk : alk. paper)
1. Money. 2. Capital. 3. Equality. 4. Economic policy. 5. Distributive justice. I. Title.
HG220.A2S62 2007
332.4--dc22
                              2007017096
The above were provided by The Library of Congress
6. Public Commons. 7. World Federation. 8. Property rights law. 9. Monopolies. 10. Monetary theory. 11. Peace. 12. Economic theory. 13. Technology. 14, Henry George. 15. Social-credits 16. Extracting wealth. 17. Unearned wealth. 18. Free enterprise, 19. Money, 20. Economic Policy. 21. Distributive justice. 22. Equality. 23. Capital

Book cover designed by John Cole, www.johncolegrf.com
This book is printed on acid free paper.

Table of Contents

Acknowledgements

I thank Henry George for giving me an understanding of economics that led to a final understanding of monopolization and its elimination across the full economic spectrum.

Special thanks go to the authors of the 50 to 60 books on money which provided the foundation for my understanding of that mystery. Specifically I have proven the validity of William F. Hixson's book title, *It's Your Money*. Professor Mieczyslaw Dobija's research revealing that money originated as an accounting unit of productive labor on the clay tablets of Sumer 5,000 years ago is priceless.

William H. Kötke, author of the classic *Final Empire*, Jana Paripovich Dr. Ekema Manga, our webmaster Anup Shah, and Mike Masters were especially helpful.

Special recognition must be made for the great help and advice of Mochamad Effendi Aboed of Indonesia. Crucial support was provided by Phil Hawes, Keith McHenry (FoodNotBombs), John Leonard, Michael Mityok, David Aronson, Edward Ongwesso, and many more

The advice and support of Professor Glen Martin and Alanna Hartzok has been crucial. I thank Ms. Sudha Menon, and Jeff & Diana Jewell, and David Kendall for their proofreading. Jeff Yalan's last minute proofing was sincerely appreciated. The advice of William Krehm of COMER is appreciated. The support of Garda Ghista (www.worldproutassembly.org) is invaluable. We welcome Professor Sidney Becker Smith to the group.

As always, I wish to dedicate this book to my children, Betty, Ada, Patti, and Cynthia, and grandchildren Sam C., Will, Stephan, Mathew, Sam O, and Susie. It is hoped this work will contribute to their understanding of the world.

Foreword

Books describing the violence, environmental destruction, and pending cataclysms of today's world abound. Books calling for the revitalization of democracy, for an end to economic globalization, and for an abstract peace with justice are not difficult to find.

But nowhere can there be found books offering a clear and comprehensive path forward for our world. Dr. J.W. Smith's present book is quite unique in this respect. In the face of a world of cynicism and despair, it offers a clear, common-sense path to a decent world order.

It is not the ideas presented here do not appear in Dr. Smith's earlier works such as *The World's Wasted Wealth* and *Economic Democracy: The Political Struggle of the Twenty-First Century*. But here they are extrapolated from these larger texts and compacted like a laser beam. The result is a masterpiece of power and clarity.

Critically aware people know that much of the ideology of "free enterprise," disseminated, for example, by *perception management* designed to cover up the unjust appropriation of the wealth produced by nature and belonging to all in roughly equal shares. Few have been able to see that we need not throw out the baby with the bath water.

Through simple common-sense changes that bring us to the creative, productive, and innovative heart of capitalism, we can create a just and prosperous world order for everyone. As Smith's magnum opus, *Economic Democracy*, points out, the final struggle if we are to have real democracy on Earth is the struggle to make capitalism democratic. *Perception management* claiming this is already so is meant to protect **exclusive titles to nature's resources and technologies, denying others their rightful share to what nature offers to all for free**; the **monopolization, wealth extraction, process** siphoning that unearned wealth into the hands of non-producers.

Over the centuries only a handful of great books, often brief and highly focused, have moved civilization significantly forward. I believe *Money: A Mirror Image of the Economy* is one of these rare books. It is a powerful, concise statement of both the next step for human civilization and how to take this step.

Glen T. Martin
Professor of Philosophy, Radford University
Author, *Millennium Dawn – The Philosophy of Planetary Crisis and Human Liberation*
Secretary-General, World Constitution and Parliament Association

Pulling this research together alerted us that roughly 95% of America's huge blocs of capital were capitalized values of unearned wealth and elimination of those monopoly values would double economic efficiency permitting each to live a quality life while reducing working hours by half or more.

This led to another realization: Most economic classics are not philosophical works on efficient economies. They are instead justifications for an *unequal property rights system* put in place by powerbrokers over the past 700-plus years. Though it is getting more difficult every day, major classics and their descendents are still justifying their *inefficient and inequitable property rights laws*. As those laws are the heart of the monopoly system, and thus the heart of the problem, any philosophy which does not challenge those unequal fundamental laws cannot be a guideline for *full and equal economic rights* for all.

Learning that most accumulations are unearned extracted wealth would be a shock to most of us. We all feel we work hard for our money. What we don't realize is that over half our labor is ground up and wasted within the superstructures managing monopolies we are told do not exist. This waste includes the military protecting the monopoly system.

Egyptians spending their labor and resources building pyramids had nothing on *monopoly capitalism* whose waste is just as massive. Powerbrokers were able to get away with the fraud, first because ever-improving technology was so enormously productive that all would gain even though their *unequal property rights laws* were grossly inefficient; and added to that were the huge amounts of wealth were being extracted from the periphery of empire and distributed within imperial centers as honest earnings. The citizenry, working hard every day, were unaware half their efforts were wasted and equally unaware that much of their wealth had been *unnecessarily* appropriated from the periphery of empire.

Quite simply, if any country or federated region successfully gained their freedom, eliminated monopolization within their internal economies, and achieved economic efficiency—as we demonstrate is possible—the impoverished world would notice and the monopolization structure, both internally and in world trade, would collapse.

The legal structure of a non-monopolized capitalist economy is very simple—*full and equal economic rights* for all through *conditional titles to nature's resources that she offers to us all for free, technologies shared by all without charge, and legislating essential services such as health care and retirement as a human right*. Under these *inclusive property rights laws*, the massive blocs of monopolized capital—previously buying and selling *capitalized appropriated values (misnamed profits) within the ethereal world of high finance*—are transposed into *equally-shared use-values*.

We are taught that these huge blocs of capital were crucial to economic efficiency. Not so. *Socially-owned* banks under social control fulfill any need for finance capital by creating essentially debt-free money for social infrastructure, including first industries. Once an economy is fully developed, infrastructure, universal health care, retirement, costs of running governments, etc, are fully funded by resource rents and the profits of a cheaper operating, socially-owned, banking system with automatic 100% reserves. Under *full and equal economic rights*, each would have their proper share of both created and circulating money (savings, finance capital) to provide a quality life and, once a society is fully industrialized, all this while working only two to three days per week outside the home.

A friend was having trouble understanding banking. So I sent her this summary: Alert and motivated leaders had just been voted in with a pledge to clean up the collapsed political and economic system. As per current law, the bankrupt banks were automatically taken over by the socially owned Federal Reserve (this is happening in this 2008-10 financial crash). A new currency was issued spendable only within the nation's borders. As the books were settled and with negotiations on currency values with other countries ongoing, newly created money was tradable for the old money (not happening in today's crash yet but it will if, or when, the dollar crashes).

You were chosen to run one of these banks. You come to work the first day, check that your share of the newly created money to operate your region was in your Federal Reserve account, and sit down at your desk. As this socially-owned bank established under this emergency operates at $1/3^{rd}$ the cost of the collapsed monopoly system you can pay higher interest rates on deposits while charging lower interest rates on loans. As it also has access to Federal Reserve created money to cover any emergency (100% reserves) and thus cannot go broke, depositors and borrowers flock to the security and profits of your bank.

You already understand depositing and loaning with your employees taking in the money and making the loans. There are minor things to pay attention to, such as how to keep your surplus invested, but that my friend is all there is to banking. All else is smoke and mirrors as the ethereal world of high finance, primarily made up of massive funds extracted from productive labor, devises devious ways to lay claim to wealth properly belonging to others.

As those huge blocs of capital pile up, more and more obscure financial instruments are devised. They are primarily a bet on values going up or down while in an honest banking-economic system values vary only slightly and there is nothing to bet on except new entrepreneurial projects which can be handled by venture capital.

Eliminate the monopolies we are told do not exist and both money and the economy becomes simple, visible, touchable, and understandable by all. Note the title of this book, *Money: A Mirror Image of the Economy*. Except for gifts, every trade is a transfer of wealth symbolized by money. You cannot have an honest banking system without first creating an *honest property rights system*. Neither can you have honest property rights without an honest banking system. One is the mirror image of the other.

A monopolized economy is just as much smoke and mirrors as a monopolized banking system. Restructure to *full and equal economic rights* and those monopolies disappear, economic efficiency doubles, poverty disappears, and if those principles are extended worldwide, wars will be relegated to history.

This is continual update, concept expansion, version 1.8, 2010. Please check www.ied.info for latest updates

Introduction: Utopian Living Through Restructuring Property Rights Law

> Environmentalists and all concerned with global warming will be interested in the huge levels of economic waste, 50% per unit of production, which can be eliminated under a philosophy of full and equal economic rights for each citizen of this world.—The author

For two years I had been inserting these words at the end of each chapter on monopolies: "Once this monopoly is eliminated through restructuring property rights, the huge blocs of capital, buying, and selling, those capitalized appropriated values (misnamed profits) within the ethereal world of high finance, are transposed into roughly equally-shared use-values." But, I still did not see the big picture.

Pulling those chapters together for this book, I took one look and said, "Good Lord! Fully 95% of the huge blocs of capital America is worshipped for, were not only unnecessary; they were reducing economic efficiency by over 50%."

The day before I would have said, "one cannot challenge classical economics," but I now realized those were only justifications for **a system of theft, unequal property rights law, as applied to nature's resources and technologies, denying others their rightful share of what nature offered to all for free, which the powerbrokers spent over 700 years putting in place, and that privatization process is still ongoing.** We will be analyzing the aristocratic roots of those property rights laws.

No one produced natural resources; it is offered to us all for free by nature; hence all are entitled to their share, and that can be efficiently accomplished through **society paying resource (land) rents to themselves; the social-fund**. That social collection of land rents converts aristocratic exclusive title to nature's wealth to conditional title. That conditional title, socially collected resource rents, providing social-credits for social needs, affirms access to land as a human right and, as you will quickly see, much more.

Land titles, being first issued by governments as "patents," acknowledge patented mechanical and chemical technologies as being a part of nature. They are, like natural resources, waiting to be discovered. With rights of all citizenry to their share—in this case paying inventors well and placing all technology in the public domain—the wealth produced by technology is equally shared through a 50% to 80% drop in the price of consumer products (see chapter 3). That savings represents the labor and resources no longer wasted and a quality living can be provided working two to three days per week.

Taxi medallions (licenses in New York City) having a capitalized rental value of $200,000 per year, alerts us they are monopolies identical to that of land; land has unearned capitalized rental value, and so do taxi medallions. The connection between them is that their values were not produced by labor, but by **exclusive titles,** which gives them unearned rental values; the **monopolization, wealth extraction, capitalization, process**. Like taxi medallions, banking, insurance, law and health care, are all technologies; they are a part of nature which must be discovered and refined over time, licensed within "**the monopoly, wealth extraction process**"; that legal structure gives them non-tangible, unearned, rental values.

Land has tangible value, but it is produced by nature and offered to all for free. Banking and insurance are social technologies, and their licenses within a monopoly structure give them non-tangible, unearned, monopoly values; all are beyond the tangible use-values produced by labor. Healthcare and law have tangible labor values (years of study), but their market prices are primarily unearned monopoly values, created by license, which is also beyond the real values created by **productive** labor. Patents have some tangible labor values, but the much greater non-tangible, unearned, monopoly values more than double costs to consumers.

Licenses per se do not have monopoly value; they are a necessity and are proper. It is the ad hoc expansion of "the monopoly, wealth extraction, process," within which they were issued, that is the problem.[a] Licenses are issued within other social structures without developing those unearned values. The ad hoc manner in which the superstructures operating these social technologies formed led to unnecessary labor and resource costs which have been factored in as normal. Those technologies are well understood today, and labor is wasted battling for market share for what is recognized as a necessity, and thus should be a social, or human, right. Converting marketing rights to banking, health care, insurance, etc, for a few, to social rights or human rights for all, drops costs by half or more. The resulting full and equal economic rights, eliminating most legal battles, are part of the cost savings.

---

[a] Best explained throughout *Mercantilism as a Rent Seeking Society* by Robert B. Ekelaun & R. Tollison (Texas A & M University, 1981).

Monopoly Capitalism's Extractive Property Rights Versus Property Rights Providing Full and Equal Rights

Money is a social technology discovered over 5,000 years ago. Banking is a part of money technology learned over the centuries. By restructuring private, monopolized, banking to a socially-owned banking system, one has applied the principle that, as such technologies are a part of nature discovered centuries ago, and have few, or no, tangible values produced by labor; each has a right to their proper share of the wealth nature produced.

Over the centuries, to protect and increase their wealth and power, power-brokers have extended the principle of monopolization of land through exclusive titles to include banking, patents, communications, insurance, health care, the legal system interpreting those rights for us, and other more minor sectors of the economy (run an Internet search for "**rent-seeking**"). To both protect their system of wealth extraction, and lay claim to even more unearned wealth, this system of unequal economic rights—the privatization of every aspect of nature's resources and technologies properly belonging to all in roughly equal shares—is being imposed upon the rest of the world (they are now pushing back).

Perception management, as to the high efficiency of an economy operating at less than half its potential, is not only hiding inequalities, violence, and lack of democracy; it is also hiding **monopoly capitalism's close connection to aristocratic law. Those aristocratic exclusive titles to nature's resources and technologies she offers to all for free, designed from their earliest beginnings to lay claim to wealth properly belonging to others, is really aristocratic law**.

Money is a social technology discovered over 5,000 years ago. Banking is a part of money technology learned over the centuries. By restructuring private, monopolized, banking to a socially-owned banking system, one has applied the principle that, as such technologies are a part of nature discovered centuries ago, and have few or no tangible values produced by labor; each has a right to their proper share of the wealth nature produced.

Each person having the possibility of owning those exclusive titles, gives the appearance of equality. But superior rights are contradictions in terms. Some will win (1% own over 90% of America's wealth), some will lose, and the aristocratic structure of a wealthy few, and impoverished many, stays firmly in place. This reality is hidden by the immense wealth stolen from the rest of the world through plunder by trade. If the developing world allies together, and demands equality in trade, Europe and America would immediately lose a large share of the wealth annually distributed among their citizenry as earnings. Demographics within those nations would quickly shrink to the aristocratic structure, from which Western capitalism never fully evolved. That aristocratic structure, **exclu-**

sive title to nature's resources and technologies, denying others their rightful share of what nature offers to all for free, is still there hiding under beautiful names—democracy, capitalism, freedom, etc.

Aristocracy fought for centuries to acquire, extend, and retain their superior rights, and a large share of violence and wars today is financial aristocracy—just as the aristocrats from which this legal structure evolved—battling to acquire, extend, and retain the same aristocratic exclusive titles to nature's resources and technologies, denying others their rightful share, in only slightly adjusted forms, as under aristocratic law.[b] Battles against those unequal economic rights are the primary struggles throughout the world today.

How is it possible to have "free thought," "free thinking universities," and a "free press" and not be aware of this **monopolization, wealth extraction, process**? Think of the centuries the common people were trained to look up to and worship aristocracy. As aristocrats were the only ones who could read and write, the first books can only have supported them. When education spread to the common people, literature still had to glorify aristocrats. For powerless people to have attacked them in books in any way would have led to very unpleasant consequences.

This system of control was retained as the bourgeoisie gained rights and power. The common people were never anticipated to have rights, and their masters had disciplinary power. Thus the classics supporting unequal property rights, with none attacking the system being permitted, amounted to firm control of what was taught. For centuries aristocracies' perception management held firm; serious alternative views challenging the system are not permitted yet today. **Aristocratic property rights hiding within current property rights, as applied to nature's resources and technologies, denying others their rightful share of what nature offers to all for free** were taught as maximally efficient while all other systems were, except on the margins, taught as dictatorial and inefficient.

Marx's philosophy is one such belief system which, due to he being a theorist for labor, gained a large following. Powerbrokers spent trillions of dollars, slaughtered tens of millions, and spent billions on perception management (funding think tanks which carried through to the media and the universities) to relegate that philosophy back to the margins. (With capitalism in deep crisis, Marx is resurfacing.) Classics and derivative works supporting the system were taught, and are taught, as the only viable philosophies, and simultaneously it was taught that all were free to think as they wish, and encouraged to do so. But those who did were

---

[b] Throughout *The Divine Right of Capital: Dethroning the Corporate Aristocracy* (Berrett-Koehler, San Francisco, 2001/2003) Marjorie Kelly addresses the aristocratic structure of current capitalism.

immediately ostracized to the margins, just as all challenging thought had been for centuries, and that scene is replayed over and over. Those marginalized understand it. Due to continued perception management (propaganda) such people are believed to be a threat to freedoms and rights, that they are radicals not to be listened to, or whatever. Meet any professor today and you will find them totally sincere, wanting to do good, and totally unaware that their thoughts are as firmly under control as those of scholars 500 years ago.

Note the complexity of classical and neoliberal economics. Note the simplicity of eliminating poverty and providing a quality life for all as we will be outlining. Note its solid logic, and note the certainty that it will be rejected by those mentally locked within the "system." However, when their children are cold and hungry those belief systems (perception management, propaganda) will be thrown aside, and one who parrots the old beliefs will be hard to find. The waste and violence of the current system is so enormous—far more wasted, destroyed, and production forgone, than consumed—; we must hope that day will be soon.

Citizens within what are touted as full democracies, but in reality are only representative democracies, are subject to laws imposed by others, primarily corporate lobbyists whose bosses claim far more than their fair share. For each to attain their rightful share of nature's wealth, full and equal economic rights for each citizen should be enshrined in a constitution. The justice of those rights will be evident as every citizen both produces and consumes their fair share. The essentials of such a constitution are laced throughout this treatise.

Once such a legal foundation is in place, laws covering disputes and changing circumstances can be decided upon by participatory direct democracy as opposed to today's representative democracies. Such laws voted on by a citizenry, as referendums will then be approved or disapproved; utilizing eye or thumbprint scans to assure honesty, this would be very viable. With direct citizen approval of important laws and constitutional changes, and though not perfect, Cuba and possibly Libya are the only such democracies today but Venezuela, Bolivia, Ecuador and other South American countries are following in their footsteps.

As opposed to a full democracy, the key laws of imperial nations are **unequal property rights, as applied to nature's resources and technologies, denying others their rightful share of what nature offers to all for free,** designed by their predecessors over the past 700-plus years, and generally addressed as "property rights law." Even though it is an unequal property rights system, individuals can make decisions, and society within the imperial centers can, due to the enormous efficiencies of ever advancing technology, rapidly develop. Those pointing out that current property rights permit stability while the enormous wealth in imperial cultures deny themselves the realization that this unequal legal structure prevents the full development of both internal and periphery economies. All societies, including those imperial-centers-of-capital, could advance much faster, and more equally, if those laws were designed for full and equal economic rights. Sector by economic sector we will be explaining how applying equal rights to (access to) nature's wealth and technologies which she offers to us all for free, will **eliminate the inequality of today's property rights law, as applied to nature's resources and technologies, reduce labor time, eliminate waste of resources, and substantially   reduce environmental impact.**

Through the greater share of the 700-plus years inserting inequality into property rights law, little consideration was given to the rights of the common person, or to their share of wealth produced by nature. Laws were written by the powerful for protection of their wealth and power, and for attaining more wealth and power. Thus the extension of aristocratic exclusive titles to land under the enclosure of the commons process, which started formally in England under the Statute of Merton of 1235, creating massive wealth for the powerful few, and colossal poverty for the many. See chapter one of *The Earth Belongs to Everyone* , 2008, by Alanna Hartzok. She goes deeply into the early privatization of the commons as a system of theft of wealth properly belonging to all.[c] Those early enclosures of the commons, and the ongoing privatizations today, are the fundamental **unequal property rights laws governing monopolization**.

Aristocrats created those first monopoly laws, and the very principle of aristocracy was exclusive title to nature's wealth, those huge blocs of land they controlled. Those exclusive titles, enclosing the commons, were only aristocratic privileges (**monopolization, mercantilism, privatization, rent-seeking**, they all mean the same thing) inserted into law to extract wealth from the politically powerless. Whenever the citizenry figured out the fraud, the power structure controlled the slight changes in political structure, gave their **rent-seeking** legal structure another name, and went right on.

Those Property rights laws dealt with rights, but in the sense of superior and inferior rights. As the masses slowly gained more rights, they were given the opportunity to purchase land (resources of nature). Quietly and slowly these unequal property rights, as applied to nature's resources and technologies, spread in step with the wealth production of the ever-increasing efficiencies of technology. The elite property owners, with their excessive rights, were the only ones educated, they held all the positions of power, and it was they, at all times, who created those laws. They poured out philosophies of high economic efficiency un-

---

[c] Alanna Hartzok is Co-Director of Earth Rights Institute. She is currently directing a 34 member International Advisory Group which is developing a program on land value capture for the UN Habitat's newly-launched Global Land Tool Network. See www.earthrights.net

der property rights as structured, aristocratic exclusive title to nature's resources and technologies, denying others their rightful share of what nature offers to all for free, and we hear that claim—"this is the most efficient economic system"—repeated in almost every classroom today. Those superior rights were continually protected and entrenched in later laws.

Superior rights, assured by aristocratic exclusive titles to nature's wealth, had a secret: Aristocracy proper was to largely disappear, but the principles of aristocracy, still protecting wealth and power, lived on in those **aristocratic exclusive titles to nature's resources and technologies.** At that time, it could not have been anticipated that the common people would ever own a part of the earth upon which they lived and worked. When the bourgeoisie, and later the common people, were brought into the flow of money to purchase land, the fortunate now had, once that purchase was paid for, a share of the superior rights once held by aristocracy. Our research exposes that hidden secret, **aristocratic exclusive titles to nature's resources and technologies, denying others their rightful share of what nature offers to all for free, is the very foundation of the monopoly, wealth extraction, process, imposed upon the world.** By giving each a chance—in reality a few a good chance, some a small chance, and most no chance of **gaining clear title**—the system is, like every game of chance, very seductive.

If you were accosted and robbed, that is obviously a criminal act, violating the rule of law. If your legislature passed a law giving an advantage to a group, or an individual, which enabled them to extract unearned income from you (it happens all the time, run a search for "**rent-seeking**"), that would be within the rule of law, but would be easily recognized as creating inequality through granting excess rights to a fortunate few.

The British Enclosure Acts addressed above, assigning exclusive land titles to lords of the land, and forcing the commoners into the city to survive in breadlines, is easily analyzed as unequal property rights law giving excessive rights to a few and taking away rights and wealth from the many. That injustice was justified by philosophical treatises, again known today as classics, stating those unemployed workers were necessary to work in the factories at the start of the Industrial Revolution.

This is a clear example of the need to philosophically justify **inequality structured into property rights law, as applied to nature's resources and technologies which is properly shared by all.** Today we know every factory ever built in either a poor country or a rich country is always overwhelmed by applications for employment. The reason is obvious; those employed can purchase more of the amenities of life. As labor has always been available in long-established, heavily-populated societies, the need to dispossess people from the land to create a labor force was only a justification, not an honest philosophical analysis.

With continued philosophical justification, the major classics, the masses' rights to the commons were forgotten, and **aristocratic exclusive titles to nature's resources and technologies, denying others their rightful share of what nature offers to all for free**, were not only accepted as normal, they were taught as imperatives for economic efficiency. We hear those justifications yet today; "this is the most efficient economic system." Even when its imperfections are recognized, it is still justified: "this is a really a bad system, except it is better than all others." Through demonstrating the enormous efficiency of a modern commons within all sectors of the economy while still retaining the efficiencies of honest capitalism, we prove such alibis have no relevance to reality.

Those rationalizations were hiding the systematic theft of other people's wealth through unequal property rights laws as applied to nature's resources and technologies. Those evicted from the commons knew they were losing rights, and the landlords were gaining rights. But, until the neocons' violent theft of Iraq's oil alerted serious thinkers, the only voices heard were those justifying that theft. Over time, current unequal property rights were accepted as normal.

An attempt was made to establish aristocratic law in America. But the expanse of land was so vast that those intended as serfs simply squatted on "empty" land—that is empty after genocidal slaughters of the natives—claimed it, and retained 100% of what they produced as opposed to half or less that a commoner would retain. At that time, and as the Industrial Revolution was forming, the American Revolution gave more rights to the common person, but, except that each had to compete for those new property rights, primarily in the same form as aristocracy, exclusive title to nature's resources and technologies denying others their rightful share. Through the French Revolution, other crises, and with the new freedoms and rights in America blowing back onto Europe, the suppressed of that continent attained more rights.

The theft of wealth throughout the colonial world, and a need for a loyal citizenry to provide the military to enforce that piracy, required a further sharing of wealth with internal labor.

With wealthy citizens throughout Western Europe and America, and the acquisition of wealth beyond anyone's dreams only three generations ago, this is taught as justification for what is obviously a profoundly unequal and unjust system. This treatise proves monopoly capitalism, misnamed capitalism, is inefficient to the extreme. Massive unearned wealth is being extracted from both societies' own labor, and from the periphery of empire. Half that wealth is ground up through the offices and labor (the superstructures) managing those monopolies. Added to that waste is the military protecting what is little more than a racket within world trade (Google United States Marine Corp Major General Smedley Butler's "War is a Racket").

As addressed above, Asia's industrialization was an accident of history. Imperial powers were seeking allies in their desperate effort to prevent honest and moral property rights from emerging to challenge their unequal and unethical legal structure. The Conclusion will address how that accident of history, a highly industrialized Asia; an awakened world may yet overthrow the unequal legal structure the West has spent 700-plus years establishing.

As much of the world now understands the fraud imposed upon them for the past half millennium-plus, those **aristocratic exclusive titles to nature's wealth, the very essence of monopolization extracting wealth,** has the possibility of disappearing into history to be replaced by a peaceful, prosperous, sustainable, federated world with full and equal economic rights, providing a quality life for all.

Contrary to those 700-plus years of justifications, by what are known today as the classics, there was never a need for exclusive titles to nature's bounty to accumulate finance capital. Avoidance of that unequal legal structure, through utilizing the mighty economic and financial engines of sharing technology, as opposed to monopolization, would have doubled economic efficiency, and eliminated poverty as fast as new technologies were invented If our early ancestors had designed a cooperative capitalism instead of monopoly capitalism, technology would have spread across the world as fast as new technologies were invented, and would have done so without poverty or war.

Aristocratic exclusive title to nature's resources and technologies, denying others their rightful share of what nature offers to all for free, is a system of theft; as proven by the 500 years of struggle against it, this was recognized as such when first being imposed. However, philosophical justifications, again those classics and their derivatives, taught in the universities and through the media, have erased that reality from the social mind. To bring up the possibility of such inequality and inefficiency in either polite society, in an academic setting, or in this book, is to create total shock. Such is the totality of the belief systems imposed upon us to hide the reality of a system designed from its origins to extract wealth from the politically weak.

Customs and laws of other societies also lay claim to wealth properly belonging to others. The caste system, now outlawed in India, but still having substantial impact, is a system of rights and entitlements, which amounts to property rights law extracting wealth, established centuries ago. Only 160 years ago in America, and in some cultures yet today; slaves and women were property. The principles are the same, superior rights for the few, and inferior rights for the many, so as to lay claim to unearned wealth. Excessive rights are easy to spot in such a system, and thus easily condemned. The monopoly system of inequality is hidden so deep in custom, in property rights laws, and protected by philosophical justifications, classical and neoliberal, through the educational system and the media, that it is not only considered normal and just, but also is deemed and taught as essential and efficient.

Social scientists must look closely. Before this latest surge of populist revolutions, large parts of the world were accepting monopoly property rights as providing equal economic rights and maximum economic efficiency. They now know better. Capitalism's mighty economic engine, and the belief system societies are encased in, hide the enormous inefficiencies and the violence imposed through unequal property rights laws installed over the past 700-plus years..

The first impositions of unequal economic rights were by violence as the commons were privatized. Major classics then justified the imposition of that system of theft. Later impositions of the belief in the justice of such thefts of others' wealth were through the university systems teaching those classics. The belief systems were so total that professors were unaware those philosophies were only justifying a system of theft imposed for centuries, and that process is ongoing yet today. Our research tells us that, in their struggle for full and equal economic rights, a large share of the world is breaking out from under those belief systems protecting unequal, monopoly, property rights.

Production of wealth is, at every turn, a utilization and transformation of nature's wealth. This treatise addresses how restructuring property rights in land (resources), technologies, money, and communications—all technologies of nature—from aristocratic exclusive titles to equal rights conditional titles, with society collecting rent values, and with social rights and human rights legislated into law, would increase economic efficiency equal to the invention of money, the printing press, and electricity. That economic philosophy would give full and equal rights, economic and political, to everyone on earth.

We are primarily addressing the internal economy of today's hegemon, America. Until checkmated in Iraq, it was their system of **exclusive title to nature's resources and technologies, denying others their rightful share of what nature offers to all for free, creating wealth and power for a few and the impoverishment of many, that was being imposed upon the world.**

The proof that monopoly property rights are systems of inequality and inefficiency would be the transformation of the massive unearned finance capital within a monopolized economy (roughly 95% of all finance capital) into equally-shared use-values through restructuring aristocratic exclusive titles to resources and technologies to conditional titles. This can only be done when a financial crash destroys most those unearned values.

Under those conditional titles, society will **pay rental values on all natural resources to themselves** (socially collected); in the case of technologies, those monopoly values are eliminated through paying inventors well, and placing their discoveries in the public domain; and, in the case of monopolization through licenses, legislate those crucial services as a social right, or a human right. Roughly 5% of today's level of private finance capital (in the form of use-values) will then, as now, build/run industry and operate the economy; the 95% of finance capital once wasted remains with those who produced that wealth. That wasted finance capital (fully 95%), now transposed to use value, had only been buying and selling the capitalized values of extracted wealth, and running the shadow economy of that appropriation process (the ethereal world of high finance).

Appropriations of wealth through aristocratic exclusive titles, no matter where or how they are invested, engender a continual extraction of more wealth. The owners of those unearned funds, searching for a safe place to invest, typically settle for buying treasuries issued to cover the costs of the federal government, and purchasing bonds issued for sewers, water systems, and other crucial infrastructure. Citizens from whom that wealth was extracted in the first place pay taxes to pay off that principal and interest. As those debt instruments are paid off, that money is again loaned back to the same people. The same citizenry, through either taxes or the purchase of products and services at excessively high prices, again pay off those debts. And that impoverishing cycle goes on, in perpetuity, interrupted only by economic collapses, such as is ongoing today, 2008-10, due to too much wealth in the hands of the few, and too little buying power in the hands of the many.

It is the potential of doubling economic efficiency through **conditional titles to nature's resources and technologies to achieve that equal sharing of nature's wealth and eliminating all appropriation of others' rightful wealth** which tags those continual repayments of extracted wealth over and over as "impoverishing cycles." Those inefficiencies under the founding principles of classical economics alert us they were only justifying a system of excessive rights; they were not laying out principles of an efficient economy. Those justifications, rationalizing unequal property rights within classical and neoliberal principles, are pouring out yet today; however, other voices are starting to be heard.

Just as customs of ancient cultures are huge obstacles for their societies to evolve efficiently, exclusive feudal property rights in monopoly cultures severely restrict the efficiency of capitalism. Those inefficiencies are not perceived because modern technologies are so efficient that the huge gains are visible, and admired; while the further doubling of consumption possible under inclusive property rights, even as employed labor time is reduced, remains unknown. We are bringing those gains out into the open for all to see.

The basic principles of monopolization under feudalism were never abandoned. Citizens living within the belief systems of monopoly capitalism have full rights only in the sense that each has a chance at becoming a wealthy monopolist while only a few gain substantial wealth.

Until the current financial collapse, those inequalities were not fully visible to Americans and Europeans because of the large percentage with a high standard of living, and thus the appearance of full rights. But, unrealized by the citizenry, and most in academia, that high standard of living is maintained only through massive additional thefts of wealth from the periphery of empire. The powerful today are fighting to retain, and expand, their aristocratic monopoly property rights; **exclusive title to nature's resources and technologies, denying others their rightful share of what nature offers to all for free.** Feudal powers fought for centuries to maintain those aristocratic exclusive titles to land which is, of course, the same wealth of nature being fought over today.

As the enormous wastes within an economy cannot be eliminated without elimination of monopolies, we will address deeply the four primary monopolies—banking, land, technology, and communications—and, with the principles of exclusion and inclusion within property rights law well established, summarize the secondary monopolies—insurance, law, health care, etc. As this is primarily a treatise on money, we will be addressing that monopoly first.

Money is a social technology discovered over 5,000 years ago. That a banking system is properly owned by society is demonstrated by outlining the enormous efficiencies, and full and equal economic rights, under that social structure. To keep everything local, each social unit—a federation of nations, each nation, each region within a nation, each state, each community, each business, and each entrepreneur—should have a constitutional right to their share of socially-created money and savings (investment capital). Except for vast overcharges, credit cards approach this ideal for consumer purposes but such full and equal economic rights have never in the history of private enterprise been applied to investment. High interest charges on those cards disappear when issued by a socially-owned banking system with **the citizenry making loans to, and paying the profits to, themselves with those "earnings" funding essential social services.**

So long as there are available resources and labor, money can be created, **up to the level of a balanced money supply**, to build social infrastructure as well as financing the early stages of industrial capital. Education systems, roads, railroads, harbors, communication systems, water and sewer systems, etc, any natural monopoly, are properly owned by society and should be built and operated with resource rents and banking profits.

History is replete with examples of creating money for wars. The populists of the late 19th century advocated printing money to loan to farmers was a replay of created money funding the economy before the Revolutionary War and within Benjamin Franklin's colony in Pennsylvania. Classical money theory is silent on the enormous potential for created money funding infrastructure and, up to the level of monetary balance, other essential social needs. Aware non-classical theorists very correctly advocate creating money for—again up to the level of monetary balance—infrastructure, environmental cleanup, communications, retirement, and universal health care.

Primary-created money (base money created up to the level of monetary balance) building infrastructure circulates within communities, regions, nations, and federations to provide the citizenry with food, fiber, shelter, health care, retirement, etc. As industrial capital is justly privately owned, later industries are built by savings; excess circulating money is destroyed by higher mandatory reserves. Once a banking system is socially owned, first industries developed, and resource rents and banking profits are funding all infrastructure and social needs; there is no need for fractional reserve banking.

Balancing an economy under a modern banking commons within an inclusive society with full and equal economic rights for all would be simplicity itself. Financial capital would then be the total savings of all, balanced by primary-created money (again base money) to fill any shortfall, or its destruction through higher required reserves to eliminate any surplus. Such full and equal economic rights would eliminate inflation and deflation and assure a quality life for all.

Eliminating offices and staff (superstructures) managing those monopolies and the wars generated protecting them eliminates well over half the economic activity of a monopoly system even as poverty disappears. Those aristocratic exclusive titles to nature's wealth, primary monopolies, and those secondary monopolies structured under unequal property rights laws, typically by license, are consuming roughly 95% of the financial capital flowing through America's financial system. Those wasteful flows of money can only be shut off by eliminating feudal monopolization firmly entrenched within economies.

Societies do not transform incrementally, necessary change occurs in revolutionary leaps. The appearances of current changes are only potentials. The actuality is the poor of both the wealthy economies and the less developed world are getting poorer as the rich got richer and only under extreme crisis, such as we are now facing, will the rights of the politically weak be considered.

The necessary restructuring can only happen when the current system collapses; this may be happening as we speak. If it does we must be ready to provide the philosophical foundation for restructuring unearned values, currently capitalized into massive blocs of unearned capital, into roughly equally-shared use-values.

The infrastructure necessary for the developing world to be efficient appears expensive. But that is only true if built by outside contractors. All costs above resource rent values are labor costs (industrial and finance capital are both stored labor). We document that most resources from which use values are manufactured are within their borders and rents from those resources properly go into the social-credit fund. Machinery and infrastructure built by a region's own companies and trained labor creates wealth equal in value to the price of that labor (which is their own). Labor spends their wages for their living while governments spend resource rents and banking profits to run governments and essential services. All those values, except that spent for imports which, when resources and technologies are equally shared will be minor, are created through a region's circulating buying power contracting local labor.

Train labor, build industries to scale for a region, build construction equipment with those industries, build that infrastructure, and the cost to a region is primarily importing modern tools for those factories. Those undeveloped regions have most of the world's natural resources and all manufactured wealth is processed from natural wealth. So, although it is necessary that the banking system be socially-owned, developing an economically viable region is primarily creating money to train and employ a region's own labor force to build the necessary infrastructure. For maximum efficiency, their currency eventually must have no value outside their borders, a **dual currency** system. Once the currencies of developing world regions and nations are protected by an honest world currency, they are in position to trade access to resources for technology.

That infrastructure and the wealth produced backs the newly-created money as it circulates producing more wealth. Surplus money is easily destroyed by increasing mandated reserves. The circulation (velocity) of base money producing and consuming within the borders of an economically-viable region year after year is the economic multiplier of a prosperous community. **Aristocratic exclusive titles to nature's resources and technologies, denying others their rightful share, of what nature offers to all for free, denies that simplicity to the world**.

Though we describe in depth that it can be done, that the world will abandon its current struggles over who will control resources and the wealth producing process, and peacefully and rapidly eliminate poverty, is not likely. But such revolutionary leaps have happened before and communications superhighways, along with the 2002-10 disastrous foreign policy of America, the hegemon currently blocking such changes, has cost them the moral high ground, greatly increased—and may have assured—the potential of another such leap.

Our concluding chapter is a theoretical example of just such a restructuring and the world rapidly developing. As banks have to fund any system—efficient or inefficient, equal or unequal—leaving monopoly property rights in place while creating a theory of either money or economics is an exercise in self delusion.

That the world will peacefully eliminate **the monopolization, wealth extraction, process**—aristocratic law hiding under unequal property rights laws imposed upon the world—is unlikely. Eliminating those monopolies would be revolutionary and the only way to address the many obstacles to peace and prosperity was to tie it to the current financial collapse and the worldwide populist revolution currently under way. So, the improbabilities aside, it is one of the possibilities, and we address it as such.

That communications superhighways will revolutionize the world is well understood. That a worldwide populist revolution is in progress is recognized by many. We hope to alert these people that capitalization of unearned values is monopoly capitalism's mighty engine wasting or forgoing production of over half a society's wealth production potential. In contrast, the much smaller, yet twice as powerful, economic engine of full and equal economic rights would eliminate that waste, eliminate wars, and would provide a quality life for all the world's citizens within 50 years.

The Community Social-Credit Process

How did such an inefficient economy as we have today evolve? Visualize a fertile valley 10,000 years ago with fruits, nuts and vegetables growing wild along with lush thatch for building shelters. The new settlers have only to pick their food, build their thatch homes, and once that home is built, relax most the day.

A cunning cabal forms to lay claim to a part of the land. They make a pact with toughies that they will share the spoils if they protect their unequal and unjust "property rights." That is our legal structure today, developed in various stages, those unequal laws are still being enacted, and the sheriff and the courts are today's toughies.

The primary cause of poverty among plenty has just been established. The meek, mild, and law abiding now have to share the food they pick with those "owners," have to build their houses, and provide other services. Those cunning go on to claim their unearned wealth on through history and those are the **property rights laws, as applied to nature's resources and technologies, denying others their rightful share of what nature offers to all for free**, that is in place today.

Your property rights laws today, as applied to nature's resources and technologies, is nothing more than aristocracy's property rights law, exclusive title to nature's wealth which she offers to all for free. We are not talking about personal property, which was built by labor and properly exclusively owned. We are talking about the wealth of nature, which was not produced by labor and belongs to everybody.

The power structure is privatizing everything in sight, and costs rise rapidly (frequently doubling) each time a piece of nature, or a part of the infrastructure of the economy is privatized. This is happening all over the world; efforts are underway to privatize highways and other social services, even Social Security.

When Bolivia's water system was privatized, costs tripled as services went down. The citizenry revolted, physically took back their water system; the results were that prices dropped, services rose rapidly, and the legal structure had to recognize and legitimize the recovery of society's basic right to water.

We can each regain our rights to our share of nature's wealth by paying land rents, meaning all resource rents, to ourselves (meaning socially collected) and using those social-credits to build roads, railroads, water and sewer systems, and electric grids (all natural monopolies). Those funds will also run governments, and provide education, health care, and retirement. This is not socialism. It is run by the people themselves; Congress need meet only a few days a month to tweak these equal-rights laws.

How did such a wasteful society with such high poverty ever develop in the first place? Visualize a fertile valley 10,000 years ago with fruits, nuts and vegetables growing wild along with lush thatch for building shelters. The new settlers have only to pick their food, build their thatch homes, and, once that home is built, relax most the day.

A cunning cabal form and each lay claim to a part of the land. They make a pact with toughies that they will share the spoils if they protect their unequal and unjust "property rights." The meek, mild, and law abiding now have to share the food they pick with those "owners," have to build their houses, and provide any and all other services.

Currently your earned money becomes monopolist's unearned money, which they then loan the money taken from your through current property rights law back to you. That unearned money—the other side of the ledger of everyone's unnecessary debts—grows greater and greater.

The huge gains from correcting today's unequal property rights laws is your share not being appropriated from you in the first place. That is done through **paying rental values on nature's wealth to yourself** (to the social-credit fund).

The ethereal world of high finance, the 95% of all finance capital, which is unearned wealth amassed through the private collection of rental values to nature's wealth and unearned banking profits, simply disappears). The full story is summarized in this 170 word, full and equal rights, economic and property rights, thesis.

Utopia: By paying land (resource) rents to ourselves (socially collected), a citizenry is quintuply repaid through those continually circulating social-credits, building roads, railroads, water systems, sewer systems, and electric grids (any natural monopoly), as well as funding governments, providing education, health care, and retirement. Infrastructure and populations, not capitalists, establish the use-value of land, other natural resources, and their rental values provide the social-credits funding essential social services. Restructure to honest capitalism, as described herein, and taxes disappear as employed working hours and consumed resources drop by half, and all enjoy a quality, secure, life. This requires sharing the "productive" remaining jobs and equal pay for equally-productive labor. Each region of the world, each nation, each region of a nation, each state, each county, each community, and each entrepreneur has equal rights to their share of both created and saved finance capital (created money and savings). With those rights, entrepreneurs (private industry) will fill

every niche within the production-distribution process. Virtually all capitalized values, those unearned monopoly values, disappear.

Incredulity disappears when one realizes all social infrastructure—roads, water and sewer systems, electric systems, and communication systems—and all social services—education, health care, and retirement—are fully funded even as a high quality life is attained with half the employed working hours. So long as there are no unearned monies, the economy automatically balances. This simple thesis would be understandable the first day of an economics class, as opposed to current economics which is falling apart worldwide as we speak (2008-10). If it had ever been broadly taught, and applied, the theft of others wealth, wars, and poverty would have quickly disappeared.

Thousands of books can be written expanding from this foundation. To avoid waste, monopolization, hunger, poverty, and war—which consumes over half our resources, wealth, and labor—an "**honest social structure**" must be built upon the principles of this simple, 170-word, economic treatise.

All the stated goals of capitalism, Socialism, and Communitarians are attained, living standards can be set within the earth's capacity to provide resources and absorb wastes. Instead of that efficiency throughout the past 800 years, powerbrokers, protecting their power and wealth, created the monopolization laws, which we function under yet today. As per the 10,000 year ago story above, and in the first Introduction, this was accomplished by avoiding the distinct difference between wealth created by nature offered to all for free, properly conditionally owned, and wealth created by labor, which is **properly owned unconditionally.**

All wealth is processed from resources, and most those gifts of nature are within the borders of the world's poorer nations. Fully 60% of the world's industrial capacity is now outside the borders of the historic imperial-centers-of-capital. Those two realities together are creating huge stresses within the imperial centers.

It is anticipated that most of the world will be relatively well developed by 2035, only 25 years away. If we are to avoid poverty and war, we must break free from **imperialism's conspicuous consumption**. As discussed on pp. 229-30 of this author's *Economic Democracy: A Grand Strategy for World Peace and Prosperity*, that will happen quite naturally when societies pay equally-productive labor equally.

As rapidly-developing Asia contracts with the resource powers of South America and Africa, as they decouple from Europe and America, and as they turn their productive capacity towards their citizenry; they will be far wealthier than when trading primarily with the old imperial-center. That is the trade structure (the dependent world breaking free) that caused both WW I and WW II. However, this time it is the entire world outside those imperial centers, not just parts of Europe or Eurasia, coming out from under the control of the imperial centers, and they are breaking free as we speak.

Global warming, shrinking water supplies, and depleting resources motivate good thinkers and moral people to look deeper into the causes of war, and poverty. We will be demonstrating how that violence can be relegated to history, and all while protecting resources and the environment.

With that knowledge fully dispersed within those imperial nations, only a fascist political structure can control free thinking, highly moral, citizens. Power-brokers know this, and the current pre-fascist structure (the Patriot Act, recording the communications of all citizens, detention without cause, no habeas corpus, torture, etc.) will, hopefully, be removed by President Barack Obama

Besides the efficiency of paying rental values on nature's resources and technologies to oneself, hidden within that theory for the two years it took to put together were three stunning supports that we wish to emphasize:

1) Over 95% of current finance capital is both unearned and unproductive; less than five percent is productive. This matches up beautifully with the unnecessary wasted labor and resources we expose.

2) There is no such thing as honest "capitalized value" within an honest economy; there are only use-values. Until that realization sank in, I, like everybody else, thought there were honest capitalized values. Study the 95% of finance capital that is unearned and unproductive, study that capitalized value disappearing as soon as monopolization is eliminated, and study those unearned values automatically becoming earned use-values. All that remains is productive capital, it also being a use-value. If any corporation reached for unearned profits, competitors would use the same, or better, technology and undersell them.

3) And note the steady expansion of this massive unearned and unproductive finance capital that is addressed no where within Western literature.

The claim will be made that this capital did rapidly develop the world. But study carefully both the plunder-by-trade story in Parts I and II, and the elimination of patent monopolies in Chapter 3. The world could have developed much faster if inventors had been paid well, and those inventions placed in the public domain for all to use. There would have been few wars; the world would have been relatively equally developed 100 years ago, and—with ten to twenty times the scientists and a far larger increase in entrepreneurs—this world would have developed even faster this last century.

Management of the perception of the world has collapsed, and the alert within the developing world are studying the work of the best minds in the world for how to restructure to a society without poverty or war.

For more of those answers, we start with the first of the four primary monopolies that must be eliminated before a peaceful and prosperous world can emerge out of this struggle, **money** and **banking**.

1. A Modern Money Commons, Citizens Paying Banking Profits to Themselves

With money creation and central bank accounting powers that other private banks do not have, commongoodbank.com plans to open its first bank this year. Check their webpage for contacts on how this charitable bank can be expanded to your community.

If one has a slave economy or a monopolized economy, the banking system will either buy and sell slaves or buy and sell monopolized values. Thus an honest money system can only be established within an honestly structured economy.

Our views of efficient banking diverge sharply from the views of those who advocate the elimination of fractional reserve banking (Google Federal Reserve Chairman Ben Bernanke wants to eliminate reserve requirements completely). Only if banks are socially owned can fractional reserves be safely eliminated; they then automatically have 100% reserves. We will first go through the ritual of the history of money.

From Barter to Commodity Money

Before the widespread use of money, trading involved the simplest form of commercial transaction--barter, an exchange of two or more products of roughly equal value. This limits most trading to persons possessing equally valuable items. Eventually cattle, tobacco, salt, tea, blankets, skins, and other items were used as a form of money. Such commodities were the most desirable because they were durable, portable, readily exchangeable, and had the most recognizable common measure of value.

Products intended for consumption typically have one to three owners on their way from producer to consumer. Those that are used as money may have dozens or even hundreds of owners. Whether a product is used for exchange or consumption distinguishes it as money or a commodity. The products listed above were imperfect as a medium of exchange. Their limited usefulness limited trade, created problems of storage, transportation, protection, and not everyone could use these commodities.

From Commodity Money to Coins of Precious Metal

Only highly desirable, useful items could become money. No one would accept a piece of paper, brass, or copper in trade for what he or she had worked so hard to produce. Such a trade would effectively rob one of hard-earned wealth.

Gold and silver have been highly esteemed and accepted as money in most cultures. The first known coin, the shekel, was minted in "the temples of Sumer about 5,000 years ago," and coins of measured value have been routinely minted from precious metals ever since.[1] Except for scarcity values, the labor required to produce a given amount of gold, silver, or precious stones was roughly equal to the labor required to produce other items this treasure could buy. As accustomed as we are to viewing gold as money, it is still commodity money: desirable, useful, and requiring roughly equal labor to produce.

Inequality of money values is inequality of exchanged labor values. When rulers became strapped for cash, usually because of war, they resorted to debasing their currency by lowering the gold or silver content and replacing it with inexpensive metals such as copper. The labor value represented by these debased coins was less than the labor value of the items purchased. Assuming the labor cost of gold was 300 times that of copper, each day's production of copper substituted and traded as gold would confiscate the value of 300 days of labor spent producing use-value. It was the universally recognized value of precious metals that became the first readily acceptable money.[2]

With gold, or any precious metal, divisible into units of measurable value, a trade could be made for any product. As it was only with handy universally accepted money that commerce could flourish, this convenience fueled world trade. However, as these precious metals had to be located, mined, delivered, stored and protected before society could have money, trades were still clumsy.

From Gold, to Gold-Backed Paper Money, to Fiat Paper Money

The use of gold as money was handicapped by its weight, bulk, and the need for protection against debasement. These problems were eventually eliminated by printing paper money that could be redeemed for a stated amount of gold or silver. This is known as the gold standard. As this paper money was backed by gold, there still remained the complication of finding, mining, smelting, and storing this valuable commodity.

The next step in its evolution was pure fiat paper money (legal tender by government decree). It was universally resorted to in revolutions, although it usually had little value once the banking systems returned to the gold standard. Benjamin Franklin had proposed fiat paper money and, while it was used less successfully in the New England colonies, it was used productively in the middle colonies promoting production and commerce while controlling deflation. The powerful of Britain recognized the threat to their control of trade and outlawed the printing of money in the colonies. This effectively dictated control of commerce, determined who would profit, and was a much more a cause of the American Revolution than the vaunted tax on tea.[3]

World War I and WW II weakened the old imperial nations and eroded the monopoly of the gold standard.[4] As most of their gold had been traded for war materiel, these countries had to keep printing money to rebuild their shattered cities and industrial plants. To return to money backed by gold would have left their economies to the mercy of U.S. bankers. Thus the monopoly of the gold standard was partially broken in these countries. The arms race that followed WW II almost totally eliminated gold-backed money as nations continued to print money wastefully for war.

Once freed from its bondage to gold, fiat paper money represented rather than possessed value. Printed at little cost, it could be traded for as much wealth as its stated value. Society now required only one product to make a trade. Those who sold their labor received in return the paper symbols of value and needed only save this money form of wealth until they wished to buy products produced by others. Fiat paper money, backed by a nation's production and not backed by gold, was true money.

Paper Money, to Checkbook Money, to Electronic Money

As simple and light as paper money was, it was still too clumsy for most trades. Most of these units of value called money were deposited in a bank, just as gold had been, and trades were then consummated with checks. These were more efficient than cash because each check was a symbol that the signer had produced, saved, or borrowed that much real wealth and that its money form, safely deposited in the bank, was now being traded for equal value in other products or services. Family, business, corporate, and international trades use these symbols of deposited savings, checks, drafts, notes, bills of exchange, etc.

Commodity money—hides, tobacco, etc—had dozens, possibly hundreds, of owners before this trading medium returned to its status as a commodity to be consumed. Gold, still commodity money, retained the status of money much longer and has thousands of owners. Gold-backed paper money traded more conveniently and passed through the hands of many tens of thousands of owners. Reserve deposit money, traded by check, via bank debits and credits, can have an endless number of owners as this representation of value produced keeps moving from owner to owner. Modern electronic money, still reserve deposit money, is but a blip on a computer drive that can be instantly debited from one account and credited to another. Though tied closely to the principle of checkbook money, electronic entries are the ultimate in efficient fiat money.

Using the symbol of money, the banking system collects all production, completes society's trades through debits and credits, and lends the surplus production, savings, to those who, at any particular moment, have capital or consumer needs greater than their savings. The Fed buys debt instruments to expand reserves (base money) and thus increase loan capacity or they create money and loan or spend it into existence. In each case this is done by crediting money to an account without debiting from another account. Except for Congressional oversight and authorization, money is no more complicated than that.

What makes money appear mysterious is the powerful having always controlled it. Its secrets are protected by governments, bankers, and in the ethereal world of high finance, finance monopolists of every shade took over that control as they siphoned others' wealth to themselves.

Credit or Trust Money

People accept money because they trust that the value represented can be replaced by equal value in another commodity or service. Credit, pure trust, is both the oldest and most modern currency. When credit is given, nothing is received for the item of value except a promise. Each month, families and businesses are provided with products or services (produced value) and then billed. This is a procedure based on trust. This illuminates the very meaning of money; it can be redeemed for full value simply by spending it.

If money is controlled with equality and honesty, there is trust. Money then exchanges freely and is easily understood. We are describing money and banking in the everyday language that would apply if all were equally paid for equally-productive labor, if they had full and equal rights to a productive job, and if they had equal rights to finance capital.

The Different Meanings of Money

Money is correctly referred to as a unit of accounting, savings, stored value, a measure of value, a standard of value, a receipt for value, a system of accounting, a deferred payment, a transferable claim, a lien against future production, an IOU, an exchange value, and an information medium. At a fundamental level, money represents the value of the final product of combining the elements of production, land, industrial capital, finance capital, and labor. In a properly structured society, money represents the value of labor, profits on stored labor (honest, productive, capital, only 5% of current finance capital) and a share of the costs of running society represented by land rent being paid to society and spent on essential social needs as outlined in the following chapter.

To the layperson, money is normally explained as a medium of exchange. This is true. However, a medium of exchange implies equality and it is precisely the inequality of exchanges which is the greatest problem. To understand these inequalities, we must have a better explanation of money.

Money is a Contract Against Another Person's Labor

Money is first, and foremost, a contract against another person's labor. Value is properly a measure of the time and quality of all productive labor spent producing a product or service plus resource rental values embedded in production costs. If the difference between the payment received for productive labor and the price paid by the consumer for a product or service is greater than fair value for expediting that trade, either the producer was underpaid, the final consumer was overcharged, or both. When intermediaries underpay producers or overcharge consumers, they are siphoning away the production of the labors of one or the other, or both.

Savings implies something has been produced and not consumed. But even if a commodity is produced for consumption, it is properly understood as capital until sold to the final consumer. It then becomes his or her wealth for consumption and is no longer capital. Some commodities, such as a meal, are consumed in minutes and some, such as homes, are consumed in decades or even centuries. Products are sold, production expenses are paid, any surplus is deposited in a bank, and that credited deposit is a redeposit within the banking system's continually circulating reserves (a nation's money supply, improperly spoken of by many as a creation of money). Banks lend that in excess of mandated reserves to others for investment or consumption. The parties who labored to create the value represented by that money are only lending their surplus production, in its money form, **honest finance capital**, with the promise to be repaid, plus interest, for what their stored labor produced. True interest, as opposed to usury, is honest finance capital's (stored labor's) share of the wealth produced.

Money Productively Contracting Labor

Because money is always controlled by those who rule, revolutionaries resort to printing money to finance their insurrections. Successful revolutionary wars, like those of the United States,[5] France, Russia, and China, were fought for freedom, were productive expenditures of labor, and were all fought with paper money.[6] Every battle for freedom requires large expenditures. Most labor is donated, but much of the weaponry, clothing, food, and medicine must be paid for with money. Money is thus a tool for mobilizing society's labor to produce great things; in the above examples it was freedom.

Other examples of money properly employing labor are seen every day in farming, in the creation of consumer products, and in the building of homes, roads, schools, shopping centers, factories, etc. The rebuilding of Europe after WW II was a productive use of labor employed as was the industrialization of Asia.

Money Unproductively Contracting Labor

An efficient economy has been judged as requiring only $3 of speculation for every $1 invested in the real economy yet currency speculation for financing world trade alone is 50 to 100 times the real economy and the notional value of the derivatives-hedge fund market, having little or nothing to do with the real economy, is now, 2010, somewhere between $1 quadrillion and $2 quadrillion, 20 to 30 times total world production. Those notional values becoming unpayable real values when counterparties go broke is the essence of the current, 2008-10, worldwide financial collapse.

Borrowing society's money capital for speculating on gold, silver, commodities, already issued stock, derivatives, hedge funds, or currency (the ethereal world of high finance) is an interception of others' wealth speculating with society's savings; there is no intent to produce anything. For example: blogs have alerted us that 1/3 of the price of oil as accounted for within the buying and selling of oil contracts. Other commodities will have similar speculation cost increases. The massive wealth extracted through those speculations, as well as the costs of those offices which produce nothing, show up in higher prices. To quote William Krehm, "the real economy is rapidly being reduced to the part of a bit player."

The uses of society's savings for corporate takeovers usually are battles between the powerful for control. Whether the takeover is successful or not, these unproductive uses of social capital continually extract wealth from the economy. All this unnecessary activity diverts money capital from its true purpose, production and distribution. More appropriately, massive speculation beyond that needed for an efficient economy is social insanity. On balance, the entire ethereal world of high finance is composed of massive wealth unnecessarily appropriated through unequal property rights law as per this thesis.

An even more nonproductive use of money occurs when labor is contracted to destroy others' capital (war). In 1800, Robert Owen, manager of a family textile mill in Scotland, began his famous social experiment of paying workers well, giving them decent housing, educating their children, and doing all this profitably. He calculated this community of 2,500 people was producing as much as a community of 600,000 did less than 50 years before.

Owen concluded much of that massive gain in wealth was being consumed by the petty wars continually fought by aristocracy.[7] The mill workers were being underpaid for their work, the customers were being overcharged for their cloth, and the production of their labor, in its money form, was being siphoned away and used to contract materiel and labor for war. Labor was being paid to fight because this generated the greatest rewards for those who controlled the use of money. This was wasteful to the rest of society, nothing useful was produced when that confiscated wealth was spent on wars, and much of the wealth which already existed was destroyed.

In the 15th century, "about 70% of Spanish revenues and around two-thirds of the earnings of other European countries" were employed in these wars.[8] The same massive waste of wealth is mirrored in most economies today.

The treasure pillaged from the Americas was but a small share of the wealth destroyed in European wars:

> Until the flow of American silver brought massive additional revenues to the Spanish crown (roughly from the 1560s to the late 1630s), the Habsburg war effort principally rested upon the backs of Castilian peasants and merchants; and even at its height, the royal income from sources in the New World was only about one-quarter to one-third of that derived from Castile and its six million inhabitants.[9]

That is the story of this book. The powerful are wasting massive wealth battling over the world's wealth yet today. Once the wastes of the monopoly system are eliminated within both internal economies and in international trade, all money will be backed by real value; both labor and resource use will drop by half or more.

Learning the Secret of Bank-Created Money

The secret of creating money was first learned by goldsmiths. Gold deposited in banks for safe keeping were usually left for a substantial period and bankers could safely make loans, in the form of receipts for gold, of many times its value.

Loans issued for several times the amount of gold on deposit was money created out of thin air.[10] Whenever Rothschild, or other early bankers, loaned 10 certificates of gold at 10% interest, for every unit of gold they owned or held for safekeeping, each year their personal net worth would increase equal to 90% of all gold on deposit. When private banks printed and loaned their own goldbacked currency, their creation of money and their profits, between collapses, were identical to that of goldsmiths. That is history; money creation today is only through central banks.

For centuries a prudent bank with $1 million in gold maintaining self-imposed fractional reserves at 10% could print $10 million in personal-signature banknotes, $9 million of that would be bank-created money. All goes well until some banks go beyond reasonable loan to gold reserve ratios leading to runs on banks and they collapse. Section 16 of the 1913 Federal Reserve Act established what was to become a single US currency, the Federal Reserve Note. As fast as banks were brought under that act they could loan only a mandated share of their deposits. In 1980 the Monetary Control Act brought all banks and credit unions within that system of government creation of money and control of bank reserves. Private banks hadn't created money for decades but now it was official; only the Federal Reserve could create America's money.

Incoming loan payments are roughly the same as the total being loaned by banks. Assuming 10% mandated reserves; a private bank can maintain $9 million in loans for every $1 million held in reserves, roughly the same as the prudent banker 100 years ago with self-imposed reserves of 10% in gold or silver backing each bank's personal-signature-bills.

As opposed to being backed by gold, the money created by a socially-owned banking system—and its circulation productively contracting land, labor, and industrial capital—is backed by the wealth produced. Having the power to create money to cover any crisis, a socially-owned Federal Reserve will be primarily creating base money and maintaining a proper money supply (the velocity of base money circulating) through raising or lowering mandated reserves.

Financial powerbrokers eventually stripped most mandated reserves out of the Federal Reserve Act. This was first accomplished, in the 1970s, through selling blocs of loans to money markets. Then, in the 1990s, required reserves were removed from all deposits except checking accounts and the 1933 enacted Glass-Steagall Act, which prohibited commercial banks from collaborating with brokerage firms, insurance companies, etc, was repealed. This, along with off the books accounting, circulated base money faster and faster and eventually crashed into the 2008-10, banking crisis.

No checkbook money or credit card money ever leaves a banking system. Both are instructions to transfer digital money from one account to another, and on average, a balance is maintained in all banks. Under the Goldsmith theory of banking, personal signature banknotes, promising to pay in gold were circulated. In that process, there was no increase in gold, the base money of those times, when certificates of 10 times those *non circulating reserves*, gold in safekeeping, were loaned and there is no increase in base money today when 10 times or 33 times (as is possible under 3% reserves) the original primary-created money are loaned and reloaned over and over and the full compliment of digital base money is, at all times, within the banking system. Gold as base money is stored, and only certificates of gold circulate. Fiat money itself is both base money and circulating money.

With the experience of colonial script not backed by gold; the 13 American colonies printed money to fight the Revolutionary War. But this power of government to create money out of thin air was not used by the US again in any great measure until President Lincoln printed greenbacks to finance the Civil

War. Though the alert will have spotted the efficiency of money created out of thin air and not backed by gold, as soon as that war was over the government started pulling those greenbacks out of circulation. This destruction of money caused bankruptcies to soar for the first 10 postwar years as wealth was again consolidated within the hands of entrenched wealth; those goldsmith theory bankers creating the nation's money backed by gold.

There was no need for those bankruptcies. If those greenbacks, backed only by the strength of the economy, had been allowed to stand—so long as there were unemployed resources, unemployed labor, and consumer needs—that money would have continued to circulate freely combining labor and industrial capital with America's immense natural resources, creating even more wealth. A healthy, wealthy, economy requires a measured and balanced creation of money to create wealth. Those greenbacks were withdrawn because their creation encroached upon private bankers self-appointed rights to create money backed by "their" gold.

As those greenbacks were being withdrawn, conservative bankers required $33.60 of gold in reserve for every $100 of their circulating currency. This was gold-backed money created by conservative private banks. But the next 40 years recorded greedy bankers loaning 20 to 50 times their reserves (called leverage today). Banks pooled their funds to cover runs on banks. But, with their depositors' money loaned out operating the economy and thus not immediately collectable (illiquid), perfectly sound banks would go under along with the "wildcat bankers" and bankrupt many farms and businesses with them.

Establishing the Federal Reserve: Base Money Circulating Becomes the Money Supply

With 13 banking panics over a period of 80 years, one every six years with the last one just ending in 1907, the U.S. decided, in 1913, to eventually eliminate goldsmith banking through the establishment of the Federal Reserve and modern fractional reserve banking. Since that act, **member banks** could only loan from their deposits of which a mandated percent must remain in reserve. This was a seismic change. Previously a supply of gold, silver, or gold certificates in reserve were necessary to establish a bank. With those "reserves," a bank then printed currency with the bank's name on it (personal signature banknotes) with a total value many times the value of their precious metals reserves. But now member banks, still privately owned, could loan only a percentage of their deposits of fiat money. Instead of loaning money they created as a percent of gold or silver in reserve, they were now loaning fiat money created by the Federal Reserve which was then redeposited over and over in the banking system, as those reserves circulated. A fraction of that circulating money had to be kept in reserve; America's **fractional reserve banking system** was being put in place.

In 1980, the Monetary Control Act brought all U.S. deposit institutions under the Federal Reserve. Creation of money has ever since been by the Federal Reserve and goldsmith banking—private banks creating money through loaning a multiple of their gold or silver reserves in the form of banknotes, though it had not been used much for decades—was officially relegated to history. Though they once did, private banks today do not create money. However, private bankers do control the Federal Reserve where all the money they need to protect their monopoly system is created, and that process is on full bore pouring money at themselves, during the current, 2008-10, financial crisis.

Due to the immense wealth that can be guided to their coffers, bankers, with the support of other extractors of wealth, deny society the enormous efficiency potentials we demonstrate are possible within a socially-owned banking system. The huge profits bankers make on high interest rates were theoretically to control inflation or deflation. But they were actually protecting the massive profits pocketed as they moved back and forth between bonds and stocks in sync with the rise and fall of interest rates and bond values. The simplicity, and instant effect, of controlling the money supply through increases or decreases in mandated reserves was ignored.

Between 1913 and 1936 each of the federally owned, but privately managed, 12 central banks created money for their regions eventually, and supposedly, backed by government-owned gold. However, from 1926 to 1929, the old guard running the New York Federal Reserve poured created money at their banks which loaned these massive funds to stock speculators. When the NY Fed heard the Federal Reserve's Board of Governors had held an all night meeting on their practice, they pulled back. The funding to support the bubble was not there, the stock market crashed, and the Great Depression was on. The problem was traced to the independence of those 12 reserve banks. So, in 1935-36, the Roosevelt administration assigned money creation decisions to the Board of Governors. America finally had its central bank that was not yet fully in place in 1913 and that Board and Congress has made major decisions on creation of America's money ever since (still theoretically backed by gold until 8/15/1971 when President Nixon closed the gold window to other countries as President Roosevelt had done to citizens in 1933).[11]

Modern Money Mechanics (MMM)[12] states, in error, that private banks create money. But when analyzed it is clear they—and many money theorists—are calling each change of control of money as it is loaned (each step in its circulation [velocity]) as a creation of money. Loan repayments closely matching loans made disproves private-banks-create-money-theorists.

MMM misnames a loan as created money when they have only moved deposited money (a credit to the bank offset by a debit in favor of the depositor) first to their loanable and spendable funds and from there to a borrower's account (debits to the bank continually offset by incoming deposits). Their statement, "checks drawn against borrowers' deposits result in credits to accounts of other depositors, with no net change in the total reserves," proves this.

MMM recognizes deposits, until they are loaned, as "excess reserves." In Section three, it states that since "lending banks expect to lose these deposits, and an equal amount of reserves, as the borrowers' checks are paid, they will not lend more than their *excess reserves*." The use of federally created base money has been accumulatively accounted for but it was already created (again as base money) and its re-loaning was only a continuation of the circulation of money.

Debts being extinguished (repaid) at roughly the same rate they are created keeps the money supply (base money circulating) in balance. An increase in the velocity of money is an increase in the money supply, but not an increase in base money. If more reserves are needed, the Fed must create that base money, now backed only by the faith and credit of the government, not by gold. By crediting those borrowing from—or selling debt instruments to—the Fed without debiting anyone's account, new money is created. Private-banks-create-money-theorists do not address base money, to do so would destroy their thesis. As the creation of base money, and its circulation, is the very essence of money, monetary theory textbooks address it deeply.

I have asked private-banks-create-money-theorists what happens to their deposits and am told "it just sits there." But there being no increase or decrease in total reserves as money is loaned out and redeposited, stated specifically by MMM and proven in their charts, belies that statement.

Private bankers tried hard to get past the U.S. Constitution, Article I, Section 8, saying that, "The Congress shall have power….to coin money, regulate the value thereof, and of foreign coin." Once money was no longer backed by precious metals, their lawyers simply could not get around those words in the foundation law of the land that, even allowing for shortcomings in that statement, only the government can create money. So, when technology advanced to money as digits in an accounting system, bankers designed an appearance of ownership of, but not actual title to, the Federal Reserve, all this to maintain their control of fiat money creation which is not permitted under the Constitution.

Except for private bankers being in charge, by 1935-36, when President Roosevelt's government assigned the authority for money creation to the Board of Governors of the Federal Reserve (in concert with the 12 regional reserve banks), America's fractional reserve banking system was brilliantly established. Creating money is the prerogative of the Federal Reserve which is—as proven by all profits, almost 98% of the Fed's gross income, being paid to the Treasury—federally owned.[a] See also John Kenneth Galbraith, William Greider, and James Livingston.[13]

The money supply is only base money's measured circulation. If the receiver of what is commonly, and wrongly, referred to as "private-bank-created money" puts it under the mattress instead of into a reserve deposit, money circulation (velocity) stops. But as soon as that person spends the money, where it is soon deposited into a reserve account, again 90% is loaned back out, that money is then committed and there is no surplus to loan until it is again deposited (typically within hours or days if the transaction was by check and instantly if by debit card) and 90% of the money continues to circulate as it is again loaned out. In the act of being accounted for each time it changes hands, the money totals increase and these increasing totals within double-entry bookkeeping make it appear that money has been created. But each trade of money for value has only been counted (and becomes a part of a nation's GDP); base money (reserve deposits) has not increased. It has only circulated. (Loan repayments roughly equaling loans made is the missing link in faulty "private-banks-create-money" theory.)

Private banks creating both money and debt when they make loans is badly misinterpreted by private-banks-create-money-theorists. A debt within the normal flow of money is just that a loan; a debt to be repaid. It is a normal function within the circulation of money.

Once spent, money has no commitments or connection of any kind to any past depositors or borrowers. Depositors look to the bank for protection of their stored labor, and that bank's protection is pledged equities or the good credit of borrowers.

A bank could have bought a bond, a business, or a vacation for its entire staff instead of making a loan and it would have had exactly the same effect as loaning money. The check written would have returned to the bank as another deposit ready to loan out or to spend. "The net effects on the banking system [by bank purchases] are identical with those resulting from loan operations," Surely money theorists will not call a bank's expenditure of money as a creation of money.

---

[a] The Bank of England was chartered in 1694 as a privately owned central bank. Government IOUs instead of Gold were used as reserves. Today all central banks create money backed by the faith and credit of the government and they ignore the ritual of gold as a symbol of value backing money.

Go to any major coin-currency show and any theorist on money creation will become humble. Counties, railroads, communities, and banks have created so many different issues of money that it requires one or more deeply-researched books for each state. Successful examples of money creation addressed in most such histories have been repeated over and over again throughout most states and the world. That those coins and bills are in collections today testify to most of those money creations as having some measure of success, many very successful.

The $850 billion the Federal Reserve had in treasuries going into the current financial crisis set the limit on how much money they could disburse without consulting Congress. Due to the rapidly deepening crisis, the Federal Reserve and Treasury went to Congress for more funds and were authorized to create virtually trillions of dollars (many trillions pledged, no one really knows how much, some borrowed through selling treasuries as nervous capital fled to safety, the rest to be created). Though the Fed is in charge once authorized to create money, when more money is needed it must again be authorized by Congress.

Private banks can only increase money's circulation (velocity) which is the final measurement of the money supply. If monetary theorists would use the term "circulating money supply;" no one would be saying, "Private banks create money." They can never create money because they cannot add a credit without accounting for a debit as they did for centuries under the goldsmith theory of banking. If enough people refuse to borrow, spend, or loan, the money supply appears to shrink even though the velocity of base money has only slowed.

Further Testing the Assertions that, under Modern Fractional Reserve Banking, Private Banks Create Money

Alternative money theorist's fractional reserve banking assertions are clear, "Deposited money sits in an account until withdrawn by the depositor and, while on deposit, it serves as reserves for the money the banks create through loaning money into existence."

So those theorists are saying, "Private banks create money by crediting it to the borrowers account and must have 10% that amount on deposit [$1,000 in reserve] to back that $10,000 creation. That $10,000 is spent, and is deposited back into a reserve account which becomes a total of $11,000 in reserve. The $1,000 remaining in the original reserves is still backing that original loan while the $10,000 deposited after that loan was spent is now additional surplus reserves for further loans."

Challenge 1 Money theorists cannot have it both ways. If that first $1,000 in reserve deposits backs a $10,000 loan, that secondary reserve deposit of $10,000 becomes reserves for a $100,000 loan which completes cycle two. Cycle three creates $1 million. Cycle four $10 million. Cycle five $100 million and four more cycles would reach $1 trillion. No bank claims that ability or that right. Such a money creation process would destroy the very meaning of both M1 and fractional reserve banking. Replace those circulating dollars with diamonds and it would be obvious their circulation would not be a creation of money.

2 Loan payments going into deposits equaling loans spent going out of deposits is as fatal to the theory of private banks creating money as bringing circulating reserves (circulating base money) into the equation.

3 The creator of money owns that representation of value. If banks could create money by making loans they would have tons of money and never go broke.

4 Competition for profits from money created with a few key strokes would competitively shrink interest rates to just that necessary to keep a bank solvent.

5 The same money theorists that claim private banks create money push for 100% reserves (cash in the vault to back all deposits). If deposits are not loaned out, as they claim, that money is still in the bank—available by check, credit card, or debit card—and 100% reserves are already in effect.

6 In the current (2008-10) worldwide liquidity-solvency crisis, banks all over the world are in trouble. Because they cannot, none have created money to solve their problem and, because it is they who create our money, central banks and national treasuries are pouring trillions of dollars at those in-trouble banks.

7 All money currently circulating within the banking system is federal fiat money where money created by private banks have always had that bank's name printed on it. As all digital deposit money is convertible to cash money, which is federal fiat money (greenbacks), no one would consider giving a private bank the right to create Federal Reserve notes and no one can point to a law giving them the right to create digital money tradable for reserve notes.

8 Historically interest was normally paid on deposited money. Bank deposits are nothing more than a loan to the bank, typically at interest, that can be rescinded by the depositor at any time. Private banks would not borrow money anywhere if they could simply create free money.

9 It is against the U.S. Constitution, Article I, Section 8, "The Congress shall have power….to coin money, regulate the value thereof, and of foreign coin." There would be no regulation of the value of money if private banks created it each time they made a loan.

10 The fundamental principles of double entry bookkeeping does not permit it. Any who attempted to create money, you or a banker, would go to jail.

11 The seal of the nation, the signature of the Treasurer of the United States and the signature of the Secretary of the Treasury on every bill and it being fiat money "good for all debts public and private," prove only the federal govern-

ment—through the Federal Reserve and under the authorization of Congress — creates digital money.

12 James Livingston, in *Origins of the Federal Reser ve,* chapters 7 & 8, John Kenneth Galbraith in *Money: Whence it Came, Where it Went,* pp 126-83, 188, especially pp 134, 144, 177-90, 195-96, 199-200, William Greider's *Secrets of the Temple,* especially pp 31, 49-50, & 280, and Paul Krugman in *The Return of Depression Economics,* 2009, p. 176, clearly say (throughout their books) the Federal Reserve is federally owned and that they create our money. They do acknowledge that between 1913 and 1936 regional reserve banks created money independently for their regions. That freedom led to the Great Depression and, as per laws enacted under President Roosevelt in 1935-36, all creation of money decisions were then placed under the authority of the Board of Governors of the Federal Reserve.

Through precious metals as reserves and the faith and credit of nations, that right to money creation had been ebbing and flowing between private banks and governments for decades. Any time money was created by private banks and loaned, wealth was extracted when that debt was repaid. As wealth represented by newly created money obviously belongs to all, over time governments created all money and theoretically, but not actually because political control still guided that free money to the powerful, just as is happening now, 2008-10, all citizens gained their share. It is time for citizens to understand that wealth represented by newly created money is theirs collectively; it does not belong to banks, governments, or monopolists extracting wealth from the economy.

There is precedent for assigning the full powers of money creation by, and for, society to a socially-owned central bank of a "National Banking System." President Abraham Lincoln felt money should be created by society and spent into circulation on essential social needs without debt.

> The monetary needs of increasing numbers of People advancing towards higher standards of living can and should be met by the Government. Such needs can be served by the issue of National Currency and Credit through the operation of a National Banking system. … Government has the power to regulate the currency and credit of the Nation [run an Internet search].

America has a socially-owned, yet private banker controlled, central bank today but does not have a socially-owned National Banking System. Private banker control can be quickly eliminated, socially-owned banks can be just as quickly put in place, and this is happening as we speak, March 2010, as states learn from Ellen Browns writings on how North Dakota with its own state bank is the only state in the nation with a balanced budget. States are realizing that all the profits of a state bank go for state services. This can happen on a large scale, when banks go broke they are, under current law, converted to public ownership.

As the cost of operating a bank is one half of one percent interest on loans, public owned banks can pay higher interest for deposits, even as they charge lower interest on loans. The Federal Reserve has been pouring money at major banks to keep them afloat. Instead, simply call in those "permanent rotating loans," a euphemism for imminent nationalization, and take over those bankrupt banks. Backed by the Fed's money creation powers, socially-owned banks cannot go broke. Depositors and borrowers will flock to that security. Already in trouble, the rest of the banks will turn in their keys as their customers disappear.

With all bank profits going into the **social-credit fund**, taxes can be reduced by at least half even as the greater share of social needs are fully funded (next chapter eliminates the rest of the taxes). That great opportunity was missed when President Obama's economic recovery team poured trillions of dollars of public money at their former employers who had created the crisis in the first place.

The Fed's Open Market Operations Hide the Simplicity of Money Creation

To maintain the secret of how simple money creation really is and to avoid the creation of debt-free money for infrastructure and essential services so as to reserve those investment opportunities for monopoly capital, designers (monopolists) conceived the Fed's Open Market Operations.

Money is created by the Fed buying debt instruments and crediting the selling bank's account without debiting another account. The reserve account of the bank where that check is cashed being credited with the amount of the sale with no debiting of another reserve account creates money. That base money circulating (plus currency and coin) is the only "real" money within modern fractional reserve banking.

Once the limit of circulation of money is reached, an increase in base money requires the Fed purchasing bonds in the market. No other bank's reserves are debited as that banks reserves are credited and money has been created.[14] If imminent failure of banks threatens to damage the economy, the Fed may, up to a certain level and under Congressional oversight, create money as a loan to banks or, in an emergency, even loan directly to industries. To do so, the Fed, when authorized by Congress, simply credits their account and debits no other account. Lowering or raising reserve requirements increases or decreases the circulation (velocity) of money (increasing or decreasing the money supply) but does not increase or decrease base money. Base money increases are the responsibility of the Federal Reserve, when authorized by Congress, and only bankruptcies or the Federal Reserve (or a refusal to accept by other societies) can destroy that money.

It would be transparent and much simpler for the Fed to credit the Treasury's account and the government to spend that money into circulation. As those just-purchased treasuries were originally printed by the Treasury, they can be destroyed rather than go through the ritual of the government paying those debts to the Federal Reserve, and, by law, the money is then promptly returned to the Treasury.

The interest and principle paid by the U.S. Treasury on Fed-purchased T-bills goes to the Fed, which returns that and a part of other profits—bonds, currency trading, priced services to banks, etc—to the Treasury. In 1994 the Fed received $19.247 billion from the Treasury as interest on bonds and paid to the Treasury $20.470 billion, or $1.223 billion more than it received in interest.[15] The dividends investors in the Federal Reserve may receive (6%) can be eliminated by buying back those misleading shares as allowed in Section 7 of the Federal Reserve Act; the same law where all profits are returned to the Treasury.

The unpaid principal and interest on those Fed-purchased, and thus government-owned, bonds are simply credits and debits on the Fed's and Treasury's books. Both are government agencies and when payments are made to the Fed by the Treasury that interest, principle, and other profits are promptly returned to the Treasury, thus proving there never was a debt. The Treasury-Federal Reserve could have openly created that money. But the simplicity of creating money and spending it into existence would be visible to all and maintaining that secret is the very purpose of the whole charade.

Private bankers politically control, but do not own, the Fed. If they really did, the Fed would pay taxes and the owners would retain both interest and principle on Fed-owned debt instruments. Their $212 million in dividends in 1994 at a mandated 6% interest rate tells us the member banks have fewer than $2.4 billion invested. Since the profits turned over to the Federal Reserve would give it a capitalized value of several hundred billion dollars, or more, it is over 99% publicly owned and less than 1% privately owned.[16]

Operation costs are paid for by charges to banks, the Fed reports to Congress, and the payment of over 99% of its profits (almost 98% of its gross income) to the Treasury is proof that the Fed is an arm of the federal government. With all this and the Fed itself claiming it is a government agency that pays no taxes; the Fed is privately owned theorists have nothing to back their claim.

In a society with full and equal economic rights for all, each unit of money represents an equal unit of use-value within the economy. In a steady state economy, value is being destroyed, by consumption and depreciation, as fast as it is created or, if you prefer, created as fast as it is destroyed. Consumption and production are in balance. Still assuming full and equal economic rights, as laid out in this treatise, the circulation of base money does this naturally.

Pointing that created money towards the ethereal world of high finance and towards war along with the failure to fully utilize the power of mandated reserves (while banks are privately owned), in balance with money creation, seriously lowers economic efficiency.

As described earlier, America had the good fortune of sincere bankers, tired of the multiple crisis of wildcat banking (one every six years for 80 years), established in 1913, and finally restructured to a true central bank in 1935-36, a modern fractional reserve banking system overseen by the Federal Reserve's Governing Board. Then they had the misfortune of corrupt bankers taking over and dismantling the beautiful system they designed. For the purpose of laying claim to more unearned wealth, they slowly repealed the protective laws of a fully functional central bank, essentially eliminated fractional reserve banking, and eliminated the Glass-Steagall act which forbid combining banks, insurance companies, and brokerage houses. The result was the current financial collapse.

Those selfish few had guided the nations wealth to their coffers, loaned those appropriated funds back to the masses, did all this on higher and higher margins (leverage), that is now collapsing (2008-10), and this has the potential of another Great Depression, WW III, or a total restructuring of the world economies such as we are suggesting.

The ease of analyzing increasing or decreasing mandated reserves as the most effective method of controlling inflation or deflation means bankers have always known this highly-efficient tool was there but chose to fatten their profits by controlling inflation through higher interest rates. Bonds and stocks rise and fall in reverse order to interest rates and the wealthy do not want to destroy that honey pot by raising or lowering mandated reserves, instead of interest rates, to control the money supply.

Very little has to be done for society to reclaim their full and equal rights to finance capital. Buy back those privately owned shares in the Federal Reserve system (roughly $2.4 billion) as allowed for in the Federal Reserve Act, remove those bankers from their undemocratic positions of power, put trained professionals in their place, mandate the creation of money for infrastructure (up to the point the money supply is in balance), and raise or lower required reserves to maintain that balance. Then run the Federal Reserve-Treasury efficiently with all regions, all states, all communities, and all entrepreneurs having full and equal rights to finance capital (created money and savings). This can be done under present law. In a financial crisis, such as the one ongoing, inefficient private banks become socially-owned and operated simply by calling in the Federal loans shoring them up.

Efficient Social-Credits Require Banking Profits and Created Monies be Paid into the Social-Credit Fund

All borrowers, consumers of the moment, are borrowing the deposits of savers of the moment. One may be borrowing from oneself, from a checking account or out of pocket, and expecting to replenish their bank account or pocket change, both are savings. The banking system keeps an account of these trades between people. Many are equal trades—in a month, or a year, most people earn roughly what they spend—but the unequal trades, more produced (earned) than spent, or more consumed (spent) than earned, are balanced by the lending/borrowing of deposited savings in banks' reserve accounts.

Monopolies per se produce no value. If money contracted only productive labor and full values were paid for that labor, money would represent real value and would become a symbol of actual wealth; its use-value. Money would then be only a tool, a symbol for the trade of productive labor, which is the mechanism that functions when we describe efficiency increases equal to the invention of money, the printing press, and electricity as an efficient and just property rights structure provides the social-credits to fund infrastructures, governments, and all essential social needs.

Under conditions of equal economic rights, each person is fairly paid for his or her fully productive labor, each has rights to a productive job, and money lent combines land, labor, and industrial capital to produce full value in needed goods and services. Neither money nor the economy can become truly efficient until all nonproductive extractions of wealth through unequal trades in both internal and world trade are eliminated. Every contracting of labor for nonproductive use must, on final analysis, be paid for by extracting value from other stakeholders.

Powerful bankers thousands of miles away have no concept of local needs and no loyalty to local people. Farmers, homeowners, and small businesses are strapped for finance capital as their locally-produced wealth is claimed by stock speculators, merger and takeover artists, currency speculators, hedge funds, and other gamblers in the worldwide market casinos.

Do away with the ethereal world of high finance and stock markets and local private capital needs can be easily financed. Simply calculate finance capital needs and assign a surcharge to all loans to go into a socially-owned capital accumulation fund kept in, and loaned from, local, socially-owned, banks. Larger banks will have a department for financing large industries. Worker-owned businesses and cooperatives financed by those larger banks would be the economic ideal of labor employing capital. Everything is then local as opposed to an ethereal world of high finance claiming title to wealth throughout the world. Capital needs of each federated region of the world, each nation, each state, each county, and each community can be calculated. So long as there are surplus labor and resources and real value is to be produced, finance capital not available from savings can be obtained through creating money. Once established, an investment fund would replenish itself through loan repayments and interest rates high enough to cover loan losses.

Remembering that governments, infrastructure, education, universal health care and retirement should be financed by resource rents and bank profits (**social-credit funds funding what amounts to a greatly expanded Bill of rights**), it is clear that wealth accumulated in the past through **aristocratic exclusive titles to nature's resources and technologies, denying others their rightful share of what nature offers to all for free**, has gone for many other things besides society's finance capital needs, primarily buying and selling the capitalized values of appropriated wealth (speculation within the ethereal world of high finance), and for extravagant living (conspicuous consumption).

Every alert entrepreneur knows the big profits end up with those who call the tune with their money. With **social-credit funds** (resource rents, banking profits, and created money) replacing those huge blocs of unearned finance capital, destined for obsolescence under full and equal economic rights, citizens with sound ideas, but no capital, would have the opportunity to realize the profits from their abilities and accumulate capital. As talent is broadly diffused, wealth, accumulated by true producers, would quickly diffuse itself relatively equally throughout the population.

Just as each individual has rights, federated regions, nations, regions within nations, states, communities, and entrepreneurs should have rights to their share of the world's finance capital (primary-created money, resource rents, and bank profits). Denying borrowed **social-credit-funds** for speculation in the world-wide gambling casinos known as stock markets (see Chapter 3), but permitting it for new speculative enterprises, would guide lending into productive channels; the real economy, as opposed to the ethereal world of high finance laying claim to wealth produced by others.

Consumer credit, within limits, should be a right quickly available, just as pioneered by computerized credit cards. Using eye patterns, thumbprints, and signature scanning, procedures now in use, along with a credit check, risks would be almost nonexistent. Each person's right to credit would be tempered by being subject to standards much as they are now, and the local credit union, an integrated member of the banking system, would be in a position to know a member's creditworthiness. Local bankers should best know the needs of the region and the trustworthiness of those who borrow to build and produce for that society. If not, they should not be bankers.

The economies of prosperous nations are dynamic due to the hopes and dreams of their citizens. The economic health of a nation requires that those with ideas, talents, and energy have access to finance capital (others' savings). With rights to credit, a nation's talented can bring together land, labor, capital, and technology at the right time and in the right place to fulfill society's needs. If there is a shortage of finance capital for productive use, and the resources are available, and can be used without destroying the environment, a nation's Federal Reserve simply creates money and the Treasury spends it into existence (up to the level of a balanced money supply, building infrastructure or providing essential services). Through social collection of resource rental values (next chapter) and the greater profits of efficient socially-owned banks paid to society (both are social earnings, neither are properly private earnings), all citizens pay their share of normal social costs through the products and services purchased with their relatively equal pay for equally-productive work.

Credit is currently rationed by the simple method of checking track records and lending up to a certain percentage of a borrower's equity, a great rule for monopolists. "Loans are made in a very impersonal way—everything depends on 'track record,' and if you don't have a 'track record' [or equity], as most young people do not—you can forget it."[17] Access to investment capital should be a right based on productive merit as well as collateralized equity. Thus credit for productive people in their first ventures and those with a vision for productive expansion would be easier to obtain.

With employees of a banking authority trained to be alert to productive investment requests, these loans would be quite simple. When a loan request was received, an evaluation would be made of its potential productive and financial success. If it looked reasonable, the loan would be approved. This is precisely how loans in America were made for the first 15 to 20 years after WW II. After the boom years were over, banks reverted primarily to loans against equity.[b]

With the disappearance of monopoly values, the much smaller loans needed would be backed by an equally smaller, secure, true value, and those values would be matched by the savings of fully-productive labor and entrepreneurs within a fully efficient economy. A loan would, of course, require financial accountability by the borrower just as it does now.

Through regional capital accumulation funds charging enough interest to cover risk, loan institutions can fund new projects. It is not necessary to lend strictly to owners who would then hire workers. Those with insight need only prepare a prospectus describing the product or service, market potential, profit expected, financial requirement, and labor needs. The loan institution would study the proposal and, assuming the ideas were sound and beneficial, would

---

[b] With the elimination of appropriated values in the various monopolies, there will not be those monopoly values against which to lend. But neither will money capital be needed to purchase those fictitious values.

approve the loan. Workers would study the prospectus, and agree to 10-20% of their wages being deducted as payments until their 60-80% of the stock is paid for. Those who planned the productive endeavor would own, and be responsible for paying for, 20-40% of that industry's value. Fully worker owned and operated industries and cooperatives should receive equal consideration. Their financing would be the economic ideal of labor employing capital. A Google search for "Mondragon Cooperative" alerts us that this is the world's fastest growing production model.

With workers owning a substantial share of industry and a share of their wages being used to pay off the loan, those owners of capital would be true producers. Society would receive useful products or services and the nation's savers and central banks, providing primary-created money (base money) when necessary, would be fully paid for their finance capital.

With these triple benefits to society, bankers should be taught to pay close attention to requests for investment credits; they are the sinews of capitalism. Most workers would stay on the job, but, once a new business was secure and their new stock had maximum value, the talented would search out another prospectus, help develop another business, train more workers, build that industry to its maximum use-value, and move on again.

Labor would be both mobile and highly productive just as capital is now and the most productive of those workers would be the accumulators of capital. This would be mobilization of labor without the dispossessions that had been the norm of past capitalization processes. Labor would have the same rights to gains in efficiencies of technology as investors now have. The talented would be in high demand by the developers of industry. Periodically, employed working hours must be lowered in step with technology's efficiency gains.

Besides collateral protection, there are three flows of money that make those loans secure, resource rents, profits, and a share of wages. Every success increases the use-value, and thus the rental value, of land. As they are sharing in those profits, society's collection of resource rents—either directly or through lower product and service costs—could, and should, permit it to accept its share of the risks of new entrepreneurs.

With these restructured borrowing rights, many more people would qualify for investment capital than under equity loans. If successful, they and their workers would own that capital honestly, as opposed to the current custom of **capitalizing values through exclusive titles to nature's resources and technologies, denying others their rightful share of what nature offers to all for free.**

Those searching for a higher return, and confident they have found good investments, could directly employ their capital. Those with the opportunity to lend their savings at a higher rate would be free to do so. But they could no longer obtain high profits by bidding on exclusive titles to nature's resources and technologies and, through that monopoly structure, laying claim to wealth properly belonging to others. The huge blocs of accumulated capital confiscated from productive labor, **roughly 95% of all investment capital, would be transformed into equally-shared use-values under these proposed conditional titles to nature's resources and technologies.**

Once restructured, a society must reduce labor time and share productive jobs. If this is not done, new mini-monopolizers, in the form of excessive job rights, will emerge. A socially-owned capital accumulation fund within a modern financial commons (finance capital comprised of created money, resource rents, bank profits, and savings) would eliminate the ethereal world of high finance composed of capitalized, unearned, rental values and the many games played within the ethereal world of high finance with this unearned, and surplus, finance capital, laying claim to ever-more wealth produced by others.

Japan operated just such a capital accumulation fund and utilized it with a vengeance to reach its current position in world trade. We do not suggest a nation's international trade capital accumulation fund be that aggressive but it would be great protection against others' predatory trade practices.

The 95% of finance capital that is both unearned and unproductive is a loss to society, while the 5% honestly earned, saved, and operating the real economy is efficient. That which was not honestly earned is inefficient to the extreme. Not only is creation of money, socially-collected resource rents and profits of socially-owned banks funding infrastructure, governments, and other essential services more efficient than when funded with unearned finance capital extracted from its proper owners, those massive funds are also floating around searching for something to own is the ethereal world of high finance laying claim to ever more of the wealth properly belonging to others.

The key to understanding an honest banking structure is that money and banking are only tools with which to produce and distribute wealth. Beyond a little brick and mortar there is nothing tangible (labor created) there to own. With automatic 100% reserves, a socially-owned and operated bank cannot go broke. Their cost of operation is only ½ of 1% on loans leaving massive profits available to assist in funding health care and retirement. An efficient privately owned bank is an oxymoron.

That exorbitant interest rates are unnecessary was demonstrated by early Scottish bankers whose thrift is so well known that even today a person careful with his or her money is called "Scotch." In the 19th century, the universal practice of Scottish banks budgeted 1% of all loans to cover banking costs. Their innovative practices are still considered a model of banking stability.[18] With the costs well established at 1% for small-volume banking using expensive hand accounting, ½ of 1% would be a proper service charge for large-volume banking using inexpensive computerized accounting.

During the stable years following WW II, the real rate of interest in the United States, allowing for inflation, hovered around ½ of 1%. Although the real rate of interest during what were considered the best years the world economy has ever known was under 2%, we believe stored labor should be well paid and will allow the highest long-term average real rate of interest for investors, 3%, as a fair rate. With interest on savings at the high end of historical norms, both industrial and honest finance capital (both are stored labor) and current labor would be well paid. People would save and those savings would be available for productive investments. Unearned, unproductive, finance capital deserves no interest.

Though the interest rate on loans could be made 1% over that paid savings, totaling 4%, an efficient economy would charge possibly 6-to-8%. In league with social collection of resource rents, those surpluses would become social-credits for essential social and human rights (funding governments, infrastructure, education, universal health care, retirement, etc). Those funding needs and the sums collected from resource rents and interest charges can be adjusted to provide all necessary funding.

In a banking system, with the exception of money created, total debits and credits will balance, withdrawals will equal deposits. With a fully integrated banking system, any deviation from that balance could be quickly corrected. The visible flow of funds would be the economic pulse of a community, a region, a nation, a federated world region, and the entire world. Any unexplained deficit in a bank, community, or region could be immediately looked into while normal deficits are balanced by others' normal surpluses.

To provide an adequate living standard for all people and still protect the world's resources and environment, a balance between a respectable living standard and the capacity of the earth's resources and ecosystems will have to be reached. Assuming centers of capital could no longer siphon the world's wealth to themselves, and then waste it battling over that wealth, societies throughout the world could then progress calmly and rapidly.

Every trade financed by money capital moving between two banks creates a change in those overseas banks' reserve accounts at the central bank for that currency. If that central bank does not honor a transaction in its currency through suspending targeted banks' access to their reserves, those banks funds are frozen.

The power to discount currencies and freeze funds of developing countries gives powerful nations effective control over currency values and thus control over others' ability to create money and control its value. Nothing is more important for a nation's or a region's economy than productive use of created money and savings, its finance capital. This requires their currency being under their control, spendable only within their borders, and an honest World Central

Bank currency; a dual currency system, handling trades between nations with a mandate to protect the value of all currencies. If economically viable regions restructure to a regional currency spendable only within that region, and a sustainable, efficient economy is established as per the 170 word full and equal rights thesis on page 16 and throughout this book, there will be no need for bank rescues; all problems are resolvable through production readjustments.

The Theory of Interest as Usury

Working on a bill to submit to the Eighth Session of the Provisional World Parliament, Professor Glen Martin of Radford University expanded upon the Biblical and Koranic principles that it is wrong to charge interest. As money and banking are social technologies understood for thousands of years, ownership is only proper for items built by one's labor or purchased with funds earned by one's labor, and banking systems are neither, they are properly socially owned.

What caught Professor Martin's attention was that, if properly structured, the elimination of the waste of monopolies and the attaining of full and equal economic rights through sharing the remaining productive jobs, with paid employment only two to three days per week, and being equally-paid for equally-productive labor, equalizes the earnings of all relative to their productivity. It also does away with the huge blocks of wealth formerly extracted from its proper owners through **aristocratic exclusive title to nature's resources and technologies, denying others their rightful share of what nature offers to all for free.**

Beyond application, approval, accounting, and brick and mortar costs, recoverable at a ½ of 1% interest rate on loans, there is no one within a banking system applying anything other than normal mental or physical labor. Therefore, though all are entitled to be well paid, no one is entitled to the unearned profits earned through 6-24% interest charges or the many other methods of bankers to extract wealth properly belonging to others. The ethereal world of high finance will have disappeared.

By raising required reserves in step with the creation of money, it is possible to create money for a developing region's first industries and infrastructure. As the economy develops, industries can be financed from savings and infrastructure from resource rents paid to society. By raising mandated reserves every two months for a year, and by creating money (increasing base money) at an annual 18% rate during that timespan, China has proved its viability. Though China may still run into trouble because her money being spendable outside her borders leaves her vulnerable to financial warfare, other developing regions will be studying that model. It will work beautifully so long as you use a currency spendable only within the borders of a region and handle trade between regions through a world trading currency as China, Russia, Brazil, India, and others are petitioning for as we speak.

Honestly-earned depositor savings are entitled to interest on their stored labor. They should be rewarded and we do so through, as outlined above, the payment of interest on savings at the high end of long term averages, 3%. Operating costs are ½ of 1%. The key is what is done with the profits of 2-to-6% earned by socially-owned banks charging modest interest rates. No one's labor is involved beyond that of well-paid managers, accountants, and clerks within the banking system and we have deemed monopolies structured through aristocratic exclusive titles to technology (their licenses) are the heart of the current monopolized banking system. So, beyond brick and mortar, there are few tangible, labor-created, values to own. Thus the proper recipient of bank interest, above operational costs, is society itself.[c]

With **society paying banking profits to themselves**, those social-credits fund universal health care, retirement and other essential services. As all funds are returned to society collectively, effectively there is, just as preached in the Bible and Koran, effectively no interest. Society has simply taxed the loan structure in the form of an annual percentage on outstanding loans. The differential between the 3% paid savers and that charged borrowers and the charges for resource rents would be balanced to cover government costs, building and maintenance of infrastructure, universal health care, retirement and other essential social costs.

Once the world is developed to a sustainable level, as we demonstrate in the Conclusion can be done within two generations, the wealthy world will have repaid the struggling world for 500 years of slavery and plunder through which the massive wealth of the imperial nations was accumulated. At that point, interest and resource rents society pays to itself should, except for those protecting against resource depletion and environmental degradation, be reduced to the level required to operate a peaceful federated world. To not federate means continual war. **To federate under full and equal economic rights for all would mean peace for all time.**[19]

The elimination of banking monopolies through socially-owned banking, with the profits **paid to society, and spent on infrastructure**, **universal health care, retirements, and other essential social needs**, engenders an economic efficiency gain equal to the invention of the printing press. This increased efficiency would require democratic and communitarian oversight to conserve the earth's resources and protect the environment (see Conclusion).

Interest can be analyzed from another direction. Industrial capital is composed of factories (a series of tools efficiently producing) and businesses which produce and distribute consumer products. Honest finance capital is only a

---

[c] We have already demonstrated that 95% of current finance capital is unearned and unproductive so it should never have been extracted from the citizenry in the first place. Though billions in interest is paid to them every day, in an honest, moral, economy none of that interest or principal would be owed.

symbol for industrial capital. Without industrial capital (tools) all a person can do is pick fruit and nuts off of trees, catch a few small animals, etc. With tools (industrial capital that can be as small as an ax, a shovel, a bow and arrow, or a wrench) one can do a lot of work and thus produce substantial wealth. Without those tools, industrial capital, nothing can be produced.

The claim is made by some monetary theorists that private banks create money by making loans but do not create the money to pay interest on those loans. We have shown that capital (both industrial and honestly earned financial capital) is just as productive as labor, actually far more so. It is stored labor; it produces wealth efficiently, and thus should be well paid. Interest on this honest capital, as opposed to unearned wealth, is a necessary cost and it earns its own way, just as does labor. The statement that no money is created to pay interest is not valid. Honest finance capital, a representation of productive industrial capital, is even more productive than labor (try producing anything without tools which is stored labor [industrial capital]), and should be well paid.

On OpEdNews.com, Ellen Brown just published "The Mysterious CAFRs: How Stagnant Pools of Government Money Could Help Save the Economy."

Many states are looking into her recent work pointing out that other states should copy North Dakota, establish a state bank, and, by law, keep state and community monies in that bank. Ms. Brown points out that most of the states are receiving almost nothing for their banked money just as you receive almost nothing for the funds sitting in your bank accounts.

If the states set up their own bank, and all government agencies banked there by law, they could receive respectable interest on their average bank balances, while charging more modest interest to government entities which need to borrow money.

What she has proposed in a modest way is exactly what we have proposed, socially-owned and operated banks. And we have said exactly what she says is possible; depositors can be paid higher interest and borrowers can be charged lower interest.

In both our theories, both Ms. Brown's and ours, is that the unearned interest going to the ethereal world of high finance is transposed into honest earnings, going into the social fund where it is available to fund essential social services.

The only difference is that Ms. Brown is proposing a modest move towards socially-owned banks as an example of how we can soften the current collapse of state, county, and community monies while we have assumed the banksters will retain control, keep pouring the bailout funds at themselves, and only after a total collapse will they be pushed aside, and a honest restructuring of the banks, and then economy, be possible.

If Ellen Brown's proposals are followed, the financial pressures on the state will be alleviated. When the public learns they would get respectable interest on all deposits, they will move their money to those state banks. If that reached its logical conclusion, state banks would either replace private banks, or private banks would pay honest interest. In either case, the unearned profits would no longer go to the banksters; it would go to the depositors as their "earned" money.

In Ms. Brown's case there would be an increase in funds for essential social services. In our proposals, going all the way, virtually every social need, infrastructure, governments, education, health care, retirement, and all other social services, all currently—and intentionally—starved for money, would be fully funded.

Both Professors Michael Hudson and William K. Black have pointed out that the financial industries share of all profits was 2% 40 years ago, and today it is 40%. Finance capital is only the money symbol of industrial capital and operating funds. Ever-more efficient technology steadily lowers industrial capital costs. Thus finance capital costs, and profits, should be lower, not higher. I thank them for quantifying the unearned, unproductive, share; it is 95% of all finance capital.

We now turn to how full and equal economic rights requires society collecting resource (land) rents to provide social-credits for funding governments, building and maintaining infrastructure; for providing education, health care and retirements, and for any other essential social service.

[1] Joel Kurtzman, *The Death of Money* (New York: Simon and Schuster, 1993), p. 11.

[2] William Greider, *Secrets of the Temple* (New York: Simon and Schuster, 1987), p. 335.

[3] John Kenneth Galbraith, *Money* (Boston: Houghton Mifflin, 1976), pp. 62-70.

[4] Ibid, pp. 167-78; Greider, *Secrets of the Temple,* pp. 228, 282.

[5] John Kenneth Galbraith, *Money* (Boston: Houghton Mifflin, 1976), pp. 62-70.

[6] S. P. Breckinridge, *Legal Tender* (NY: Greenwood Press, 1969), cha 7; Galbraith, *Money,* pp. 72-75.

[7] *Carl Cohen, Editor, Communism, Fasism, Democracy* (New York: Random House, 1962), pp. 13-14; Paul Kennedy, *The Rise and Fall of Great Powers* (NY: Random House, 1987), p. 53.

[8] Galbraith, *Money, pp. 18-19.*

[9] Paul Kennedy, *The Rise and Fall of the Great Powers. New York: Random House,* 1987, p. 53.

[10] E.K. Hunt, Howard J. Sherman, *Economics* (NY: Harper & Row, 1990), pp. 491-93, 505-508.

[11] William Greider, *Secrets of the Temple: How the Federal Reserve Runs the country* (NY: Simon & Schuster, 1987) throughout but especially pp. 49-50, 380; James Livingston's *Origins of the Federal Reserve System: Money, Class, and Corporate Capitalism, 1890 to 1913* (Cornell University Press, 1986), chapters 7 & 8; and John Kenneth Galbraith, *Money: Whence it Came, Where it Went,* (Boston: Houghton Mifflin, 1995), pp. 176-83, 188, especially pp. 134, 144, 177-90, 195-96, 199-200

[12] MMM, http://landru.i-link-2.net/monques/ mmm2.html or run a Google search.

[13] William Greider, *Secrets of the Temple: How the Federal Reserve Runs the country* (NY: Simon & Schuster, 1987) throughout but especially pp. 31, 49-50, 280; James Livingston's *Origins of the Federal Re serve System: Money, Class, and Corporate Capitalism, 1890 to 1913* (Cornell University Press, 1986), chapters 7 & 8; and John Kenneth Galbraith, *Money: Whence it Came, Where it Went,* (Boston: Houghton Mifflin, 1995), pp. 176-83, 188, especially pp. 134, 144, 177-90, 195-96, 199-200

[14] Hixon, *Triumph,* chapter 5.

[15] Ibid.

[16] Ibid

[17] Robert Swann, *Need for Local Currencies* (Great Barrington, MA, E.F. Schumacher Society, 1990), p. 6.

[18] George Tucker, *Theory of Money and Banks Investigated* (NY: Greenwood Press, 1968), pp. 219, 255.

[19] Errol E. Harris, *Earth Federation Now: Tomorrow is too Late* (www.ied.info: the Institute for Economic Democracy, 2005; Glen Martin, *Basic Documents of the Emerging Earth Federation* (www.ied.info: the Institute for Economic Democracy, 2006).

2. A Modern Land Commons, Citizens Paying Resource Rents to themselves

Land, minerals and other aspects of nature's wealth are subtly monopolized by private collection of rental values on what nature offers free to all. This monopolization of social wealth started centuries ago as the powerful structured superior rights into ownership of land. These first privatizations laid the base for the theft of your and my wealth today. As British Prime Minister Winston Churchill said, land is "by far the greatest of monopolies—it is a perpetual monopoly, and it is the mother of all other forms of monopoly."[1] This chapter is essentially Henry George's thesis.[2] Monopolizations of industrial and social technologies, banking etc, were patterned off land monopolies but go well beyond his writings.

When resource rents are privately collected, it is "an extraction of uncompensated value" (run a Google search for **rent-seeking**) properly belonging to all in roughly equal shares. As society collects its full due in resource rents (meaning **the citizens are paying those rental values to themselves**) all private-property use rights are retained. As the initial cost of land drops to zero, ownership of land for homes, businesses, and production will be a human and community right. With resource rents and banking profits replacing all taxes and fully funding all essential social services, land for homes and businesses would, on balance, cost nothing. Those rental values coming back to all citizens as social-credits financing infrastructure, health care, retirement, running governments, and other essential services, means society is quintuply repaid for restructuring to **paying resource rents to themselves** (to the social fund). Eliminating monopolization would not only increase your right to land and the profits from its productive use, it would ensure that human right.

Reclaiming Your Share of Wealth Produced by Nature

If a person were born with fully developed intelligence, physical ability, and judgment, but without social conditioning, one of the first confusing realities he or she would face is that all land belongs to someone else. Before one could legally stand, sit, lie down, or sleep, he or she would have to pay, or have the implicit permission of, whoever owned that piece of land. This is absurd. Air, water, and land nurture all life and each living thing requires, and is surely entitled to, living space on this earth. No person produced any part of it, it was here when each was born, and their share of its bounty is everybody's common right:

> The first man who, having enclosed a piece of ground, bethought himself as saying "this is mine," and found people simple enough to believe him, was the real founder of civil society. From how many crimes, wars, and murders, from how many horrors and misfortunes might not any one have saved mankind, by pulling up the stakes, or filling up the ditch, and crying to his fellows: "Beware of listening to this impostor; you are undone if you once forget that the fruits of the earth belong to us all, and the earth itself to nobody."[3]

Jean Jacques Rousseau, in A Discourse on the Origins of Inequality, was outlining the injustice of one person having exclusive title to another's living space. This practice is only social conditioning (spin, perception management) locking society within belief systems. Being thoroughly conditioned, and having never experienced or imagined anything else, few realize that, under exclusive ownership of land and other aspects of nature's wealth—including mechanical, electrical, chemical, and social technologies—they do not have all their rights. Instead, the possibility of eventually owning one's piece of land, or a license to practice within a monopolized structure—banking, insurance, law or other social technologies—is viewed as full rights. Being conscious of the not-so-distant past when common people did not have even those rights; citizens view and celebrate these limited rights as full rights.

Mark Twain recognized that same alienation of nature's gifts in unrestricted private title by one person and loss of rights for others: "If he owned the entire world, all the wealth of the world would be his and all the world's citizens would be his slaves."

While one's lack of full and equal economic rights is difficult to visualize when a person is accustomed to exclusive ownership to what nature provided free for all; it is easy to see if one uses a gift of nature, such as air, that has not yet been alienated from the commons. Air is one of nature's gifts and if a group could claim title to it (when windmills were invented such efforts were made), each person would have to pay for the right to breathe just as now they have to pay for the right for a place to live.

Water was still free long after land was fully claimed. As population density increased and water became scarce, it has become profitable to claim exclusive title to water. With those exclusive titles to water recorded at the courthouse, water sources develop high capitalized values, society becomes accustomed to paying dearly for its drinking water, and more unearned wealth is banked.

Instead of society wasting that wealth paying non-producing monopolists, each one's proper share of nature's bounty should be paid by, and distributed right back to, all citizens through socially-collected resource rents providing the social-credits to fund infrastructures, education, universal health care, retirement, running governments, etc. The secondary monopolies—again insurance, health care, law, etc—are social technologies with only modest amounts of tangible, labor-created, values, but high monopoly values. Each one's proper share of values to which they have a natural right is assured by replacing marketing rights (licenses within a monopolized structure) with social rights or human rights to those services.

Pride in Ownership Must be Maintained

Land is, unquestionably, social wealth. However, the right to one's space on this earth, the pride it returns to its owner, and the care normally given to one's personal property, are compelling reasons to keep land under a conditional form of private ownership. If equal rights for all to a share of the production of land are acknowledged through society collecting resource rents, private ownership is socially efficient and fully justifiable. What is unjust is the unrestricted monopolization of the natural resources that nature freely provides on, above, and under, land. It is necessary to keep private ownership of land and resources while eliminating monopolization and its unavoidable inequities

The Feudal Origins of Land Titles

Societies have battled for title to land for millennia. One society's violent claim to land is another society's violent loss. Today's landowners are the descendants of the winners of the latest clashes of cultures. After the collapse of the Roman Empire at the hands of the Germanic tribes, the common people regained their rights to the land, and the use of nature's wealth in common again developed a powerful following.[4] Their belief in freedom and natural rights resembles our belief (but not our practice) in these principles today.

However, this reversion to social wealth in public ownership came under attack by powerful clans. Petr Kropotkin, a unique historian, describes the repression of these rights as the origin of the modern state: "Only wholesale massacres by the thousand could put a stop to this widely spread popular movement, and it was by the sword, the fire, and the rack that the young states secured their first and decisive victory over the masses of the people." Those people were struggling against imposition of a legal structure (privatization) which protected aristocratic exclusive titles to land, and all the resources on and under the land, previously owned and used by all in common.[a]

---

[a] In *The Earth Belongs to Everyone*, chapter 1, published by this institute, Alanna Hartzok addresses the formalization of the privatization process into modern law as starting with the Statute of Merton in England in 1235. Many other authors address important aspects of

As described by Kropotkin, the medieval roots of our culture grimly parallel the massive slaughter in many countries of the emerging world today. People in these countries are fighting to retain, or reclaim, their right to a fair share of the earth's wealth, those resources now owned by the cultural descendants of earlier violent thefts of land. The resemblance here is not a coincidence; current struggles are a continuation of that medieval battle over who shall have rights to nature's wealth and, as we have stated and will be demonstrating further, today's land titles are feudal exclusive property rights. However unjust, if legal title to land or any other gift of nature can be established (the privatization process) those with unrestricted title can, through the collection of rental values or various overcharges, lay claim to wealth produced by others.

In the 14ᵗʰ century, the sharing of social wealth in common was still practiced by local communities. But, tragically, that century saw the beginning of a 300-year-effort by the aristocracy of Europe to erase all trace of communal rights. Kropotkin explains:

> The village communities were bereft of their folkmotes [community meetings], their courts and independent administration; their lands were confiscated. The guilds were spoilated of their possessions and liberties, and placed under the control, the fancy, and the bribery of the State's official. The cities were divested of their sovereignty, and the very springs of their inner life—the folkmote, the elected justices and administration, the sovereign parish and the sovereign guild—were annihilated; the State's functionary took possession of every link of what formerly was an organic whole. Under that fatal policy and the wars it engendered, whole regions, once populous and wealthy, were laid bare; rich cities became insignificant boroughs; the very roads which connected them with other cities became impracticable. Industry, art, and knowledge fell into decay.⁵

Though privatization of the commons started with the Statute of Merton in 1235, the continued efforts to alienate the individual from common use of the land are documented in Britain by the nearly 4,000 enclosure acts passed between 1760 and 1844 that effectively gave legal sanction to this theft.⁶ Those en-

that system of theft of wealth produced by others. The privatizations ongoing today are extensions of that same process, read *Shock Doctors,* by Naomi Klein. The rule of thumb is that privatizing the commons more than doubles costs and creates a mega wealthy class as it impoverishes the masses. The 50% overcharges today (those doubled costs) are the same 50% of a serf's production paid to aristocracy 300 to 800 years ago. Modern imperial law is only aristocratic law hiding under the beautiful words of capitalism and democracy. Lawmakers today are continually expanding those aristocratic rights and deferring to the rights of the masses only when the threat of ballot box revolutions is high.

As Co-Director of Earth Rights Institute, Alanna developed an online class on the social collection of rental values of land and resources (see www.earthrights.net).

closure acts were the continued privatizations which, in turn, are the continuations of **rent-seeking** legal structures (monopolizations) appropriating wealth properly belonging to others.

For the powerful to protect their aristocratic exclusive titles further, it was necessary to erase from social memory all traces of the earlier custom of social ownership of social wealth. Kropotkin points out, "It was taught in the universities and from the pulpit that the institutions in which men formerly used to embody their needs of mutual support could not be tolerated in a properly organized State."[7] Classics for the past 400 years justified that injustice and we hear those justifications yet today: "This is the most efficient and proper social structure."

The classic descriptions of the evolution of capitalism explain how trade and industrial capital usurped the preeminent position of nobility with their historical title to all land. Yet in parts of Europe an elite social class still owns large tracts of land. As late as 1961, the Duke of Bedford, the Duke of Westminster, and the British Crown owned the most valuable sections of London, and large estates still abound throughout the countryside. In fact, at the turn of the 20th century,

> the English upper class consisted ... of around ten thousand people drawn almost entirely from a core of 1,500 families.... The aristocracy owned great estates and houses and works of art—but, above all, they owned land. Well over ninety percent of the acreage of Britain was theirs.[8]

Today's neoliberal philosophies are the ongoing efforts to prevent a rekindling of mutual support beliefs and social wealth held in common. Today we are taught, by those who parrot the original disinformation, that an efficient economy requires all property being privately owned with each individual a "free" bargaining agent.

Our disagreement with current property rights law is that title to land, or any other gift of nature, including mechanical, chemical, electrical, and social technologies, should—since no person built this natural wealth and all are entitled to their share—be conditional. Exclusive title as opposed to conditional title is that remnant of feudal law which is the primary cause of today's inefficient economies creating a wealthy few, an impoverished many, and the many wars protecting power and wealth.

Private Ownership of Social Wealth Moves to America

Parts of America's land ownership were originally structured under the same aristocratic property rights as in Europe. The "manorial lords of the Hudson Valley" owned huge estates "where the barons controlled completely the lives of their tenants." One such estate in Virginia covered over five million acres and embraced 21 counties.[9] Such excessive greed contributed to the widespread dissatisfactions that fueled the American Revolution.

> Under Governor Benjamin Fletcher, three-quarters of the land in New York was granted to about thirty people. He gave a friend a half million acres for a token annual payment of 30 shillings. Under Lord Cornbury in the early 1700s one grant to a group of speculators was for two million acres.... In 1689, many of the grievances of the poor were mixed up in the farmers' revolt of Jacob Leisler and his group. Leisler was hanged, and the parceling out of huge estates continued.[10] [B]y 1698, New York had given thousands of acres to the Philipses, Van Cortlands, Van Rensselaers, Schuylers, Livingstons and Bayards; by 1754, Virginia had given almost three million acres to the Carters, Beverleys, and Pages—an early example of government "aid" to business men.[11] [Spanish land grants were even more extensive]

Despite the egalitarian rhetoric of the American Revolution and an attempt to place a proclamation in the Declaration of Independence for a "common right of the whole nation to the whole of the land," the powerful looked out for their own interests by changing the wording of Locke's insightful phrase: "All men are entitled to life, liberty and property." This powerful statement that all could understand, especially if they replaced the word property with "land," coming from a highly respected philosopher was a threat to those who monopolized that natural wealth. So they restructured those words to "life, liberty and [the meaningless phrase] pursuit of happiness." The substitution in America's Declaration of Independence of phrases which would protect every person's rights to nature's wealth for words that protect only the monopoly rights of a few should alert one to check the meaning, and purpose, of all laws of all societies carefully. Only portions of the huge estates described below were confiscated, and "speculations in western lands were one of the leading activities of capitalists in those days":[12]

> Companies were formed in Europe and America to deal in Virginia lands, which were bought up in large tracts at the trifling cost of two cents per acre. This wholesale engrossment soon consumed practically all the most desirable lands and forced the home seeker to purchase from speculators or to settle as a squatter. "[Moreover, observes Beard], as the settler sought to escape the speculator by moving westward, the frontier line of speculation advanced."[13]

Some of America's famous leaders were deeply involved:

> In the Ohio Valley a number of rich Virginia planter families, amongst whom were counted both the Lees and the Washingtons, had formed a land company and this, the Ohio Company, founded in 1748, was given a crown grant of half a million acres.[14] [And with] every member of the Georgia legislature but one [having] acquired a personal interest in the speculation schemes, [they sold thirty-five] "million

acres to three ... land speculating companies for a total payment of less than $210,000.[15] [That is six-tenths of a cent per acre. Thus,] as the frontier was pushed back during the first half of the nineteenth century, land speculators working with banks [and corrupt legislators] stayed just ahead of new immigrants, buying up land cheap and then reselling it at high profits.[16]

Those who participated in these later land grabs knew the route to wealth lay in claiming exclusive title to land so those who followed would have to buy or rent it from them. Whether rented, or sold at high capitalized values, a share of the wealth produced each year would be siphoned to those owners without expenditure of their labor.

Individuals, such as the butcher's son John Jacob Astor who had title to much of Manhattan Island, became immensely wealthy. Matthew Josephson, in *Robber Barons*, and Peter Lyon, in *To Hell in a Day Coach*, document the greatest land grab in history when the railroads, through control of state and federal governments, obtained unrestricted title to 183 million acres of land, 9.3% of the land in the United States. By the turn of the century this included "more than one-third of Florida, one-fourth of North Dakota, Minnesota, and Washington and substantial chunks of 25 other states."[17]

> The state of Texas was the most generous of all: at one point they had actually given away about eight million more acres than they had in their power to bestow; as it finally turned out, they forked over to twelve railroad companies more than thirty-two million acres, which is more real estate than can be fitted inside the boundaries of the state of New York.[18]

Those to whom this land was parceled out had taken care to buy Congress and codify their aristocratic exclusive titles in legal statutes, inequality structured into unequal property rights law. The arrival of the railroads provided easy access to these lands and made them valuable. Instead of immigrants being allowed to choose land on a first-come first-served basis and using its rental value to develop social infrastructure, the land-hungry poor were forced to buy from these profiteers. Land sales by speculators were contracts siphoning to the speculator a part of the future labor of those who bought the land.

America's celebrated Homestead Act of 1862 came after most of the choice land had already been claimed by speculators. Some 600,000 pioneers received 80 million acres under this act, but this was less than half that allotted to the railroad barons, who were only the latest in a long line of profiteers. These new lords of the land thoroughly understood the legal mechanics of siphoning wealth properly belonging to others to themselves. They knew all the surplus land had to be owned before their land could have significant value, thus the Homestead Act was vital to their plans of attaining great wealth.

Saleable Land Titles Permitted the Mobilization of Capital

Once land had been confiscated from the masses in the Middle Ages, it belonged permanently to the lord of that land, and could only be lost through war. When English law changed to permit the sale of land, this created the foundation for modern monopoly capitalism. When an entrepreneur wished to speculate by building a factory or ship, land could be mortgaged for that venture. Monetizing (capitalizing) the value of land provided a broader base of wealth for loans than loaning against potential profits from monopoly trade rights issued to favored friends by royalty.

The privatization of land and resultant mobilization of capital was a key stage in the development of capitalism that expanded rights to more people. However, those exclusive titles to nature's wealth still maintained the **aristocratic legal structure** which permitted nonproducers to claim wealth that should have been social-credits (those rental values) funding essential social needs.

An efficient economy will have neither those capitalized appropriated values (misnamed profits) nor the huge blocs of unearned capital currently buying and selling capitalized unearned values. When those exclusive titles are restructured to conditional titles, societies paying those rental values to themselves, the monopoly values (the 95% of finance capital that is unearned) are transposed into equally-shared use-values. There are no longer any unearned values for it to represent but money, once created, stays in existence until destroyed. The remaining 5% runs the economy efficiently. Thus, before a society can restructure, that massive, unneeded, finance capital must be destroyed by financial collapses.

Slave labor was also a method to accumulate capital and pockets of slavery remain today. Export platforms in the emerging world that avoid taxes and pollution laws and pay dimes per hour for workers to produce items for sale in the developed world, where workers with the same qualifications are paid $9 to $35 an hour, is a simple capital accumulation scheme akin to slavery.

The forced acceptance of opium sales to China a century ago, and the turn-a-round sales of drugs to the developed world today, accumulates capital. Charging Japan's well-paid citizens triple the price for Japanese manufactures or food as the same item would cost in Europe or America is also a capital accumulation scheme.

The "Robber Barons" of the late 19th and early 20th centuries accumulated capital at great cost to all others in America. That cost is not acknowledged because, even with massive destruction of natural wealth, timber, topsoil, etc, the remaining vast resources could still provide a good living for the relatively small population. The timber burned to clear the land could have provided a fine set of hardwood furniture for every family on earth, and topsoil could have been preserved to feed people for millenniums.

Through hard work, frugality or good fortune, a family owns a valuable piece of land. When the breadwinner's buying power decreases or ceases due to death, tracts of land are sold off piecemeal to maintain the accustomed standard of living. All money from land sales deposited within the banking system as savings become part of the nation's privately owned finance capital. Eventually all the tracts of land are sold, some of the money becomes accumulated capital, and the part spent to maintain the family, that also could have been accumulated capital if that person had worked for his or her living, becomes consumed capital.

John Jacob Astor's aristocratic exclusive titles to a large share of—and piecemeal sale of—Manhattan Island, is probably America's leading example of wealth accumulation through land monopolization. As tracts of land became smaller and smaller, and their capitalized (monopoly) values, rose higher and higher. The values unrealized (potential capital), the capital wasted through high living of heirs, and the enormous monopolized values encroaching others' rights, tells us transposing privately collected rental values into social-credits is far more efficient.

A simple adjustment in the law, paying resource rents to themselves (resource rents paid into a social fund), and those funds building infrastructure and providing other social needs attains those rights. The "mother of all monopolies," the private taxation of land, will have been eliminated; each will have rights to their share of the wealth produced by nature.

Profound Thinkers Who Believed in Society Collecting Resource Rent

The French Physiocrats were the originators of laissez faire, the philosophy of little government interference. They held as a cornerstone of their beliefs—extended from the work of Jean Jacques Rousseau, John Locke, William Penn, and Richard Cantillon 50 to 100 years earlier—that society should **pay resource rents to themselves** (to their government). One of their most respected members, Mirabeau the Elder, held that this would increase social efficiency equal to the inventions of writing or money. Note: These theorists were royalists who would point those rental values towards the king and their thesis is only of value if those rental values are returned to the citizenry in the form of economic infrastructure and social services.

David Ricardo formulated the law of rent which supports the logic of Mirabeau's statement. Put in simple terms, Ricardo's law of rent means all income above that necessary to sustain labor will be claimed by the owners of the land without the expenditure of "their" labor. A land monopolist retains ownership of land until some innovative entrepreneur sees its potential for more productive use. The high price demanded effectively siphons a part of the wealth produced by that entrepreneur to the previous owner, now the holder of that mortgage and sales contract. Ricardo, not theorizing the proper recipient of resource rents being society itself, testifies to his being a "justifying" philosophy.

Adam Smith's statement "every improvement in the circumstances of society raises rent" tells us he knew titles to land claim much of the wealth produced by the increased efficiencies of society.[19] The respected economist John Kenneth Galbraith, although questioning changing tax policy at this late date, accepted the justice of society collecting resource rents. In 1978, the conservative economist Milton Friedman stated, "In my opinion the least bad tax is the property tax on the unimproved value of land."[20]

Earlier philosophers who believed in the free enterprise philosophy of the Physiocrats—"society collecting the land rent"—include Thomas Paine, who is credited with proposing much of the Bill of Rights; William Penn, Herbert Spencer, the noted philosopher in his classic Social Statics; Thomas Sperry of the Newcastle Philosophical Society; and philosopher John Stuart Mill. These early economists were not radicals. They all "believed in the sacredness of private property, particularly land."[21]

Besides Henry George, the leading theorists on the subject, the Robert Schalkenbach Foundation lists over 100 more famous thinkers —including Confucius, Moses, Thomas Jefferson, Mark Twain, Henry Ford, John Maynard Keynes, Albert Einstein, President Eisenhower, and several popes—who recognized the principle that the natural product of the land belongs to all citizens. Also listed are various places in the modern world where these policies have been, at least in part, implemented.[22]

Commercial Land

As David Ricardo and Henry George taught us, the closer one approaches to the center of commerce, the higher the price of land. Every transit line from the suburbs to a commercial district raises commercial land values a calculable amount. This high value represents the cheapness and the quantity of trades within any population center and that savings, efficiency of trades, is recognized by the price business is willing to pay for that land.

Because rent lays claim to a large share of the wealth produced by commerce, land values are very high in large population centers. Land values gradually lower as the distance from the center of population becomes greater and the trades become less frequent and more expensive. In a matter of minutes on an acre in the middle of a city there would be millions of dollars' worth of trades in grain, diamonds, stocks, land, finance capital, or consumer products. A share of each trade is remitted to the landowner as rent, thus the high value of land within population centers.

It is not unusual for commercial land to be valued at three, four, or even 10 times the value of the buildings placed upon it. Probably the highest priced acre in the world was in the center of Tokyo, valued, before prices dropped over 75%, at $1.5 billion. The space of one footprint in Tokyo was valued at $8,000. The land area of the 23 wards of Tokyo was equal in monetary value to the entire land area of the United States. The land upon which the emperor's palace sat was valued at the price of all the land in California. All the land in tiny Japan was worth four times as much as all the land in America. "In fact, the real estate value of Tokyo [in 1989] at $7.7 trillion [was] so high that, once collateralized and borrowed against (at 80% of [the then] current value), it could buy all the land in the United States for $3.7 trillion, and all the companies on the New York Stock Exchange, NASDAQ and several other exchanges for $2.6 trillion."

Farm Land

The quality of farmland depends on rainfall, growing season, fertility, and accessibility to markets. Once the quality has lowered to where one can earn only the wages expended in production or distribution at the margins, meaning the economic edge of profits, the land's value reaches zero.

By exporting food to countries that—if their lands, resources, and trade were not monopolized—could just as well feed themselves, and by farming the public Treasury, agriculture in the United States has made handsome profits and evaded Ricardo's law of rent. Resource rents from the monopoly created by those laws, are capitalized into, and maintain the unearned capitalized value of, farm land. Under Ricardo's law, but without subsidized sales to countries able to feed themselves if this cheap food was barred from their shores, the price of the current high priced farm land of America would be almost zero.

Home Sites

In smaller cities of America, a typical $240,000 house will be on a $120,000 lot. In major population centers, it is not uncommon for the same house to cost double, triple, or even 10 times that price. In Honolulu and parts of California a comparable home would be over $1 million and in Washington, DC it would be $1.6 million. As labor and material costs are relatively equal, the price differentials are the costs of land functioning under Ricardo's law of rent. The price of land accurately measures the resource rents collected by landowners without the expenditure of their labor.

The powerbrokers took from Locke, the Physiocrats, and others, only that which protected and further extended their wealth and power. As historically most members of legislative bodies were large landholders, naturally they did not accept that society should collect resource rents. If that were to happen, everyone would have a right to their share of nature's wealth. The "divine rights" of private ownership of social wealth, siphoning large amounts of wealth to those who did no productive labor (those who owned those monopoly values bought and sold on the markets), would be converted to "conditional rights" where only those who produce are paid.

Take homes for example: real estate taxes are currently levied mostly on the improvements and only a small part on the land. That tax structure is the key to land monopolization. Removing all taxes on the house and society charging full rental value on all lots, used and empty, drops home-site land prices to zero.

As the monetized (monopolized) value of the land disappears, its use-values increase. The purchase price would be only the value of labor and material that built the house. The initial capital required to purchase a home would drop to the cost of building the house, or the depreciated value of an older home.

The social collection of resource rents eliminates all other taxes, and lowers the purchase price of homes and businesses 50 to 90%. Those socially-collected rents—along with banking profits[b]—transpose into social-credits building and maintaining a nation's infrastructure, running governments, providing education, universal health care, and funding retirements. That is at least a quintuple gain over monopolists collecting those rental values and loaning that unearned money back to those from which it was extracted.

Though the purchase price of home and business sites are zero, each paying annual land rents to the social-credit fund, lowers the monthly purchase cost of homes and businesses to slightly less than current costs. However, former unearned profits are now social-credit funds, taxes have disappeared, and all social needs (not personal needs) are fully funded; thus the quintuple gains through society paying resource rental values to themselves.

Occasionally a city council person will become aware of the social efficiency of taxing unused land within their jurisdiction. If that idle land is properly taxed it will quickly be put to use. But these alert officials quickly find that powerbrokers have inserted restrictions into state constitutions and passed state laws on local communities' ability to tax land.

Land held in unrestricted private ownership entitles the owners to large rental values which create high capitalized (monopoly) values. True free enterprise, economic efficiency, and fully funded social needs, requires society collecting

---

[b] The private collection of land rent is "The extraction of uncompensated value from others." Because there are few tangible (labor produced) values within banking proper, so is the private collection of banking profits.

those natural resource rental values. Distribution of land by price (capitalized value) would then be replaced by distribution of land by rental value paid to society and that money returned to the citizenry through paying for the social services described above, all taxes eliminated, etc. The initial cost to the homeowner would be slightly lower, much lower if Mason Gaffney and Fred Harrison's estimation of 35% of national income being resource rent is correct, and there would be no interception of others' labor through private collection of rent on what nature provided to all for free; thus the gains have quintupled.

Oil, copper, iron and other ores are land and can very properly be privately owned so long as the resource rents are returned right back to society in the form of social-credits funding social needs. The world has adequate reserves of most of these minerals. It is only richer deposits and cheaper labor in the emerging world that make their minerals more available. Under Adam Smith's unequal free market philosophy, the developed world's more expensive deposits are not mined until the "**resource powers**" cheap deposits are exhausted.

Developing land—clearing, drainage projects, shaping the land, irrigation dams, canals, and so forth— require special consideration. Those who invest in such improvements should be well paid. However, unconditional title to land development becomes exclusive title to the land. Currently the government pays a substantial share of development costs. Investor-developers can be fully reimbursed by liberal deductions of the remaining costs from resource rents.

The market measures the rent value of land. The resource rents paid by society would be slightly less than that now collected both publicly (taxes) and privately (interest). The price spread of resource rents between the choice sites and lower-valued sites must be maintained. The current private resource tax, both interest and rent, are converted to socially-collected land rent that would be slightly lower than the former combination of taxes and land payments.

Society Paying Resource Rents to Themselves and Taxes Disappearing is Key to the Community Social-credit Process

According to Gore Vidal:

In 1986 the gross revenue of the government was $794 billion. Of that amount, $294 billion was Social Security contributions, which should be subtracted from the National Security State. This leaves $500 billion. Of the $500 billion $286 billion went to defense; $12 billion to foreign arms to our client states; $8 billion to $9 billion to energy, which means, largely, nuclear weapons; $27 billion to veterans' benefits, the sad and constant reminder of the ongoing empire's recklessness; and finally, $142 billion to loans that were spent, over the past forty years, to keep the National Security State at war, hot or cold. So, of 1986's $500 billion in revenue, $475 billion was spent on National Security business.... Other Federal spending, incidentally, came to $177 billion ... which is about the size of the deficit, since only $358 billion was collected in taxes.[23]

In 1929, federal government expenditures were 1% of GNP and at the peak of the Cold War they were approximately 24%.[24] David Stockman calculated that after deducting bureaucratic waste and payments to

> law firms and lobbyists and trade associations in rows of shining office buildings along K Street in Washington; the consulting firms and contractors; the constituencies of special interests, from schoolteachers to construction workers, to failing businesses and multinational giants, all of whom came to Washington for money and legal protection against the perils of free competition ... that leaves seventeen cents for everything else that Washington does. The FBI and national parks, the county agents and the Foreign Service and the Weather Bureau—all the traditional operations of government—consumed only nine cents of each dollar. The remaining eight cents provided all the grants to state and local governments, for aiding handicapped children or building highways.[25]

As those valuations are no longer kept, extrapolating from 1990 land values of $3.7 trillion,[26] we can safely say 2010 values of land were well over $10 trillion. Resource rents at 4% of value would be over $400 billion per year. That is over three times the percentage of GDP that ran the peaceful American government in 1929[c] and to that must be added the resource rents from oil, minerals, timber, etc. To those rental values we must add profits collected once banks are socially-owned. Obviously, society will have adequate funds for all essential services.

When necessary to regulate commerce, other taxes are proper, but those funds should also be returned to society through social services. For example, ecological taxes can support pollution-free energy development and resource conservation. The proper level of sin taxes, alcohol, tobacco, etc, would lower disease through lowering consumption and the funds collected would offset health care costs incurred from such habits.

Machinery and inventory are relatively easy to obtain; it is the price of land that restricts ownership of farms, businesses and homes. While land prices would drop close to zero, use-values and productive ownership rights would increase. Commerce would flourish as business people, farmers, and other entrepreneurs, all true producers, would be able to start businesses with only the

---

[c] The 2007 budget was $2.4 trillion. But Social Security is a paid-for insurance, not rightly part of that budget, and that also applies to health care. With costs hidden in other parts of the budget, the actual cost of the military is far above the $439.3 billion listed. Assuming Stockman's estimate that only 17 cents of each budget dollar will operate "all the traditional operations of government," those needs in that year's budget were $470 billion.

capital necessary to buy buildings, machinery, and inventory. They do not have to purchase monopoly values that, now in the form of much lower use-values, belong to everyone.

Resource rent being paid to society out of cash flow means only hard working and talented people would own farms and businesses. Labor costs to industries and businesses would be reduced by whatever taxes labor previously paid. The elimination of all taxes, and a lowering of finance capital costs makes replacing all taxes with socially collected resource rents and banking profits a bargain for any business.

Although society would be enormously richer, land will not have monetized (capitalized [monopolized]) value against which money can be loaned. The sale value would be calculated as the rental value one pays to society monthly or, as in the case of farmers, annually. Society, not the landowners, puts that value there by increased population, education, roads, water systems, sewers, electricity, communication systems, etc. Resource rents, profits of socially-owned banks, and all other rental values from nature's resources and technologies would be returned to the people through the cost of social services—measured in employed labor time to provide it—dropping at least 50%. Opportunities to extract wealth from its proper owners will be almost nonexistent, and all would be well cared for, even as all the functions and services of government (universal health care, retirement, infrastructures, etc.) are well funded.

When society collects the rental values of the land and natural resources, which nature offers to us all for free, the huge blocs of capital, previously buying and selling those capitalized appropriated values must be destroyed. The high values they represented, have been transposed into much lower, equally-shared, use-values. Each now has a human right to their share of land and resources for homes, businesses, or industries. If the remaining productive jobs are shared, and labor paid equally for equally-productive work, those quintuple gains from abandoning the private collection of rental values (rights to land at no initial costs as a human right, those socially-collected social-credits building economic infrastructure, and no taxes to pay) will become even greater gains by employment outside the home lowering to two to three days per week. Each citizen of that society, or the world if so applied, will have the opportunity for a quality life.

Michael Hudson and Baruch A. Levine, in *Privatization in the Ancient Ne ar East and Clas sical World*, trace the 5,000 year history of privatization of nature's wealth. Restructuring those aristocratic exclusive titles to conditional titles, as applied in this thesis, has, in one stroke, retained the claimed efficiencies of privatization—private property, individualism, competition—even as it restores, in modern form, the commons that was the original economic structure for every people on earth. A study of the five books on property rights law in this footnote will alert one that this subject is in continual discussion in America's courtrooms and collective rights trump private rights if it can be shown as imperative and just.[d]

---

[d] Laura Underkufler, *The Idea of Property: Its Meaning and Power*; Janet Dine, Andres Fagan, editors, *Human Rights and Capitalism;* Marjorie Kelly, *The Divine Right of Capital: Dethroning Corporate Aristocracy*; Stephen R. Munzer, *A Theory of Property;* Jeremy Waldron, *The Right to Property*

---

[1] M Gaffney & F Harrison, *Corruption of Economics*, (London: Shepheard-Walwyn, 1994), pp. 13, 193.

[2] All works of Henry George and many authors writing on him are available from the Robert Schalkenbach Foundation, 41 E 72 St, NY, NY 10021 (212.988.1680)

[3] Michael Parenti, *Power and the Powerless* (New York: St. Martin's Press 1978), pp. 184-85, quoting Jean Jacques Rousseau, "A Discourse on the Origins of Inequality," in The *Social Contract and Discourses* (New York: Dutton, 1950), pp. 234-85.

[4] Kropotkin, Petr, Mutual Aid, (Boston: Porter Sargent Publishing Co., no date) p. 225.

[5] Ibid., p. 226

[6] Ibid., pp. 234-35

[7] Ibid., p. 226. Read also George Renard's *Guilds in the Middle Ages* (New York: Augustus M. Kelley, 1968), chapters 7-8.

[8] Lewis Mumford, *The City in History* (New York: Harcourt Brace Jovanovich, 1961), p. 264; Angela Lambert, *Unquiet Souls* (New York: Harper and Row, 1984), p. 6.

[9] Charles A. Beard, *Economic Interpretation of the Constitution* (New York: Macmillan, 1941), p. 28; Howard Zinn, *A People's History of the United States* (New York: Harper Colophon Books, 1980), p. 48.

[10] Zinn, *People's History*, p. 48. See also Howard Zinn, *The Politics of History* (Chicago: University of Chicago Press, 1990), pp. 61-68.

[11] Herbert Aptheker, *The Colonial Era* (New York: International Publishers, 1966), pp. 37-38.

[12] Zinn, People's History, p. 83; Herbert Aptheker, The American Revolution (New York: International Publishers, 1985), p. 264, quoted in Beard, Economic Interpretation, p. 23; Petr Kropotkin, The Great French Revolution (New York: Black Rose Books, 1989), p. 143.

[13] Beard, *Economic Interpretation*, pp. 23, 27-28, quoting C.H. Ambler.

[14] Olwen Hufton, *Europe: Privilege and Protest* (Ithaca, NY: Cornell University Press, 1980), p. 113.

[15] Herbert Aptheker, *Early Years of the Republic* (New York: International Publishers, 1976), p. 125; Abraham Bishop, *Georgia Speculation Unveiled* (Readex Microprint Corporation, 1966), in forward.

[16] James Wessel, Mort Hartman, *Trading the Future* (San Francisco: Institute for Food and Development Policy, 1983), p. 14.

[17] Quoted by Peter Lyon, *To Hell in a Day Coach* (New York: J.B. Lippincott, 1968), p. 6. See also Edward Winslow Martin, *History of the Grange Movement* (New York: Burt Franklin, 1967); Joe E. Feagin, *Urban Real Estate Game* (Engelwood Cliffs, NJ: Prentice-Hall, Inc., 1983), pp. 57-58; speech by U.S. Representative Byron Dorgan, North Dakota, the statistics researched by his staff and quoted in *The North Dakota REC* (May 1984).

[18] Lyon, *To Hell in a Day Coach*, p. 6.

[19] Adam Smith, The Wealth of Nations (NY: Modern Library Ed, Random House, 1965), pp. 247, 647, 773-98.

[20] *101 Famous Thinkers on Owning Earth* (New York: Robert Schalkenbach Foundation); Durand Echeverria, *The Maupeou Revolution* (Baton Rouge: Louisiana University Press, 1985), p. 182; Guy Routh, *The Origin of Economic Ideas* (Dobbs Ferry, NY: Sheridan House, 1989), p. 62; John Kenneth Galbraith, *Economics in Perspective* (New York: Houghton Mifflin, 1987), chapter 5, especially pp. 55, 168; Mark Blaug, *Great American Economists Before Keynes* (Atlantic Highlands, NJ: Humanities Press International, 1986), p. 86.

[21] Herbert Spencer, *Social Statics* (New York: Robert Schalkenbach Foundation, 1995 unabridged edition); Dan Nadudere, *The Political Economy of Imperialism* (London: Zed Books, 1977), p. 186; Phil Grant, *The Wonderful Wealth Machine* (New York: Devon-Adair, 1953), pp. 416, 434-38; Hufton, *Privilege and Protest*, p. 113.

[22] 101 Famous Thinkers.

[23] Gore Vidal, "The National Security State: How To Take Back Our Country," The Nation, June 4, 1988, p. 782.

[24] E.K. Hunt, Howard J. Sherman, *Economics* (New York: Harper and Row, 1990), p. 511.

[25] Wm Greider, The Education of David Stockman and Other Americans (NY New American Library, 1986), pp. 6, 17.

[26] Samuelson, " Great Global Debtor," p. 40.

3. A Modern Technology Commons, Consumers Saving Fifty Percent or More

The original meaning of a patent was, "A grant made by a government that confers on an individual fee-simple title to public lands." This affirms our analysis that **patent monopolies were patterned after aristocratic exclusive titles to land.** Copying the legal design of land and patent monopolization, later monopolies were established through licenses.

Before the advent of industrial and finance capital, all sustenance for life and all wealth were processed directly from land. Finance capital is the money symbol for industrial and distribution operating capital, and these factories and distribution systems are only extremely efficient tools to process and distribute products from the land. So the monopolization of finance capital and industrial capital are only extensions of the monopolization of land. When wealth began to be produced by industrial capital as well as land, powerful people undertook to lay claim to (monopolize) those tools for the production of wealth just as historically they had monopolized land to lay claim to the wealth it produced.

If you claim technology is produced by labor and is not a part of nature, put yourself in the position of the rest of the world when denied its use even if independently invented. Or consider technology thousands of years old, patented within monopoly capitalism's unequal property rights laws, and denied its free use even to those who have used it for those millenniums.

We addressed a money system as a social structure known for centuries so, unless it is monopolized to lay claim to unearned wealth, and thus create a capitalized value, there is little there to own. All technologies are a part of nature waiting to be discovered and thus honest ownership can only be under conditions protecting the rights of all to their share of the wealth produced by efficient production and distribution technology.

Communication systems are a natural monopoly in the same sense as are sewers, water systems, electric systems, natural gas, roads, railroads, and garbage collections. It is well understood that duplicating such services through competing private ownerships is highly wasteful economic nonsense.

Social technologies are also a part of nature and such key knowledge has been monopolized whenever possible, money and banking for example. Systems of government are also social technologies and any thought of monopolizing governments would be ridiculed. Yet most governments are monopolized through power, witness the firm control of imperial governments throughout history by the very monopolies we are exposing.

For centuries, as modern economies developed, the hidden hands of the alert and powerful were busy structuring property rights to gain, or retain, title to wealth-producing sectors of the economy. Patent laws were being structured to monopolize technology; stock markets were being structured to both harvest those profits and further monopolize industries.

That stock markets are crucial to raising investment capital in a modern economy is a myth. Most stock traders have no contact with new issues of stock and those who do are primarily taking an already established private company public. Most corporate investment needs are financed from profits, liberal depreciation schedules, and borrowing. A stock is taken public primarily to put those values in play to join in the game of making money betting on whether stocks will go up or down, which is really gambling, not producing.

Expanding markets means increased profits capitalized into the value of a company's stock and, with the potential for profits thoroughly analyzed by the market; those capitalized values are claimed before those profits are banked. "Behind the abstraction known as 'the markets' lurks a set of institutions designed to maximize the wealth and power of the most privileged group of people in the world, the creditor-rentier class of the first world and their junior partners in the third."[1] Restructuring exclusive patent laws to pay inventors well, and place those patents in the public domain, would erase those centuries of carefully crafted monopoly laws. The purpose is to create unearned values above and beyond intrinsic values created by labor; in short, to monopolize values created by nature.

Under that simple legal change to conditional patent titles, the inventors are well paid and their patents placed in the pubic domain. The monopoly structure—85% of the offices and labor within stock markets where those profits are collected—disappear, and the price of consumer products drop by at least half (we are confident it is closer to 75%). Current capitalized, non-tangible, values of corporations have been transposed into much lower use-values.

Combining those social savings with free trade between equally developed regions, with managed trade between unequally developed regions, and dropping protections in step with the harmonization of previously unequal economies, would protect both labor and capital worldwide. The masochistic destruction of jobs and capital under current internal economic and world trade structures based on monopolization of technology and control of resources would be eliminated.

Capital Destroying Capital Within Internal Economies

Moving factories offshore for low-paid labor sharply reduces buying power. The profits from lower cost production sold on the high-priced markets of the imperial centers go into corporate coffers become capitalized profits distributed to owners of stock, corporate managers, and stock traders. Those increased profits, higher capitalized values, which—so long as there is broad ownership of stocks and an increase in taking in each other's wash, cooking each other hamburgers, or giving each other heart transplants (service industries) to maintain the circulation of money— temporarily replaces buying power once earned by labor.[a]

By expanding productive capacity without expanding equal buying power, capital destroys capital. It is unrealistic to assume this will be the first time in history those rising stock and real estate values, that have been providing a substantial share of consumer buying power, will not go down and collapse the imperial center's buying power. It is happening as we speak (2008-10).

Japan's industrial capacity operated at 65.5% of capacity for 15 years and by 2010 much of the industrialized world was producing at two-thirds capacity. Michael Moffit quotes Stanley J. Mihelick, executive vice-president for production at Goodyear:

> Until we get real wage levels down much closer to those of Brazil's and Korea's, we cannot pass along productivity gains to wages and still be competitive." With factory wages in Mexico and Korea averaging about $3 an hour, compared with U.S. wages of $14 or so, it looks as if we have a long way to go before U.S. wages will even be in the ball park with the competition. That the decline of U.S. industry is the natural and logical outcome of the evolution of the multinational corporate economy over the past twenty-five years has been a bitter pill to swallow, and it will become increasingly distasteful as time goes on. *One consequence will be a nasty decline in the standard of living in the United States....* [W]e have the outlines of a true vicious circle: the world economy is dependent on growth in the U.S. economy but the U.S. domestic economy is [now] skewed more towards consumption than production and investment, and this consumption is in turn sustained by borrowing—at home and abroad.... The deal with surplus countries essentially has been as follows: you can run a big trade surplus with us provided that you put the money back into our capital markets.[2]

---

[a] Forty years ago the United States economy was 30% services and 70% industrial. In 2008, it was 15% industrial and 85% services.

The excessive accumulations of capital by stateless corporate imperialists, and the denial of capital to the world's powerless, are two sides of the same coin. There is too little buying power among the dispossessed to purchase all the production of industrial capital. When there is already an excess, capital building more industry without developing more consumer buying power, capital will destroy other capital:

> So long as global productive capacity exceeds global demand by such extravagant margins, somebody somewhere in the world has to keep closing factories, old and new.... South Korea will be losing jobs to cheap labor in Thailand and even China may someday lose factories to Bangladesh.[3]

Several auto companies appear headed for bankruptcy as we speak (2010). When China (which is considering buying in-trouble auto companies) and other developing nations develop brand names, and sells cars, and other consumer products, on the world market 40% below current prices, both overseas and home profits of auto makers, and the producers of other consumer products, will disappear. So will American and European jobs.

Labor Should Employ Capital

That capital is properly owned and employed by labor is recognized by Adam Smith. His bible of capitalism, *Wealth of Nations*, states: "Produce is the natural wages of labor. Originally the whole belonged to the labourer. If this had continued all things would have become cheaper, though in appearance many things might have become dearer."[4] The "appearance of becoming dearer" is because each worker would have been fully paid. Things would have been cheaper because the purchasing power of those fully-paid workers would have advanced in step with productive capacity. If that philosophy had been followed, those who currently make their living through extracting wealth from labor would have to move into the ranks of productive labor. Those well-paid workers will purchase more from other fully-paid workers; with that increased buying power, others would produce more to take advantage of that market.

In short, purchasing power, which is so hard to generate under monopoly rules, would have developed in step with the productive power of easily-built industrial technology. If monopolization had been avoided, labor would have been fully paid and the world would have developed rapidly, without destructive wars, without poverty, and without financial and economic crashes such as the world currently faces.[b]

---

[b] This cannot happen until democracy is established. A restructuring to full and equal, inclusive, property rights will eliminate those monopolies.

If labor owned the capital it produced, then labor would employ, rather than be employed by, capital. When monopolized, capital's use can be denied to labor at any time, and it will be denied if no profit, earned or unearned, is made. The natural order of labor employing tools (capital) is reversed. If land and capital (both industrial and financial) were not monopolized, land, labor, and capital could freely combine to produce social wealth, workers would receive their full wages from what they produced, and the owners of industry would receive full value for use of their capital. Elimination of the monopolization of technology under current stock market and patent structures would increase social efficiency equal to the invention of money.

As all people are stakeholders in their nation's—and the world's—economy, no economic sector should have excessive rights (**monopolization, structured within property rights law, denying others their rightful share of what nature offers to all for fre**e). Just as with land, we are accustomed to wealthy people claiming ownership of the nation's industrial capital. We are taught this is the proper and most efficient social arrangement. Therefore we do not recognize the obvious; capital is social wealth, composed of all tools of production which were produced by labor. Thus honest capital, both industrial and financial, is but stored labor. Those technologies, industrial capital, are only a part of nature that has been discovered, and all should be entitled to the opportunity of employing that capital, or being employed by it, and receiving a fair share of what is produced.[c]

Capital, however, is often more productive under private ownership and, when this is so, private ownership is justified. In such cases, entrepreneurs, whose special talents lead to increased production, properly buy industrial capital, at a fair price, from those who produced it. A substantial share of society's capital has been justly claimed in this manner. Capital that is obtained by means other than trading useful labor—physical, intellectual, innovative, or special talent—is an unjust interception of wealth produced by others. Those natural values are properly distributed to all through patents placed in the public domain sharply lowering consumer prices.

---

[c] This thesis is easily tested. Factories are only a series of tools. Without tools you must pay a shop to repair anything. Most homes have simple tools and carry out simple repairs in a few minutes at no cost. Monopolize those tools in the same manner as industrial technology is monopolized, and you have to pay someone else to do those repairs. Likewise, eliminate the monopolization of technology through the patent process, and other communities and societies can produce their own consumer products. Two massive wastes have been eliminated, preventing others' use of technologies, and the superstructure—the unneeded share of stock markets—managing that monopoly. This first is proven by the rest of the world quickly industrializing under those just rules and the second by the roughly 50% (very possibly 75%) drop in price of consumer products and services that would occur.

Capital which is more efficient under social ownership belongs to all society, with all citizens receiving the profits. For example, no profits are directly distributed from the increased wealth produced by highways, airports, harbors, or post offices. But the wealth society is able to produce and distribute, through the common use of these natural monopolies, is many times more than construction and maintenance costs. Just as each ones' share of the use-value of land, in a modern commons, is realized by all through socially collected resource rents, the efficiency gains of socially-owned natural monopolies are distributed to all, silently and efficiently. Through far cheaper production-distribution costs, and elimination of massive amounts of labor and resources being wasted; none of the wealth properly belonging to all in roughly equal shares will be claimed by monopolization.

Much of what is properly social capital,[d] "honest" private capital, and "fictitious" capital are all currently lumped together and collectively treated as private capital. Ownership of capital is considered proof it was justly earned, and that the owner deserves compensation for its use. Below we distinguish between social, private, and fictitious capital. Once identified, the proper owners can claim their capital and the profits it produces. Fictitious capital, like that in banking and land monopolization, can be replaced by socially collected, and thus socially owned, finance capital.

Efficient Socially-Owned Capital

The difference between what is properly social capital and private capital is that everybody uses social capital. It forms a natural monopoly, while proper private capital is used only to produce products or services for specific needs of specific people. Capital required for society's basic infrastructure, is properly part of a modern commons through a modern legal-social structure. This includes not only highways, airports, harbors, and post offices, but also railroads, electric power systems, community water systems, banking and communication superhighways. Most recognize these natural monopoly infrastructures should be socially owned.

Although such facilities and services are publicly held in most societies, U.S. citizens are unaccustomed to railroads, electric power systems, banking, and communications being socially owned. These are natural monopolies and all claims of efficiency under private ownership are rhetorical covers to hide the siphoning of the fruits of others' labor to those who hold title to those economic crossroads.[5]

---

[d] Social capital is also used by some to refer to the unquantified—but real—value of social interconnections that aid the functioning of society, typically meaning a higher education level.

Almost 24% of America is served by consumer-owned electric utilities, 13.4% are publicly owned and 10.2% are rural cooperatives. Privately-owned companies charge 42.5% more for electricity than those publicly owned. Yet, since they serve population centers with the highest density of customers per mile, privately-owned electricity costs should be far lower. The difference in electricity costs between privately-owned and publicly-owned electric companies is even greater than these statistics show. Not only do they sell cheap electricity to private companies, the publicly-owned utilities also provide enough profits for some of those communities to build swimming pools, stadiums, and parks.[6]

Matthew Josephson's classic *Robber Barons*, Peter Lyon's even more profound *To Hell in a Day Coach*, and Edward Winslow Martin's *History of the Grange Movement* cover how the American railroads were built at public expense. As much as half the funds collected for building them were pocketed and over 9% of the land in the United States was deeded to these railroads. The pocketing of those funds, claiming title to these natural monopolies, and being deeded that land, were little more than thefts of public wealth. Martin describes the building of the Union Pacific Railroad as perhaps the most flagrant example but the pattern was typical:

> Who then was Crédit Mobilier? It was but another name for the Pacific Railroad ring. The members were in Congress; they were trustees for the bondholders; they were directors, they were stockholders, they were contractors; in Washington they voted subsidies, in New York they received them, upon the plains they expended them, and in the Crédit Mobilier they divided them. Ever-shifting characters, they were ubiquitous—now engineering a bill, and now a bridge—they received money into one hand as a corporation, and paid into the other as a contractor. As stockholders they owned the road, as mortgagees they had a lien upon it, as directors they contracted for its construction, and as members of Crédit Mobilier they built it.... Reduced to plain English, the story of the Crédit Mobilier is simply this: The men entrusted with the management of the Pacific road made a bargain with themselves to build the road for a sum equal to about twice its actual cost, and pocketed the profits, which have been estimated at about thirty millions of dollars—this immense sum coming out of the taxpayers of the United States.[7]

"By 1870 the states alone had given $228,500,000 in cash, while another $300,000,000 had been paid over by counties and municipalities." Of course, those millions of 19th century dollars would be hundreds of billions in inflated 21st century dollars. In the process of building those railroads, promoters skimmed off possibly one-half of this public investment and stockholders' capital, while simultaneously claiming 9.3% of the nation's land through land grants.[8]

With enforced privatizations through imposition of Reaganism-Thatcherism, the first heavy promoters of this philosophy, on the successfully destabilized former Soviet Union, social wealth was being placed under exclusive private ownership in the 1990s at a rate that makes America's robber barons of the late 19th and early 20th centuries look like country bumpkins. Those defeated nations were paid pennies on the dollar to give up title to their natural wealth, their banks, and their industrial capital. The citizenry, of course, had little to say. In many cases, if not most, one member of these less-than-honest groups, to put it mildly, would be signing as government agent and another was the buyer.

Obviously there is no savings to society from the private ownership of a natural monopoly such as education, railroads, electricity, post offices, power systems, sewers, water systems, communication systems, etc. And, as shown in chapter 5, the true cost of a communications superhighway, when properly structured under a public authority and used in common, would be only pennies per dollar of current costs.

The basic infrastructures addressed above are integral to a nation. Society is a machine; even though these basic facilities do not directly produce anything, society cannot function without them. They are an integral part of production, and are just as important to social efficiency as modern factories.

To demonstrate this, compare the labor costs of a society with an undeveloped infrastructure to those of a developed society. Vacation to any wilderness park, hike for a day, and calculate how efficient virtually any economic activity, such as sending and receiving mail, would be from there. In the 18th century, a letter traveling by U.S. mail from New York to Virginia, 400 miles, took four to eight weeks and cost 60 cents a page.[9] Today it is 44 cents, possibly equal to less then a penny 200 years ago, for several pages anywhere in the nation and that letter normally arrives within one to three days. When China built a road into the almost inaccessible Tibet, the price of a box of matches dropped from one sheep to two pounds of wool.[10]

Efficient Privately-Owned Capital

Commercial activities producing for variable individual needs, rather than everybody's needs, are properly privately owned. Thousands of personal preferences—clothes, furniture, jewelry, hobbies, recreational activities, etc—cannot be provided efficiently by a public authority. Such personal needs can only be assessed by perceptive and talented individuals close enough to recognize and fulfill those needs. The capital to provide such services is more productive under private ownership.

Most of the construction and production for basic social infrastructure operated under public authority is quite properly provided by tens of thousands of privately-owned industries. This free-enterprise, privately-owned, capital can, under contract, accommodate the needs of public institutions. We see this every day in contracts to build infrastructure.

Fictitious Capital

Few economists agree on exactly what constitutes capital. Most include all wealth that produces a profit—titles, stocks, bonds, etc. But, although this paper has a firm claim on what is rightfully part of society's income, much of it was skimmed off and resurfaced in another investment. The earnings of the skimmed off share of those first certificates is properly defined as "wealth extracted through fictitious capital." Bonds used to construct harbors, deepen riverbeds, and build railroads represent true capital. But, if 50% were pocketed and reinvested elsewhere, that leaves two dollars in claims against each dollar of value of the original infrastructure contract.

In the previous example of building the Union Pacific Railroad, half the money was used to build; the other half was pocketed and reinvested elsewhere. That share of those certificates claiming a part of social production and yet had produced nothing was fraudulent. This fictitious capital may represent wealth to the owners, but it is not, on balance, increased wealth to society.

There are three physical foundations to production—land, labor, and capital. Land commands rent, labor is paid wages, and honest interest can only be for the productive use of honestly earned capital (stored labor). Patent monopolies capitalize stock values far above tangible values (use values), and those fictitious values demand profit equality with real values. Through excess profits on unearned wealth, the production of others' labor is siphoned from those who produce to those who do not. The share of finance capital demanding payment, and yet produces nothing (the 95% of current finance capital which is the primary subject of this Part III), is properly labeled "fictitious capital."

Restructure to a modern commons throughout the economy and those huge blocs of capital currently buying and selling capitalized unearned values disappear, and all that remains are equally-shared use-values. The doubling in economic efficiency (employed hours and resource use drop by half, and the reasons for war disappear) proves those huge blocs of wealth should never have been extracted from their proper owners in the first place.

Yes a large share of appropriated capital built industries and infrastructure. But that infrastructure, plus essential social services—education, health care, and retirement—should have been paid for by the unearned money—resource rents and banking profits—those monopolists were banking.

That it is necessary to appropriate huge blocs of capital to finance infrastructure, industry, or any other aspect of an economy, is a cover story to justify unearned wealth. If technology had been shared the past 500 years instead of monopolized, it would have spread rapidly across the world and there would have been little poverty and few wars.

Banking is a social technology which would have spread to the rest of the world right along with mechanical, chemical, electrical, and other technologies. Being far more efficient, thus producing far more wealth, each technological leap can be financed by savings or created money. The increased wealth, both the industry and its production, backs that investment.

Invention, a Social Process

> There is no isolated, self-sufficing individual. All production is, in fact, a production in and by the help of the community, and all wealth is such only in society. Within the human period of the race development, it is safe to say, no individual has fallen into industrial isolation, so as to produce any one useful article by his own independent effort alone. Even where there is no mechanical cooperation, men are always guided by the experience of others. —Thorstein Veblen

These words from an eminent philosopher of massive waste within our economy are well spoken. The long march of technology leading up to the present sophisticated level is based upon thousands of earlier discoveries—fire, smelting, the wheel, lathe, and screw—and untold millions of improvements on those basic innovations.[11] Many primitive, but revolutionary, technologies were discovered by Asian and Arab societies. Greek, Roman, and other cultures, improved upon these methods, which were, in turn, used by later cultures. As social processes build upon the insights of others, Stuart Chase's list of inventions of 5000 years ago barely touches the subject:

> The generic Egyptian of 3,000 B.C., though unacquainted with iron, was an expert metallurgist in the less refractory metals. He could smelt them, draw them into wire, beat them into sheets, cast them into molds, emboss, chase, engrave, inlay, and enamel them. He had invented the lathe and the potter's wheel and could glaze and enamel earthenware. He was an expert woodworker, joiner and carver. He was an admirable sculptor, draftsman and painter. He was, and is, the world's mightiest architect in stone. He made sea-going ships. He had devised the loom, and knew how to weave cotton to such fineness that we can only distinguish it from silk by the microscope. His language was rich, and he engrossed it in the handsomest system of written characters ever produced. He made excellent paper, and upon it beautiful literature was written.... He had invented most of the hand tools now in existence.... He had worked out the rudiments of astronomy and mathematics.[12]

There were also wedges, drills, wheels, pulleys, and gears; all were necessary before modern machines were possible. There had to be countless earlier inventions, back to the control of fire, before the Egyptians could have reached even that level of technology.

Not only does every modern invention rest on millions of insights going back to antiquity, its development also requires thousands of people with special talents. For example, a British scientist's accidental discovery of penicillin has benefited almost every person in modern civilization. More people worked to develop and produce this antibiotic for the wounded in WW II than worked on the atomic bomb, and they were all funded with public money. Yet the drug was patented by an American who recognized by obtaining a patent he would have a monopoly with a capitalized value that would lay claim to vast wealth, although he had neither created, nor produced, anything.[13]

Every innovation is a part of nature. Just like land, oil, coal, iron ore, or any of nature's wealth, if something is to be discovered it had to have been there all the time. As technology is a part of nature that has been discovered, everybody should share its fruits. Inventions not only use the insights of millions of people throughout history and prehistory, they also require the support and skills of millions of present workers as well. Stuart Chase estimated at least 5,000 people were involved in contributing data to the writing of his book and they depended on others for their knowledge.

These people provided tools, materials, and services: pencils, paper, graphite, rubber, lead, typewriters, telephones, cars, electricity, typing, printing presses, book distribution, banking, and so forth. The people directly involved in Chase's knowledge required educators, authors of textbooks, and their educators, ad infinitum. Every one of these consumer items required the labor and skills of thousands of people, some in distant parts of the world such as producers of rubber or tin. Though the labor charge of some is infinitesimal, each is real and definite. Collectively they accumulate a substantial, though incalculable, value.[14]

While the contribution of any one person to the pool of social knowledge is truly small, the unearned wealth diverted to those who own the patents to social knowledge can be substantial. It has been estimated that, if the emerging world were industrialized to the level of the developed world, the royalty claims would be $1 trillion a year. These royalties would normally be going to people who "own" these efficient technologies but neither invented anything nor labored productively for this wealth. They are designed commercial chokepoints structured into unequal property rights law, denying others their proper share. This is the monopolization of these tools of production, technology, permitting huge overcharges that siphon wealth, properly belonging to all in roughly equal shares, to owners of patents.

Consider how expensive consumer products would be if the use of wheels, levers, gears, fire, and thousands of other early inventions could not be used without the payment of royalties. The current huge overcharges create excessive stock market values which become the blocs of capitalized unearned wealth owned by monopolists that—through restructuring aristocratic exclusive titles to nature's wealth, patents in this case, to conditional titles—disappear as they are transformed into efficient, relatively equally-shared, use-values. Fully 85% of the stock market, where those unearned sums are collected, will disappear if patents were placed in the public domain.

Inventors rarely receive much reward for their discoveries and innovations. The few who are compensated receive but a small share of the tribute charged by those who own this social wealth. That a small number of powerful people monopolize inventions, and ever afterwards siphon to themselves unearned wealth properly providing quality living to others, defies both decency and justice. This was well known to prominent inventors and industrialists such as Thomas A. Edison and Henry Ford. Both "agreed all patent laws should be repealed since they benefit the manufacturer and not the inventor."[15]

Patent laws should be redesigned to be a part of a modern commons, inclusive and equal property rights, in which any person can use that technology by society paying those inventors well and placing those patents in the public domain.

Capitalizing Actual and Fictitious Values

> Inventions are a "more or less costless store of knowledge [that] is captured by monopoly capital and protected in order to make it secret and a 'rare and scarce commodity,' for sale at monopoly price[s]. So far as inventions are concerned a price is put on them not because they are scarce but in order to make them scarce to those who want to use them."[16]

The current patent structure capitalizes value far above tangible values (labor values/use-values), through those unearned profits, and without expenditure of productive labor, intercepts wealth that should be funding living standards of productive labor. Where inventions once went unchanged for decades or even centuries, many, if not most, patents are now obsolete before their 20 year life expires. Due to the efficiency gains of the new patents, the owners control both the latest technologies, and the expired patents, of support technologies. Honda's exclusive ownership of patents on the stratified charge engine, even though the basic principles for this crucial technology were invented 100 years ago, makes all this quite evident.

Corporations are in such powerful bargaining positions that only occasionally will a new invention pose a threat to them. As corporate control of other critical patents limits the inventor's options, these patents are bought for a fraction of their true value, or they are patented around, and the inventor receives nothing. Controlling patents is integral to controlling markets:

> Any move by the neo-colonial state to revoke the patent law as a defensive measure would have very limited results since the market belongs to the monopolies. This becomes quite clear when it is realized that the other markets to which such products would be exported would still have such legislation protecting the same pat-

ents, and the transnational corporation would be in a position to require compliance. The mere ownership without the actual know-how which is guarded by the monopoly at headquarters would be useless. This is the whole point about monopoly. The world imperialist monopoly market would not exist if such a system of market control were not in operation.[17]

We view the inventions of 400 to 1100 years ago as primitive, yet in their time these simple inventions could produce, with less labor, both more and better products. Someone powerful enough to control these new techniques could trade one day's work for two, three, five, ten or as many days' production of other people's labor as the efficiency of his invention and political power allowed.

If the invention of the windmill could have been monopolized, its owners could siphon to themselves the production of large amounts of others' labor. This potential created a dispute between the nobles, priests, and emperor "as to which one the wind belonged."[18] A 17th century French patent granted just such a right to selected owners of windmills."[19]

However hard they tried, claiming ownership of the wind was quite difficult. But it was not so with other technologies. The water mill, first used in Europe during the 10th century, permitted one worker to replace as many as 10 others. A stone planer eliminated seven workers out of eight. One worker with an Owens bottle machine could do the work of 18 hand blowers.[20] Modern technology has created even greater efficiency gains. Many credit the steam engine with the greatest single increase in productive efficiency. Stuart Chase cites a study by C.M. Ripley of work, costing $230 done by hand labor, which would cost only $5 using electric power.[21] Modern electric furnaces and continuous casting have brought the direct labor expended in the steel industry down to only 1.8 hours per ton of steel produced.[22]

The owner of that first water mill was able to trade his single day's work, grinding grain, for seven days' labor of a woodworker or blacksmith. In effect he was paid for seven days while working one. The owner of a patented stone planer would likely gain five days' value for only one of his own. Owning a patented Owens bottle machine would probably have claimed 12 days' pay for each day's labor. If the manufacturer in Ripley's study had been able to patent that efficiency, he could have charged 20 to 30-times the labor value in his product. However, just like claiming ownership of the wind, it would be difficult to claim exclusive title to electricity and accounts for the drop in costs in Ripley's study.

Whether a market is in land, or corporate stock, what is being bought and sold under current property rights are primarily values produced by nature, or an aspect of nature, properly belonging to all in relatively equal shares. That value has been confiscated by the cunning and powerful through exclusive titles to the various aspects of nature's wealth, and those unearned values are then capitalized in the markets by a factor of 10 to 30 times. Modest use-values, properly shared by all, have been converted to massive, unearned, capitalized, values owned by a few.

Royalty Conferring Monopoly Trading Rights is the Origin of Patent Royalties

That the owners of patents are entitled to royalties exposes the feudal origin of the term. Patent rights to land and inventions were conferred upon favorites by kings and queens, with the understanding that the person so favored would share the earnings (royalties). In short, the origin of patents is indistinguishable from paying bribes for the privilege of doing business. Such bribes were the precursors of today's patent royalties.[23] Aristocratic exclusive title to patents, as opposed to conditional title, is the remnant of feudal patent law which must be restructured to attain full rights for all, a human right to the full benefits of evermore efficient technology.

The Ever-Increasing Efficiencies of Technology

In final analysis, the foundation of most law is power expressed through military strength. Long before governments protected patents, they were protected by violence. "The struggle against rural trading and against rural handicrafts lasted at least seven or eight hundred years.... All through the fourteenth century regular armed expeditions were sent out against all the villages in the neighborhood and looms or fulling vats were broken or carried away."[24] Those early claims to technology, enforced by violence, were the forerunners of today's industrial patents. Those who would control technology have just become more sophisticated. They encode these exclusive rights in legal titles. Today, being accustomed to it, and unaware of society's large losses, we accept this as normal.

The growing efficiency of textile machinery started the Industrial Revolution. Primitive looms were improved upon by inventions such as Kay's flying shuttle, Hargreave's spinning jenny, Crompton's "mule," and the power loom. Between 1773 and 1795, the labor time to process 100 pounds of cotton went from 50,000 hours to 300 hours, an efficiency gain of 16,666%.[25] That efficiency gain, within a time span of only 22 years, exposes how the owners of these technologies quickly dominated world trade. Quite simply, technology was not shared; it was monopolized through restricting the rights of production to the owners of patents.

The widespread use of machine weaving came about only because the technology was copied and the patents ignored. That 16,666% gain in 22 years is dwarfed by 150 power looms, in Formosa, weaving 24 hours a day under the watchful eyes of only one agile female operator on roller skates.[26] This is a gain of hundreds of thousands, if not millions, of times in efficiency. The labor component in the price of a yard of cloth produced by modern industry is small. This includes the labor to smelt the ore, and to fabricate the machines, which is stored in that industrial capital.

The economically powerful will say, "They are not claiming the production of anyone else's labor as there is hardly any labor involved." But this is exactly how wealth is siphoned to those who monopolize the tools of production. The price charged for those products, by the holders of exclusive titles to nature's wealth, is far above the cost of production, and others are forced to trade large amounts of their labor for what was produced with a small amount of labor.

All society is denied the full benefit of cheap industrial goods when labor is charged more than they are paid to produce and distribute that product. If a product requires one hour's labor to produce and distribute, and then sells for three hours' of labor value, it effectively siphons away the value produced by two hours of labor value. If production is traded at the same value to a country where equally-productive labor is paid one-third as much, it siphons away nine hours of labor value, see chapter one of this author's *Economic Democracy: A grand Strategy for World Pe ace and Prosperity*. Standard economics and accounting do not measure this overcharge because it shows up in stock prices far beyond intrinsic (labor created) value. If that cloth were priced relative to the price paid labor within the region sold, including fair interest and depreciation for the stored labor value represented by that machinery, then it would be priced within reach of the world's low-paid labor.

A bushel of wheat required three hours to produce in 1830 but only 10 minutes in 1900.[27] A call to Montana State University in Bozeman revealed that in 1986 it took only 3.2 minutes of labor to produce one bushel of dryland Montana wheat. Other crops have similar efficiency gains.

Railroad labor costs per ton-mile in 2010 were roughly 2% that required 95 years earlier, and that efficiency gain is dwarfed by the five million percent gain in transportation efficiency over the horse and wagon only 180 ago.

The public did receive a large share of the labor savings in textiles, agriculture, transportation, and other technologies. With the common people's newly won rights, the U.S. Constitution and Bill of Rights, and with the enormously wealthy and sparsely inhabited lands of the Americas, the gains were just too great for the powerful to claim them all. However, due to the failure to increase the buying power of all labor in step with the productivity of capital, there is more production forgone and wasted than that which society so gratefully receives.

Ownership of a key technology, the telephone, was Bell Telephone's advantage when that monopoly was established. Inventions not controlled by Bell, such as the dial phone, were suppressed for many years. The telegraph and telephone reduced communication costs by an amount comparable to the savings created by new technology in textiles and transportation. These efficiency gains of technology, protected by patents, produced the monopoly profits that established Bell Telephone, a corporation larger than any in textiles or transportation. At 10 times the capacity for 10% the cost (1% the cost per unit of capacity), and assuming powerful low frequency spectrums able to pass through mountains are reserved for social use, a communication superhighway has the potential of reducing communication costs to 1% that of today. Under those efficiencies, still advancing rapidly, the whole world has the potential of gaining their freedom.

Henry Ford's assembly line was a milestone in industrial technology that rapidly picked up the pace of the Industrial Revolution:

> The factory is not a new tool but an organization of production that eliminates the periods of idleness in the use of tools, machines, and human beings that are characteristic of agrarian and artisan production. In the artisan's shop the saw, chisel, file, and so forth are idle while the hammer is being used. In the factory all the tools are simultaneously in use in the hands of specialized workers; production is "in line" rather than "in series." But production in line requires a large scale of total output before it becomes feasible. The division of labor is limited by the extent of the market, as Adam Smith told us. But transportation, urbanization, and international trade provided a market of sufficient scale.[28]

During 1913 alone, the time required to assemble an automobile dropped from 728 minutes to 93. Until that year, the wage rate averaged $2.50 for a 10-hour day. Ford doubled the daily wages of his workers and reduced their hours from ten to eight, all while lowering the price of his cars.[29] This was unheard of in those times and drew much criticism from business and the press.

What Ford knew, and others did not, was the profits were so large that, with that 800% efficiency gain, the wages could have been increased to almost $20 per day. Ford was strongly opposed by his managers and other investors. But Emerson had reached Ford on the morality of not maximizing the profit potential of his monopoly.

However, there were attempts to monopolize the emerging auto industry. George Baldwin Seldon, a patent lawyer, understood that, as the law was structured, patents laid claim to wealth properly distributed to others. In 1899,

> he set his mind to working out the precise legal definition and wording of a patent that would give him the sole right to license and charge royalties on future automobile development in America.... Seldon had gone into partnership with a group of Wall Street investors who saw their chance to cut themselves in on the profits of the growing American car industry.[30]

The near success of Seldon, and his partners, in patenting the automobile, illustrates the basic injustice of the current patent structure. Neither Seldon, nor these investors, had anything to do with the invention of automobiles. The first ones had been built in Europe 14 years earlier, and virtually hundreds of auto companies were already in existence. Yet, if anyone had succeeded in patenting the process of building automobiles, every purchaser of an automobile would have had a part of the production of his or her labor siphoned to the owners of that patent who had invented nothing, and had done no productive work.

Seldon's attempt at patenting the principle of the automobile is being successfully accomplished today in the patenting of processes. Corporations are being formed to patent embryo transfers, gene splicing, other advanced medical procedures, even title to human genes and genes of plants domesticated by primitive societies thousands of years ago. Any doctor who wishes to use these new procedures, and any farmer who grows a patented plant, has to obtain a license and pay a royalty.[31] Totally new, manmade, identifiable, synthetic cells are being patented as we write.

The current race to patent human genes clearly outlines the monopoly cost of patent laws. There are thousands of human genes directly affecting human health. As patent laws now stand, some corporation is going to have a patent on, and thus own, each gene. Let us say that there are 300 genes to be studied in a standard gene test and the royalty to be paid to each patent holder only $1 per gene. If a couple wishes to test themselves for defective genes before conception, or their unborn child shortly after conception, the cost would be $300. Sixty minutes, July 29, 2001, suggested the possibility of $1,000 royalties.

This added tax, though common to medical equipment and drugs, has not previously been added to the cost of an operation or food crops. If ownership of procedures and food plants had been established years ago, every bill for an operation, and the cost for every plate of food, will have royalties added, and thus reduce the rights of everyone else, some to the extent of death or hunger. Only those licensed by the patent holder could perform operations or raise crops. Every improvement in patented surgical procedures, or improved crop strains, would also be patented and, as technological improvement is ongoing, the patent's monopoly would never run out. Thus Microsoft's tens of billions of dollars of software overcharges, all built from purchasing the DOS computer operating system for $3,000 and patenting it, led to later patents eventually valuing Microsoft at hundreds of billions of dollars. The cost to society can be imagined if each producer or service provider had to pay a patent holder for the use of fire, wheels, wedges, levers, and gears. Inversely, the savings are evident in their free use when in the public domain.

About 7,000 patents worldwide are based upon indigenous knowledge of India. After spending millions to get one plagiarized patent invalidated, India is creating a tens-of-thousands-page Traditional Knowledge Data Library (TKDL) to be available to every patent office in the world.[32]

There is one recent and remarkable exception to this rule. In parts of Africa, "as many as sixty percent of the people over age fifty-five were partly or completely blind" from becoming infected with a parasitic worm. Possibly 18 million people were affected. The pharmaceutical corporation Merck and Company owned the patent on a drug, Ivermectin, used to kill worms in animals. In October 1987, Merck announced they would provide this drug free of charge for Africans afflicted with this parasite. The company chairman, Dr. P. Roy Vagelos, noted, "It became apparent that people in need were unable to purchase it."[33] Here the loss to society from aristocratic exclusive title was so obvious, and devastating, these corporate executives made a moral decision to save the sight of millions of people. The cost to them was negligible; the gain to society was beyond measure.

Cuba restoring vision to 4.5 million treatable blind Latin Americans by 2015 without charge, 40% of Cuba's 70,000 doctors at work in many impoverished areas of the world, Cuban education equaling the best in the world, and Venezuela and Bolivia in the early stages of copying Cuban successes, are further examples of how cooperation can quickly alleviate poverty while monopolizations only entrench it deeper.

An intense battle was fought over life saving drugs for AIDS victims. These drugs can be produced for a tiny fraction of the monopoly prices currently asked. Even at that fractional price few in the impoverished world can afford those essential drugs and, at the monopolized price, almost no one can afford them. Drug companies have reneged on agreements to lower prices for Aids victims in Africa, and that struggle for what is obviously a human right is still on-going (2008-10).

There is a loss to society from exclusive control of any technology, but it is usually not as obvious as in these dramatic examples, where the patent rules of exclusive use were abandoned. These examples demonstrate the original morality of the medical community when "to patent an essential medicine was considered morally indefensible."[34] It is also morally indefensible for other inventions crucial to society. The Gaviotas community, regenerating the primeval Amazon forest of Colombia's barren Los Llanos plains, while building a model community using modern production methods to live off the land, does not believe in patenting technology. Its inventions, such as a cheap, 100-pound, wind-mill driven water pump, and a cost-free, maintenance free, air conditioning technology, are spreading throughout Latin America.[35]

Innovation and technology thus create large reductions in labor costs in all segments of the economy. Most are more modest than the previous examples, but reductions of 90% are common. Average increases in efficiency of 30% per decade[36] while labor's pay remains static, or even shrinking, exposes capital as banking all efficiency gains (plus a part of what once went to labor) as capitalized profits.

This alerts us that, if technology had been shared instead of monopolized, the entire world could have industrialized in step with the increased efficiencies of technology. Throughout those centuries, assuming equal rights to the fruits of nature had been taught, as opposed to the teachings of Adam Smith's winner take all philosophy; there would have been little poverty, and few wars. With each enjoying full and equal use rights, the world would have been, at all points in time, many times richer in use-values than under monopoly capitalized values.

Most wars and poverty throughout the world today have their origins in millions of unequal property rights laws the past 700-plus years, through which the powerful monopolized technology. Two of the most obvious were: 1) Kaiser Wilhelm buying technology wholesale from his grandmother, England's Queen Victoria and cousin, King George V.[37] That breach of monopolist's absolute rule to never transfer technology to any other nation was the direct cause of WW I. 2) The massive suppression of the world's breaks for freedom the past 65 years. That this is conscious policy is again proven by providing technology to the defeated nations, Germany and Japan, and to Southeast Asia, so as to halt fast expanding socialism with their more equal property rights laws. Corporations fleeing high-paid labor led to an abandonment of the rule to not share technology with other cultures. That accident of history, technology developing outside the imperial-centers-of-capital, again proves the waste and inefficiency of the monopoly system.

Overcharges cannot exist if labor is fully paid for their work. It only appears proper because people are accustomed to a subsistence wage for most labor, equally accustomed to all increased profits going to owners and management, and unaware of how rapidly that technology would spread around the world if capital were accumulated along the guidelines in this treatise—conditional patent titles, labor fully and equally paid, and productive jobs shared by all. Under those restructured rights, workers would have buying power, and technology would be regionally available to produce desired products. Capital will have been accumulated to finance it all simply through the emerging world, federated into viable economic regions, safely creating their own money, and they being fully paid for their resources and labor.

Wealth is Extracted by Titleholders Through Capitalizing Unearned Values

Shares in corporations are sold with the price based on how profitable they are expected to be, their capitalized value. This idea proved to be a real bonanza. Where conservative business people typically estimated the capitalized value of the company at 10 times yearly profits, the stock markets, anticipating future increases in profits, capitalized these values far higher, frequently 20 to 30 times annual profits and occasionally even more. It is not uncommon for the price of stock going public, called IPOs (initial price offerings) to jump 500% the first week. This capital accumulation bonanza claims a share of a nation's loans and the money supply must be expanded, either more base money created or money circulating at a higher velocity, to sustain those values.

All in one stroke, an individual or group can lay claim to the efficiency of a technology through capitalizing its value and selling shares to investors. This claiming of wealth properly distributed to other, through the mechanism of unearned capitalized values, concentrated rightful wealth of the many into the hands of a few, was christened accumulated capital, and gave capitalism its name.

Through carefully structured laws, the hidden hand of the wealthy and powerful kept claiming an ever-larger share of the wealth produced. Labor, just as naturally, tried to retain, or reclaim, what they produced. The rights gained in the American Revolution, enshrined in its Constitution, and the natural justice of those rights, eventually increased the power and income of labor. This, and the expansion of unnecessary labor in the service industries, as summarized in the next chapter, led to more people retaining a greater share of society's wealth.[e]

By eliminating monopolization, sharing the resultant fully-productive jobs, and paying labor fully for what it produces, measured values (now tangible, labor-created, use-values instead of monopoly values) would equal the rental value of nature's resources used, the value of productive labor, and the earnings and depreciation of industrial capital (stored labor) producing that wealth.

The Stock Markets are Primarily Extracting Wealth

As that is where the unearned profits from aristocratic exclusive titles to patents are collected, the battle for corporate ownership is centered in the stock market. Millions of hours are spent by speculators; they call themselves investors, trying to figure out which company is going to increase its capitalized value. The game is calculating profits that will translate into increased capitalized value. It is viewed as a simple method of keeping score. But claiming wealth, properly be-

---

[e] A large share of the massive wealth distributed had been appropriated from the periphery of empire by imposed inequalities in trade and outright theft.

longing to others as technology continually replaces labor, is the underlying theme.

Values, properly shared by all through lower prices, are claimed by the shareowners of industrial technology. Unearned values claimed by monopolists are capitalized, sold or borrowed against, the Federal Reserve creates more base money (reserve deposits) which will circulate buying and selling those unearned values, and a capitalized multiple of that annual wealth extraction (capitalized value) becomes finance capital. Through restructuring exclusive titles to patents to conditional titles, eliminating intangible values, and creating a modern technology commons in the process, those monopolized values and huge blocs of finance capital are, in the form of consumer prices dropping by 50% to 80% (measured in productive employed labor time to purchase), transposed into relatively equally-shared use-values.

Lester Thurow explains that the impoverishment of many while wealth is accumulated by a lucky few is due to "the process of capitalizing disequilibrium," distortions of trade, either internal or external, and thus distortions of values, and that "patient savings and reinvestment has little or nothing" to do with generating large fortunes.[38]

> at any moment in time, the highly skewed distribution of wealth is the product of two approximately equal factors—instant fortunes and inherited wealth. Inherited fortunes, however, were themselves created in a process of instant wealth in an earlier generation. These instant fortunes occur because new long-term disequilibriums (sic) in the real capital market are capitalized in the financial markets.... Those who are lucky and end up owning the stocks that are capitalized at high multiples win large fortunes in the random walk. Once fortunes are created, they are husbanded, augmented, and passed on, not because of "homo economicus" [economic man] desires to store up future consumption but because of desires for power within the family, economy, or society.[39]

Of course, the small fortunes accumulated by the upper middle class are from these same disequilibria in the value of land and capital. Except by violence or trickery, **those aristocratic exclusive titles to the resources and technologies, denying others their rightful share of what nature offers to all for free,** how else can wealth beyond what one produces be accumulated? The income demanded by those unearned appropriated values, derived from non-tangible values (capitalized monopoly values), is a private tax upon the rest of society, and quite accurately labeled air. "By reducing air to vendability, scarcity could be capitalized. Business would be richer—and every man, woman and child in the country would be poorer."[40]

A study of the market, over a full boom and bust cycle, will find these fictitious values developing in most stocks. The reasons given may be many, but the underlying cause is clear: the steady rise in the nation's efficiency is captured by, and mirrored in, stock and land values created through extracting wealth which should have been, and under a modern commons would have been, relatively equally shared by all.

Every speculator dreams of becoming wealthy by owning some of these stocks or land. The powerful and cunning, with better than even odds, buy and sell in rhythm with the inflation, and deflation, of stock and land prices to lay claim to much of this unearned wealth.

Those who win the gamble on who will own the world's land and industrial and distributive technology are freed from the necessity of laboring for their living. This is not a contradiction, their speculative efforts are certainly labor; however, when unnecessary, that labor is fictitious, and such earnings are appropriations of wealth. Through the stock markets, those unearned values are automatically capitalized to 10 to 30 times annual earnings.

Capitalizing values is necessary to decide the sale price of a business. However, not only should everyone involved receive proper compensation for his or her labor, innovations, and risk; society should receive its share and there should be no waste of labor or resources. Society not only provided tens of thousands of necessary preceding innovations; it also provided the schools, skills, tools, labor, markets, and infrastructure. Nature provided the resources, including the inventions waiting to be discovered, and each citizen is properly entitled to their share of the rental value of all nature's wealth.

There is a necessity for a stock market. However, that the stock market's primary purpose is financing the nation's business is pure fiction; trades in the stock market have little to do with capital investment:

> Buying a stock from a broker does not add one red cent to the corporate treasury and provides no investment capital except if the stock is newly issued. But new issues by major corporations are fairly rare because issuing new stock dilutes equity and depresses stock prices. As a result, the bulk of shares now traded on the stock markets were issued twenty or fifty years ago. Since then the shares have passed through many hands, and their prices have fluctuated over a wide range. Yet all these transactions have been strictly between the buyers and sellers of stocks, aided and abetted by stockbrokers trying to eke out a modest living.... [S]peculators are not really interested in the company whose stock they temporarily own. They want to take their profits and get out. They are not investing in the proper sense of the word; they are simply gambling. Ownership of corporations has become largely a game of chance in which the individual players try to guess what the other players will do.[41]

Market Bubbles and Crashes

Speculators are unaware their gains are unearned. If the market wipes them out, they feel they have lost earnings when actually it was just the odds of the gamble and their turn to lose. Like the casinos they are, the stock markets are primarily a mechanism for the redistribution of wealth upwards towards the already wealthy and powerful, not its production. It is a gambling game in which the rest of society's members are spectators who continually have their share of the nation's increased wealth thrown on the table of a game of chance they are not playing. The danger of gambling with the nation's wealth was addressed by *Business Week's* cover story, "Playing with Fire":

> By stoking a persuasive desire to beat the game, innovation and deregulation have tilted the axis of the financial system away from investment toward speculation. The U.S. has evolved into what Lord Keynes might have called a "casino society"—a nation obsessively devoted to high-stakes financial maneuvering as a shortcut to wealth.... "Speculators may do no harm as bubbles on a steady stream of enterprise. But the position is serious when enterprise becomes the bubble on a whirlpool of speculation. When the capital development of a country becomes a byproduct of the activities of a casino, the job is likely to be ill-done."[42]

What is normally spoken of as a market "bubble" is only the claiming of wealth, properly belonging to others, which has gotten out of hand. History is replete with examples. Charles Mackay, in *Extraordinary Popular Delusions and the Madness of Crowds*, describes the tulip craze that broke out in Europe in the 17th century. Before that insanity dissipated, one particular tulip bulb cost "two lasts of wheat, four lasts of rye, four fat oxen, eight fat swine, twelve fat sheep, two hogsheads of wine, four tuns of butter, one thousand lbs. of cheese, a complete bed, a suit of clothes and a silver drinking cup."[43]

One wonders at the variety of commodities traded for one flower bulb, but their total value of 2,500 florins serves as a guideline to the money value paid for other bulbs. During this period, prices ranged from 2,000 florins for an inferior bulb to 5,500 florins for the choicest varieties. "Many persons were known to invest a fortune of 100,000 florins in the purchase of 40 roots."[44] Although tulips are not stocks, the principle is the same.

At the turn of the 18th century, John Law implemented a plan to sell stock in gold mining in the Mississippi wilderness to pay off the huge debt of the French government. Though this scheme was seriously flawed, the French economy prospered. The plan went awry when the money rolled in. Those selling paper were so busy getting rich they neglected to invest in production anywhere; they merely reinvested in more paper. In a speculative frenzy, fortunes changed hands as people sold, and then bought back, nothing but paper.

The stock had no value because there was no investment in production and thus no wealth produced. Law's scheme was borrowed from cunning financiers in England who had sold stock in a South Seas venture, known today as the "South Sea Bubble." Although Spain controlled most of South America, and the

English had limited trade rights within it, stock companies were set up to trade within this territory. Visions of wealth stirred up a speculative fever, companies were formed for very unlikely endeavors, and the money rolled in as speculators dreamed of getting rich. Soon, so many joined the game that it got out of hand, and the government had to call a halt to new issues. The intention of most of these promoters can be summed up by one audacious proposal; this promoter touted "a company for carrying on an undertaking of great advantage, but nobody to know what it is."[45]

Since the organizers of these companies had no intention of producing anything, their capital was 100% fictitious. Proof this capital was not real was when the speculative bubble collapsed. There were no tangible assets, production, or services to back the value of the stock; there was only the transferring of wealth from the naive to the cunning, or lucky.

When wild speculation breaks loose, there is no relationship between value and price. Even when the stock market behaves normally, there are always stocks whose prices defy logic. This activity can only be attributed to crowd psychology, as described by Mackay, although sly promoters pull strings at every opportunity.[f]

Options, Futures, Derivatives, and Hedge Funds are Extractors of Wealth

The markets for stocks, bonds, commodities, futures, options, currencies, mortgages, money markets, virtually every exchange market anywhere in the world, are now one huge market. Options, futures, swaps, forwards, other derivatives, all tools of hedge funds, are only the buyers, and sellers, betting something will go up or down; neither has a stake beyond the gamble. They appear to have a legitimate purpose in takeover schemes, but in that role, until a bubble tops out; they are not even gambles. The psychology of the market almost guarantees the stock price will rise when word gets out a takeover is in progress. This increase in valuation backs the money required for the takeover.

All aspects of the markets "have become chips in a casino game, played for high stakes by people who produce nothing, invent nothing, grow nothing and

---

[f] Major banks lost trillions, markets were seizing up around the world, and several trillion dollars worldwide were, up to this point in time, distributed to the gamblers. Possibly $30 trillion of value has disappeared worldwide and this could yet be a Nikolai Kondratieff 50 year depression. Those bankrupt banks, hedge funds, and derivative traders, already having made massive sums as the bubble inflated, had their bets down for making even more, and lost that wager; then, in 2009, they earned record profits off the several trillion dollars of public funds poured at them.

service nothing." As these gamblers go broke in the current 2008-10, financial crash, they may be bringing the world down with them.

"One-third, [or more], of the cost of oil is due to speculative buying of oil contracts." That, and the same practices in other markets, is another form of harvesting unearned profits. Sharp traders have leveraged world markets with stock and currency options, futures on options, meaning options on options, futures on interest rates, warrants, a form of option, credit default swaps, and other bets (derivatives) designed to lay claim to wealth without doing any productive labor.

Hedge funds are, at this time, 2010, betting $2 trillion (backing $1 quadrillion to $2 quadrillion in notional values, 20 to 30 times world GDP) in the derivatives market. As this is five times the size of the derivatives market which triggered the 2008-09 collapse, the world should be holding its breath.

The collapse of the housing bubble in America with its valueless collateralized debt obligations (CDOs), structured investment vehicles (SIVs), etc, sold to the world triggered the crisis. While the legal debt equity (leverage) ratio was 12:1 or less, much of the world's economy was leveraged 20, 40, 70, and even 280:1 (Citibank). As most banks' derivatives bets were off book, all this was kept secret as the Federal Reserve bought up those CDOs close to their book value so as to recapitalize the banks.

Those "permanent rotating loans," bankers' language for imminent nationalization, were like sand against incoming waves. Trillions were thrown at those waves, and they are still coming at us as we go to press. As values fell, and just as all financial crisis for centuries, the value of normally sound banks, companies, and industries fell below the value of debts owed.

In the early 1990s, Wall Street bankers used derivative tools to crash the Japanese land and market bubbles, but Japan's control of investment and management did not permit others to gain title to Japanese companies. Later, Vulture funds bought up Southeast Asian properties after those etherealworld-banker engineered crashes. By printing ¥35 trillion in 2003-04, equaling $50 for each person on earth, which was converted to dollars to buy US treasuries, Japan partially evened the score.[46]

We have yet to see if a fascist financial and military fix will protect the current monopolizers of capital, or whether the oppressed world will break free as the ongoing worldwide populist revolutions build strength. President Barack Obama's sincere dedication to change should reduce the chance of a drift towards fascism, but that hope has not yet materialized (May 2010).

Bringing the World's Markets Under Control

Buying and selling investments is the legitimate purpose of stock markets; any activity beyond that is gambling. Eliminating monopolization through restructuring primary monopolies—money, land, technology, and communications—into a modern commons and eliminating secondary monopolies, next chapter, through full and equal economic rights for all will eliminate those massive appropriated funds which are reducing economic efficiency fully sixty percent. The ethereal world of high finance disappears, economic efficiency doubles; if that were to happen, poverty would soon be history.

Equal and Efficient Patent Laws Within the Community Social-credit Process

At least two millennia ago, the Chinese were producing massive amounts of iron and steel, including stainless steel. They had invented the compass, and rudders for large ships. They had paper, movable type, and the printing press. They built suspension bridges. They had matches, wheelbarrows, wheeled metal plows, mechanical seeders, horse collars, rotary threshing machines, and a drill to tap into natural gas. They knew the decimal system, negative numbers, and the concept of zero. And they once knew how to produce primary tools of world conquest, gunpowder and large ships.[47] But that technological knowledge was forgotten because of disuse, and the lack of a recording system, such as today's patents.

Inventions and innovations are the cornerstones of prosperity. To establish them in social memory, those technologies must be recorded and used.[48] It is necessary to reward those who had the original innovative ideas, and those who first put them to work.

The present policy of restricting access to technology should be changed to one of easy access—with proper compensation for inventors, developers, and producers—while returning the maximum savings to society. The patent system could do all that, be far simpler, and administration costs lowered to almost nothing, by evaluating the value of a patent, paying inventors and developers a reasonable "earned" value, and placing their innovations in the public domain. This creates a modern technology commons, conditional titles to nature's wealth; all may use these technologies without charge. The inventors and developers would be well paid, and there would be no cost for accounting or for disbursing royalties. Those royalties have been paid, in advance, to the inventors.

Most inventors would want their inventions to have maximum use and opt for instant cash, recognition, and free use by all. Inventions not originally recognized as valuable, a frequent occurrence, would be proved by developers who would then file development patents, they too would each be paid an "earned" value, all patents would be in the public domain, and inventors, developers, and consumers would all be well paid.

Businesses and communities would no longer have to shut down because their markets were overwhelmed by a competitor with a patent monopoly, capital destroying capital. Communities, and its citizens, would be secure as all gained maximum benefits from the newest technologies.

Those huge blocs of finance capital owned by monopolists, currently buying and selling appropriated monopoly values, will disappear, and be replaced by, much smaller, relatively equally-shared, use-values.

Those unearned patent monopoly profits are collected through the stock market, the superstructure of patent monopolies extracting wealth produced by technology. With each having full and equal rights to these fruits of nature, the need for 85% of the offices and staff overseeing, and the businesses and labor servicing, the patent-stock market industry disappear; the productive remainder becomes as stable as bond markets in a non-monopolized, efficient, economy.

Economic efficiency gains from these relatively small changes, but huge effects, in property rights, establishing a modern technology commons, would, assuming buying power is protected through sharing the remaining productive jobs, be equal to the invention of electricity.[49] Such massive economic efficiency gains require democratic, communitarian oversight to prevent stripping the earth's resources, to protect the environment, and to rebalance the human psyche to the massive free time available under those full and equal rights.

Again it must be pointed out that, wealth extracted from truly productive labor, through exclusive title to nature's technologies, is loaned back to its proper owners, to, as society is currently structured, finance their living. Through taxes, overpriced products, services, and those debt payments, including interest, those unnecessary debts are paid for again and again on into perpetuity. That impoverishing cycle is broken only by economic collapses, such as the one currently ongoing, 2008-10, due to the wealth having been concentrated into too few hands, and leaving the majority without adequate buying power, The elimination of those huge blocs of extracted wealth and the resultant large increase in economic efficiency and elimination of poverty is the essence of inclusive property rights laws.

Patent marketing rights (monopolization) are replaced by a social right, the right of all to use any technology. Privately imposed monopoly costs are transposed into equally-shared use-values priced 50% to 80% less than current monopolized values; all these gains are due to greater freedoms, fiercer competition, and full and equal economic rights.

A study of the four books on property rights law in this footnote will alert one that property rights are in continual discussion in America's courtrooms and collective rights trump private rights if it can be shown as imperative and just.[g] Though those court cases do not go, and cannot go, to the depth that this thesis does, the principles are all there. A legislature can go to this depth, and we can only hope they will if this current crisis deepens into a full fledged depression.

Before we analyze the 4th primary monopoly, which is the technology of communication superhighways through which our rights can be reclaimed, we will address secondary monopolies.

---

[g] Laura UnderKufler, *The Idea of Property: Its Meaning and Power* (NY, Oxford U Press, 2003); see also Janet Dine and Andrew Fagan, Editors, *Human Rights and Capitalism.* (North-Hampton, MA, 2006); Marjorie Kelly, *The Divine Right of Capital: Dethroning Corporate Aristocracy* (San Francisco, Berrett-Koehler, 2007; Stephen R. Munzer, *A Theory of Property* (); Jeremy Waldron, *The Right to Private Property* (NY, Oxford U Press, 1988).

---

[1] Doug Henwood, *Wall Street* (New York: Verso, 1997), p. 7.

[2] Michael Moffitt, "Shocks, Deadlocks, and Scorched Earth," *World Policy Journal* (Fall, 1987), pp. 560-61, 572-73.

[3] William Greider, *Who Will Tell the People?* (New York: Simon and Schuster, 1992), pp. 378-79, 399-400.

[4] Adam Smith, *Wealth of Nations* (New York: Random House, 1965), p. 64.

[5] John D. Donahue, *The Privatization Decision:* (New York: Basic Books, 1989).

[6] *Public Power Directory and Statistics* for 1983 (Washington, DC: American Public Power Association, 1983); Jeanie Kilmer, "Public Power Costs Less." *Public Power Magazine*, May/June 1985, pp. 28-31; the late Montana Senator Lee Metcalf and Vic Reinemer, *Overcharge* (New York: David McKay, 1967).

[7] Edward Winslow Martin, *History of the Grange Movement* (New York: Burt Franklin, 1967), pp. 62, 70.

[8] Matthew Josephson, *Robber Barons* (New York: Harcourt Brace Jovanovich, 1962), p. 92; Joe E. Feagin, *The Urban RealEstate Game* (Englewood Cliffs, NJ: Prentice-Hall, 1983), pp. 57-8; Peter Lyon, *To Hell in a Day Coach* (New York: J.B. Lippincott, 1968), p. 6; see also Martin, *Grange Movement.*

[9] Wilfred Owen, *Strategy for Mobility* (Westport, CT: Greenwood Press, 1978), p. 23.

[10] John Prados, *The Presidents' Secret Wars* (New York: William Morrow, 1986), p. 152.

[11] Lewis Mumford, *Pentagon of Power* (New York: Harcourt Brace Jovanovich, 1964), pp. 134, 139; Stuart Chase, *Men and Machines* (New York: Macmillan, 1929), chapters 3-4.

[12] Chase, *Men and Machines*, pp. 42-43.

[13] PBS, *Nova* (September 2, 1986).

[14] Stuart Chase, *The Economy of Abundance* (New York: Macmillan, 1934), chapter 8.

[15] Phil Grant, *The Wonderful Wealth Machine* (New York: Devon-Adair Co., 1953), pp. 301-06.

[16] Dan Nadudere, *The Political Economy of Imperialism* (London: Zed Books, 1977), p. 251, quoting in part from E. Penrose, *The International Patent System*, 1951, p. 29.

[17] Ibid, pp. 186, 255.

[18] Karl Marx, *Capital* (New York: International Publishers, 1967), volume 1, p. 375, footnote 2.

[19] Nadudere, *Political Economy of Imperialism*, p. 38, quoting Leo Huberman, Man's Worldly Goods, pp. 128-29.

[20] Lewis Mumford, *Technics and Civilization* (New York: Harcourt Brace Jovanovich, 1963), pp. 227-28, 438. Read also Nadudere, *Political Economy of Imperialism*, pp. 51-55.

[21] Chase, *Economy of Abundance*, p. 166.

[22] Lester Thurow, *Head to Head: The Coming Economic Battle Among Japan, Europe, and America* (New York: William Morrow, 1992), p. 187.

[23] Grant, *Wonderful Wealth Machine*, pp. 301-306.

[24] Karl Polanyi, *The Great Transformation* (Boston: Beacon Press, 1957), p. 277, quoting from Pirenne, *Medieval Cities*, p. 211.

[25] Marx, *Capital*, volume 1, pp. 372-74, 428, 435, 562; Eric R. Wolf, *Europe and the People Without History* (Berkeley: University of California Press, 1982), pp. 273-74, 279.

[26] Richard Barnet, *The Lean Years* (New York: Simon and Schuster, 1980), p. 260.

[27] Howard Zinn, *A People's History of the United States* (New York: Harper Colophon Books, 1980), p. 277.

[28] Herman E. Daly, John B. Cobb, Jr., *For the Common Good* (Boston: Beacon Press, 1989), p. 11.

[29] Robert Lacey, *Ford* (New York: Ballantine Books, 1986), pp. 118-40; also Juliet Schor, *The Overworked American* (New York: Basic Books, 1991), p. 61.

[30] Lacey, Ford, pp. 105-06; Brian Tokar, *Redesigning Life? The Worldwide Challenge to Genetic Engineering* (London: Zed Books, 2001).

[31] Tokar, *Redesigning Life?;* Stanley Wohl, Medical-Industrial Complex (New York: Harmony Books, 1984), pp. 69-71; Ivan Illich, *Medical Nemesis* (New York: Bantam Books, 1979), p. 245.

[32] "India Protects its Heritage Against Privatization Theft," *COMER* (February 2006), p. 8. Taken from Globe and Mail (December 12, 2005)

[33] Stephen Budiansky, "An Act of Vision for the Developing World," *U.S. News and World Report* (November 2, 1987), p. 14.

[34] Jean-Pierre Berlan, "The Commodification of Life," *Monthly Review* (Dec. 1989), p. 24.

[35] Alan Weisman, "Columbia's Modern City," *In Context*, No. 42, 1995, pp. 6-8; *Los Angeles Times Sunday Magazine*, September 25, 1994.

[36] E.K. Hunt, Howard Sherman, *Economics* (New York: Harper and Row, 1990), p. 166.

[37] Kurt Rudolph Mirow, Harry Maurer, *Webs of Power* (Boston: Houghton Mifflin Co., 1982), p. 16.

[38] Thurow, *Generating Inequality*, p. 149.

[39] Ibid, p. 154, (emphasis added).

[40] Chase, *Economy of Abundance*, p. 165.

[41] Rolf H. Wild, *Management by Compulsion* (Boston: Houghton Mifflin, 1978), pp. 92, 94-95.

[42] Anthony Banco, "Playing With Fire," *Business Week* (September 16, 1987), p. 78.

[43] Charles Mackay, Extraordinary *Delusions and Madness of Crowds* (New York: Farrar, Straus and Giroux, 1932), pp. 90-97.

[44] Ibid, pp. 1-45; Lester Thurow, *The Future of Capitalism: How Today's Economic Forces Shape Tomorrow's World* (England: Penguin Books, 1996), p. 221; John Train, *Famous Financial Fiascoes* (New York: Clarkson N. Potter, 1985), pp. 33-41, 108-89.

[45] Mackay, *Delusions*, pp. 46-88; see also Train, *Fiascoes*, pp. 88-95; Charles P. Kindleberger, *Manias, Panics, and Crashes* (New York: Basic Books, 1978), pp. 220-21.

[46] Ellen Hodgson Brown, *Web of Debt* (Baton Rouge, Third Millennium Press, 2007) pp. 253-54, 387-89, primarily on the crash in Japan and Southeast Asia.

[47] Lester Thurow, *The Future of Capitalism: How Today's Economic Forces Shape Tomorrow's World* (England: Penguin Books, 1996, p. 15; Lester Thurow, *Building Wealth: The New Rules for Individuals, Companies, and Nations in a knowledge-Based Economy* (New York: HarperCollins, 2000), pp. 85, 102.

[48] Michael Goldhaber, *Reinventing Technology* (New York: Routledge & Kegan Paul, 1986), p. 185.

[49] For another study see Vandana Shiva's *Protect or Plunder: Understanding Intellectual Property Rights*.

4. The Productive Roles, and Extractive Roles, of Secondary Monopolies

The American health care, insurance, legal, and welfare systems, taxi medallions, etc, are exclusive marketing-rights-monopolies which built up ad hoc due to a lack of those services as a social or human right. Prisons, law enforcement, and other protective industries are not monopolies per se but they grew to the huge proportion of the economy that they are due to the inequalities and lack of rights within the monopolized sectors of the economy (3.7% of adult white Americans, 15% of adult Latinos, and 35% of adult African Americans, have been in jail).

All social structures—governments, banking systems, retirements, other insurances, a legal system, health care, etc—are all social technologies (wealth producing, distribution, and governing tools) discovered and put in place over the centuries. That they are ineffectively overseeing "rights" within an unequal system is instinctively understood. The threat of ballot box revolutions due to periodic economic collapses led to Social Security, unemployment insurance, and in almost 50 countries, universal health care becoming social tools to fulfill human rights and social rights.

That these rights were given only during economic crises, and are typically partially withdrawn during good times, proves the power structure is protecting their wealth and power. Even the novice can't help noticing it would be much easier to fund those economic changes during prosperous times than during an economic crisis. Yet reforms are put in place primarily during a periodic crisis, and are partially, and steadily, withdrawn by power and wealth in good times. Hard right think tanks are gearing up to cut back, or even eliminate, Social Security as we speak.

In the early to middle stages of designing democratic societies, as imperial societies slowly evolved from Feudalism, the wealthy were so few, and those producing their daily subsistence needs within their family unit—primarily from the land—were so many, that not even the most alert could conceive of rights for all to retirement income, universal health care, home insurance, unemployment insurance, support for the incidentally, or accidentally, impoverished, etc. They were all social technologies (social tools) of the future made possible by the enormous efficiencies of advancing industrial, chemical, electrical, and medical technologies.

As imperial industrialized societies formed, ad hoc, labor-intensive, capital-intensive, monopolized, and expensive, social structures arose to fill the needs of the citizenry as they were slowly brought into the flow of money within a monopoly capitalist system. This is the process addressed two paragraphs above which prevented expansion of rights during good times.[a] Ever-increasing efficiencies of technology increased rights rapidly, but those same rights (living standards) would have been put in place many times faster if technology and wealth had been shared instead of monopolized. Power and greed caused the past centuries of poverty and war, and neither social rights, nor human rights, are yet fully in place.

The masses within a subsistence economy could have been quickly brought within a money economy, except it was seldom their rights under consideration. A society with full and equal economic rights for all could have, and likely would have, established a banking, land, and technology commons under inclusive and equal property rights principles. But the powerful, the ones creating those laws, would quickly calculate this would limit each to accumulating only earned wealth. Thus, **power structures world wide protected their power and wealth through continually refining exclusive-titles to nature's resources and technologies, which rightfully belong to all in roughly equal shares.**

Not only were aristocratic property rights designed to maintain wealth and power within national economies, they were also designed to claim the wealth of the peripheries of empires. This is the reason for the covert destabilizations of emerging countries as they attempted to break out of the strait jacket imposed by empires. If they were permitted their freedom, and full and equal economic rights, others would notice their rapid rise in living standards, and quickly restructure to full and equal property rights, social rights, and human rights, laws.

Excessive rights for a few and lack of rights for the many, structured into unequal property rights being the very heart of the monopoly system, stands exposed as we lay out the simplicity of transposing monopoly rights into use rights relatively equally shared, and utilized, by all.

The insurance industry extracting wealth within the monopolization process: Security is a necessity and, in most developed nations, some form of Social Security (retirement insurance) is now a human right. As it is recognized as such, the powerful, though they continually try and those efforts are intensifying, find it difficult to reduce life-sustaining guarantees for those final years.[1]

Health insurance, car insurance, and home insurance are necessities for most. Yet none are a social right anywhere, and the insurances we do have are,

---

[a] Expansion of excessive rights is a regular occurrence within legislatures through special-favor laws and termed it rent seeking. Starting out as a service, secondary monopolies expanded into rent seeking. Most those secondary monopolies can be eliminated through that service becoming a social or human right.

roughly, only 50% productive. With the masses not having all their social rights, ad hoc insurance industries sprang up. Instead of a social right to insurance, similar to Social Security, being established by society, a "market" for insurance evolved, and stock markets simultaneously expanded to buy and sell the capitalized values created by those massive appropriations of wealth; roughly half that extracted wealth was ground up in the process.

The annual profits of insurance industries are capitalized 10 to 30 times in the stock markets. As Social Security has proven there are no needs for insurance companies, thus no need for their costs or their profits, insurance industries are strictly a monetization, money creation, social structure for "creating money out of thin air."

A society with full and equal economic rights creates money to create wealth while current capitalist economies monopolize nature's wealth and technologies to create money. At least 95% of America's huge blocs of finance capital accumulated through that process is unearned wealth. The capitalization process made those unearned values transportable and transferable (saleable). Wealth rightfully belonging to each and all is appropriated, capitalized, sold, and banked; as if by magic, a lack of rights for the masses transposes into our many unnecessary insurance industries; we explain further below.

In the banking, land (resources) and technology chapters we theoretically eliminated wasteful monopolization by apportioning the rental values on wealth produced by nature and all wealth produced by labor directly to the citizenry. These secondary monopolies are unique in that the maximum efficiency is gained by totally replacing their marketing structure with a social right (insurance) or a human right (universal health care and retirement).

Having rights or lacking rights is the crucial difference between a highly efficient sector of an economy and a highly labor-intensive, monopolized, wasteful sector, extracting wealth from others, capitalizing the profits on those non-tangible values, and buying and selling those unearned values on the markets.

Rights can be given any time a power structure decides. But, not understanding the enormous power of a modern economy to take care of everyone's needs, and with heavily-funded think tanks pouring out perception management belief systems (spin) protecting the powerful's excess rights, rights for all are actually preached as a loss of rights (which it is for those with excessive rights). Thus retirement funds, accepted as a human right today, were typically given only when the market economy broke down, people were starving, a revolution was imminent, and the leaders, those who had been continually blocking such key expansions of rights, stood to lose both wealth and power. True to our thesis, with 60 years of good times, those powerful have been working furiously to roll back Social Security and other social and human rights within today's unequal property rights, all under the rhetoric of protecting your rights.[2] As this crisis deepens (2008-10), and especially after the year-long-battle over expanding health care, more rights for the people are spoken of even on main stream news.

Under the threat of a ballot box revolution, American citizens were given Social Security as a human right in the Great Depression. Annual management costs are less than 1% of premiums collected through payroll deductions. In contrast sales, management, and profits of insurances in the market economy typically cost 50% of premiums paid. Insurances negotiated by unions, and given as a social right to those select few, typically cost only 6% of premiums.

Social Security is insurance and it is much larger than any two or three insurance companies put together. Yet few people have ever seen their efficient regional Social Security office. Restructure health, auto, and home insurances to a social right and those insurance offices—along with the office furnishings and those wastefully employed—are replaced by a fully productive regional office that, like Social Security, you seldom see; those insurance companies simply disappear.

Your home insurance premiums paid when you pay your mortgage payment should be almost half their current costs. No fault auto insurance, paid as a percent of the price of gas, would greatly lower costs as each person pays equally, relative to the gas used. Universal health care, such as at least 12 states are discussing becoming law, all developed nations—except the US—already have, and over 5000 physicians were petitioning for, can be handled under payroll deductions at 40% today's cost, or it could be covered by socially collected resource rents and socially owned and operated bank profits at no visible, our of pocket, cost.

If one's insurance needs fall outside those parameters, simply sign up, pay the premium, and pocket the savings. That is, if the powerful will ever permit such social rights to be allotted to the citizenry. The wasted labor and capital once operating the highly inefficient insurance sectors of the economy are now available for truly productive uses.

The legal structure also extracts wealth: In a society with full and equal economic rights, both crime and the need for legal resolutions would drop to a very small fraction of today's epidemics of lawlessness and battles over divisions of wealth. In 2006, a radio show host in Boston, incensed at the murders each week by drug dealers, blurted out, "Give me a call. I will find you a job." Within a week 10 of those battling for turf on the drug scene were enrolled in a cooking school. That violent life was not what they wanted; they simply did not have rights to a job of any kind let alone one with equal pay.

With each having full and equal rights to their share of nature's wealth, rights to a productive job through a radical reduction in working days, being paid equally for equally-productive labor, and considering a total restructuring of society (see Conclusion), the daily struggle for survival would be replaced by an efficient, calm, inclusive economy with each having security and a quality life.

Assuming inclusive full and equal economic rights were sincerely put in place, which means each having the opportunity for a respectable identity and a secure life; the 2.4 million American prisoners now increasing 47,000 per year would shrink to infinitesimal levels. Those building and guarding prisons, the police, private guards, the personnel operating the justice system, and its brick and mortar infrastructure would shrink accordingly.

But the savings go far beyond the criminal justice system into the civil courts. We quote from Fred Rodell's classic, *Woe Unto You Lawyers:*

> It is the lawyers who run our civilization for us—our governments, our business, our private lives....We cannot buy a home or rent an apartment, we cannot get married or try to get divorced, we cannot die and leave our property to our children without calling on the lawyers to guide us. To guide us, incidentally, through a maze of confusing gestures and formalities that lawyers have created....The legal trade, in short, is nothing but a high-class racket.[3] The lawyers—or at least 99 44/100 per cent of them—are not even aware that they are indulging in a racket, and would be shocked at the very mention of the idea. Once bitten by the legal bug, they lose all sense of perspective about what they are doing and how they are doing it. Like the medicine men of tribal times and the priests of the Middle Ages they actually believe in their own nonsense.[4]

Fred Rodell knew that expensive divorces were replaceable by each party agreeing to how property is to be divided, each fill out and file a prescribed form, the judge questions each party to ascertain each were fully aware, that the settlement was fair, and grant the divorce.

Some states have enacted such laws, and the savings, in both emotional distress and money, were everything Rodell predicted. Special care is taken when children are involved but typically they too are rescued from the trauma of a messy, expensive, divorce. Most trauma and expense before those legal changes were because citizens were denied a right, in this case the right to a simple, agreed-upon, divorce.

Probating wills were, and many still are, subject to lawyers milking estates of the deceased. In contrast, living trusts and beneficiary deeds take effect with almost no cost upon his or her death when changes are no longer possible. As soon as papers of the trustee's death are filed, the heirs have full control of his or her share of the estate.

Legal forms are really a checklist of items that have to be addressed by all who wish to enter into a contract with each other, or with themselves. Most legal transactions are procedures requiring only the filling out of these ready-made forms. How else could it be? If most dealings between people were not based on custom, there would be chaos. This simplicity is blocked by the present legal system, which makes simple transactions complicated and tedious, thus expanding labor and time to justify large compensations. That is all wasted time, money, and resources.

Rosemary Furman, legal secretary and court reporter, estimated, if the public were given access to standardized forms, about 70% of the legal work could be eliminated. With this access, and guidance from the clerks of court, literate adults could easily handle uncontested divorces, name changes, debt collections, tax matters, bankruptcies, real estate transactions, adoptions, patents, wills, trusts, and many other legal matters. Furman charged twenty-five to fifty dollars for these services while lawyers received three hundred to five hundred dollars. But whenever citizens use a prepared form, and handle their own transactions; there are no costs beyond filing fees. "Everything I do," said Furman, "is the responsibility of the clerk of court."[5]

Over half the compensations for accidents, product liability, and malpractice are claimed by lawyers. In New Zealand, the "Accident Compensation Corporation oversees the claims process. Injured people file claims whether their injury happened at home, at work or at play, and compensation is provided fully and fairly."[6] This process is equally applicable to product liability and malpractice suits. Divorce, accidents, and liability constitute at least 80% of all civil suits and in each it is possible to almost totally eliminate lawyers.

Early lawyers were paid by the word. This led to the current unnecessary legalese that few can understand:

> It has been the custom in modern Europe to regulate, on most occasions, the payment of the attorneys and clerks of court, according to the number of pages which they had occasion to write; the court, however, requiring that each page should contain so many lines, and each line so many words. To increase their payment, the attorneys and clerks have contrived to multiply words beyond all necessity, to the corruption of law language of, I believe, every court of justice in Europe. A like temptation might perhaps occasion a like corruption in the form of law proceedings.[7]

Lawyers extract more than their share by keeping secret the simplicity of everyday common agreements. Once language is simplified and the public has access to legal forms, the practice of law via, obscurantism and hocus-pocus, disappears.

And we can go on and on: Conflict Resolution Law, corporate mini-trials, etc, are all examples of how to eliminate the current unnecessary expense of the legal system.

Most within the criminal class only lack rights. Though most the wealth consumed in the legal industry is wasted labor, wasted office space, wasted protective forces, wasted courtroom space, etc, huge profits are still made and those appropriated values—claimed by private prisons, law firms listed on stock markets, incorporated but unlisted law firms, etc—create unearned, high capitalized, values which are bought and sold.

Extracting wealth through health care: April 18, 2006, the American Medical Association released their study that, by U.S. Department of Justice guidelines, health insurers were effectively monopolies. Among the 50 most developed nations, only the United States and South Africa do not have universal health care. U.S. citizens pay out of pocket 38% more than the Canadians, 39% more than the French, 42% more than the Swedish, 53% more than Germans, 62% more than Italians, 78% more than Australians, 90% more than the Japanese, 100% more [actually 130% more] than the British, and 466% more than the Cubans.[8] Universal health care for many of these countries equal or, when one considers that all their citizens receive medical care, exceeds that in the United States.

Markets for health care are far from efficient. The more products sold, whether needed or not, or even if they may be harmful, the more profits that can be made. Such wasted labor and resources of secondary monopolies are not the result of intent. As a distribution mechanism, these unnecessary marketing territories expand relentlessly in all the service segments of the economy. Businesses must operate at their maximum to maximize profits and people must maximize their labor time to earn a good living. Thus, without full and equal economic rights, the service sectors of the economy continually expand.

In their book, *Frogs into Princes,* psychiatrists Richard Bandler and John Grinder explained the process. One of their fellow psychiatrists treated patients in a state clinic and averaged six visits per client. "In his private practice he is apt to see a client twelve or fifteen times...and it never dawned on him what caused that....The more effective you are the less money you make because your clients get what they want and leave and don't pay you anymore."[9] All sectors of the United States economy mirrors this psychiatrist's practice of, in part producing wealth, but in the greater part only extracting of wealth.

An episode of the *Sally Jesse Raphael Show* featured young women who, at fourteen years of age, were unjustly institutionalized.[10] With remarkable insight, these young women figured out the fraud, and outwitted the system. A patient advocate, a member of the Minnesota Mental Health Association instrumental in freeing these young ladies, pointed out that, when hospital occupancy declined they expanded into child care, and both "hospitals and psychiatrists were preying upon parents and children." The "cures and discharges came miraculously when the insurance ran out."

The Children's Defense Fund suggests at least 40% of these juvenile admissions were inappropriate, while a Family Therapy Network youth expert put the figure at 75%.[11] Few experiences could be more damaging to the self image of a youth than institutionalization during those crucial formative years. On balance, in the search for profits, the psychiatric industry can only have been doing far more harm than good.

A study by Rand Corporation found 40% of hospital admissions as being inappropriate because they involved simple procedures that could have been handled just as well in a doctor's office. Thirty percent of operations have been deemed unnecessary. Localities with fewer doctors had lower mortality rates and during hospital strikes in the United States, Canada, Great Britain, and Israel, the death rates went down. In the Israeli and New York strikes, the hospitalization rate dropped 85%. "It was as if the population was in better health when medical care was limited to emergencies."[12]

Canada is listed among those countries with lowered mortality rates when doctors were on strike. Yet "Canadians get bypass surgery half as often as Americans."[13] When exposed, the installation of pacemakers under promotions reminiscent of staying in style was a disgrace.[14] This author listened on the evening news to Dr. David Graham, who blew the whistle on Vioxx, pointing out that, "The patients that Vioxx was killing [44,000] equaled the death rate of two to four airliner crashes a week and there were five more drugs he knew that were highly suspect." Running an Internet search for "drugs, whistleblower" or "trans-fats, Denmark" will alert one the problem goes far beyond drugs. In each case addressed above, gaining markets, whether there was a real need or not, occasionally even if the process or product was lethal, was the game. Unneeded sales through market creation are springing up all the time. The recent lowering of the recommended cholesterol levels was surely for millions more patients to take prescribed statin drugs. TV ads on "restless leg syndrome" are to create a whole new syndrome requiring treatment with high-priced and dangerous drugs.

We could go much further but that is enough. This message, emailed to me, was sincerely appreciated: "I am a doctor and everything you said is true." David Himmelstein and Steffie Woolhandler are doctors at Harvard Medical School. In 2001, along with Dr. Ida Hellander, they wrote *Bleeding the Patient: The Consequences of Corporate Health Care*.[15] Here one will read 238 pages of unsettling facts on the American Health care system paralleling that just described.

Universal health care as a human right, paid from socially-collected resource rents and socially operated banking profits, with private doctors paid well yet all incentive for unnecessary treatment eliminated (like Britain, pay doctors bonuses for keeping patients healthy), would quickly drop health care costs by 60% even as all citizens receive quality care. A serious food and nutrition study and citizen education, if not dominated by food and drug corporations, would drop those costs another 50%, up to the last three years of life, while increasing life spans substantially. Example: Three years after the alert on the dangers of transfats, the evening news said, "There has been a dramatic rise in life expectancy and the experts do not understand why." Corn syrup and other cheap, high glycemic, sweeteners that the body cannot metabolize will prove to be just as dangerous.[b]

Welfare disappears when the wealth extractive processes are eliminated: In an inclusive society with full and equal economic rights, the only welfare necessary would be for those mentally or physically incapacitated.

By right, the first jobs for which they are qualified should go to the functionally impaired—answering services for the blind, accounting and secretarial work for those in wheelchairs, janitorial and assembly work for the learning disabled, etc. Surely there are jobs for most of these 14 million disadvantaged people, whose self-esteem would soar if only they could achieve self-sufficiency.[c]

The Americans with Disabilities Act (ADA) makes it illegal to discriminate against the physically or mentally disadvantaged in jobs they can handle. The severely impaired should have the opportunity, but—since any evaluation would be arbitrary—not the obligation, to work. It is those who have been faced with dependency who can best appreciate the need for the pride, equality, independence, and self respect, achievable through productive labor.

When handicaps result in a lack of productivity, employers being compensated by society as they maintain their employment, a right already in law, would eliminate most of the welfare bureaucracy. Those once working in the welfare industry can now move to productive jobs.

Others would have the right to a job, much as they do now—through talent, education, tests, interviews, contacts, seniority, etc. The major change would be a dramatic cut in the workweek, by law, which would—considering a total restructuring of society, open up space for realization of that human right. Who would object to over a 50% reduction in employed hours with no loss of living standards?

Rights to equal pay for equally-productive labor, a productive job, land, one's share of the fruits of technology, universal health care, retirement as a human right, honest insurance, the elimination of legal hocus-pocus, a public taught responsibility for its own health, and social safety nets for disastrous events that deny a person the ability to care for their family as a social right is the foundation of a truly democratic, all-inclusive, peaceful, productive, society with need for welfare only in cases of mental or physical incapacitation.

---

[b] Run a Google search for Bountiful Baskets.org. There one can buy healthy fresh fruits and vegetables for half the cost as in supermarkets. This simple distribution of quality food, as opposed to processed foods, would add years to one's life span.

[c] Mary Lord, ("Away With Barriers," *U.S. News & World Report* [July 20, 1992]: p. 60) says 43 million. Fourteen million is the lowest figure I have heard.

Where the foundations for primary monopolies are various forms of titles to nature's wealth, secondary monopolies evolved filling a need that citizens should be entitled to, a right which powerbrokers neglected (refused) to establish in law. Doing so would eliminate their market monopolies which currently waste over half our labor and resources.

Waste within those monopoly structures, as addressed above, expanded through the sale of unnecessary services. Eliminating monopolization through legislating those necessary services into a right typically reduces service costs over half even as citizens are better served. Unnecessary infrastructure—monopoly insurance structures, excess prisons, excess law offices, excess courtrooms, etc, and all currently wasted labors and resources—can be turned to productive use.

Agriculture within the community social-credit process:

On July 4, 2005, *Der Speigal* pointed out:

> When there's a drought in a region of Kenya, our corrupt politicians reflexively cry out for more help. This call then reaches the United Nations World Food Program – which is a massive agency of apparatchiks who are in the absurd situation of, on the one hand, being dedicated to the fight against hunger while, on the other hand, being faced with unemployment were hunger actually eliminated. It's only natural that they willingly accept the plea for more help. And it's not uncommon that they demand a little more money than the respective African government originally requested. They then forward that request to their headquarters, and before long, several thousands tons of corn are shipped to Africa ... Corn that predominantly comes from highly-subsidized European and American farmers ... and at some point, this corn ends up in the harbor of Mombassa. A portion of the corn often goes directly into the hands of unscrupulous politicians who then pass it on to their own tribe to boost their next election campaign. Another portion of the shipment ends up on the black market where the corn is dumped at extremely low prices. Local farmers may as well put down their hoes right away; no one can compete with the UN's World Food Program. And because the farmers go under in the face of this pressure, Kenya would have no reserves to draw on if there actually were a famine next year. It's a simple but fatal cycle.

Zambia had 40 small industries producing clothes for Zambians. A flood of used clothes from America undersold those producers, those industries closed down, the economic multiplier went into reverse, and the number of impoverished Zambians rose rapidly.

The wealthy world feasts on chicken breasts while boatloads of imported chicken wings and drumsticks, supported by the high price the wealthy will pay for those breasts, undersell and devastate the economies of weak nations. Not only are poor countries unable to compete against subsidized imported food and consumer products, they are also unable to export to the wealthy world due to both high supports and tariffs.

At times, the imperial centers sell items for roughly half the cost of production. But the money spent producing that item circulates within an exporting economy, roughly 15 times. This is the economic multiplier. Each million dollars worth of exports sold at half the cost of production, in this case $500,000, still generates $7.5 million of economic activity in the wealthy country year after year even as the same multiplier, now in reverse, eliminates the same value, $7.5 million, of economic activity annually in the importing country. The entire $1 million chicken business in the importing country disappears plus another $6.5 million dollars worth of business through which that money once circulated.

Let's reverse this process: If American farmers were undersold by subsidized agricultural surpluses from another society or that imported food was given to American consumers, U.S. farmers could not sell their crops. They would go broke, the tractor and machinery companies would be bankrupt, the millions of people depending on these jobs would be without work, resources and production of remaining industries would have to be sold to other societies to pay the import bill, and America would quickly become impoverished.

In a country not yet industrialized, their natural resources must be sold to pay for subsidized food, and other consumer products, from the industrialized world, and debt traps are put in place to maintain that dependency.[16] This process created a disaster in Mexico. As their food imports rose to 60% of their needs, wages fell drastically, industrial production shrunk, and debt and hunger increased dramatically. And it will get worse. Businesses that moved to Mexico for $3.50 an hour labor under that trade agreement are now moving to Asia for even cheaper labor and, along with those traders banking those massive profits instead of sharing, caused, in part, the current 2008-10 economic crisis.

Subsidiary monopolies follow this pattern: Through licenses to provide services within a monopoly structure, the citizenry are denied full and equal economic rights, doubling their costs, even as services are reduced. Give citizens full and equal economic rights—including insurance, health care, a just legal structure, etc—as social and human rights and those monopolies disappear, even as the quality of services rise rapidly. Elimination of monopolization extends both social and human rights substantially further than the Universal Declaration of Human Rights. Values, equal to the massive blocs of capital that once bought and sold by those monopolized service industries, have been transposed into relatively equally-shared use-values.

Again we point out that unearned wealth extracted through unequal property rights, is capitalized by a multiple of 10 to 30 times, sold, and becomes a bloc of capital which is loaned, in one way or another, back to those from whom it was extracted. Through taxes or consumer purchases, the citizenry repay that principal, plus interest, over and over on into perpetuity, and that impoverishing cycle continues, interrupted only by economic collapses (which appears to be happening as we speak) caused by too much unearned wealth in the hands of the few, and too little buying power in the hands of the many.

As soon as the services of these secondary monopolies are declared a right, the social structures can be put in place to care for those newly declared social and human rights at half the cost, or less, even as the quality of care rapidly rises. The efficiencies of monopoly capitalism are fiction.

We now turn to a modern information commons through which these rights can be realized.

[1] Greider, *Secrets of the Temple*, p. 630; Christian Miller, "Wall Street's Fondest Dream: The Insanity of Privatizing Social Security," *Dollars and Sense*, November/December 1998, pp. 30-35; Edward S. Herman, "The Assault on Social Security," *Z Magazine*, November 1995, pp. 30-35; Bernstein, Merton C., Joan Brodshaug Bernstein, Social Security: The System that Works (New York: Basic Books, 1988).

[2] **Naomi Klein, The Shock Doctrine: The Rise of Disaster Capitalism (New York: Metropolitan Books, 2007).**

[3] Fred Rodell, *Woe Unto You Lawyers* (Littleton, CO: Fred B. Rothman & Co., 1987).

[4] Rodell, *Woe Unto You Lawyers*, pp. 16-17.

[5] Katherine J. Lee, "Justice Has Broken Down," *Americans For Legal Reform* 4/2 (1985), p. 5; and other issues of *ALR*.

[6] George Milko, "It's Hassle-Free Down Under," *Americans for Legal Reform* 6/3 (1986): p. 3.

[7] Adam Smith, *The Wealth of Nations*, Modern Library ed. (New York: Random House), p. 680.

[8] Thomas K Grose, "Free Health Care for All," U.S. News (March 24-April 2, 20070), p. 65; Rasell, "A Bad Bargain," p. 6; Robert Weil, "Somalia in Perspective: When the Saints Go Marching In," *Monthly Review* (Mar. 1993): p. 10. Others have somewhat different statistics: Tom Shealy, "The United States vs. the World: How We Score in Health," *Prevention* (May 1986): pp. 69-71; Ernest Conine, "U.S. Should Take a Tip from Canada," *Missoulian* (Apr. 2, 1990): p. A4; John K. Iglehart, "Health Policy Report: Germany's Health Care System," *The New England Journal of Medicine* (Feb. 14, 1991): pp. 503-08 and *The New England Journal of Medicine* (June 13, 1991): pp. 1750-56; Victor R. Fuchs, PhD., and James S. Hahn, A.B., "How Does Canada Do It?" *The New England Journal of Medicine* (Sept. 27, 1990): pp. 884-90.

[9] Richard Bandler and John Grinder, *Frogs Into Princes* (Moab, UT: Real People Press, 1979), p. 102.

[10] *Sally Jesse Raphael Show* (May 30, 1988). Patient advocates Bill Johnson and Tom Wilson.

[11] "Kids in the Cuckoo's Nest," *Utne Reader* (Mar./Apr. 1992): p. 38.

[12] Sale, *Human Scale*, pp. 267-68; André Gorz, *Ecology as Politics* (Boston: South End Press, 1980), p. 161.

[13] Hurwit, "A Canadian-Style Cure," p. 12.

[14] Donald Robinson, "The Great Pacemaker Scandal," *Reader's Digest* (Oct. 1983): p. 107.

[15] Himmelstein, David, Steffie Woolhandler, Ida Hellander, *Bleeding the Patient: The Consequences of corporate Health Care* (Common Courage Press, 2001)

[16] See Bhagirath Lal Das, *WTO: The Doha Agenda: The New Negotiations on World Trade* (London: Zed Books, 2003) and his many other books. See also: Vandana Shiva's *Stolen Harvest: The Hijacking of the Global Food Supply* (Cambridge: South End Press, 2000).

5. A Modern Information Commons, Education at 5-to-15% the costs of Brick and Mortar Schools

Restructuring the developed world is prevented because information is monopolized by the financial power of four primary monopolies—land, Finance Capital, technology, communications—and the secondary monopolies, insurance, law, health care, etc.

Control of information, primarily the economic classics and the corporate media, protects monopolies. This ensures that wealth will remain in the same channels going to the same class of people.

Use-values are produced by combining labor, capital, and resources. Through **exclusive titles to (monopolization of) nature's resources and technologies, others are denied their rightful share of what nature offers to all for free.** The unearned share, of those values are claimed by capital which capitalize (monetize) those profits, both earned and unearned, by 10 to 30 times. These values, again both earned and unearned, circulate among monopolists as they each jockey for position within the ethereal world of high finance, maximizing their extraction of wealth, as opposed to the production of wealth.

Unequal property rights, as applied to nature's resources and technologies, locks each into the system. Through monopolization of the communications industry, perception management keeps belief systems firmly in place and it requires no conspiracy. Each one does just what we would do; fiercely protect the source of our livelihood.

The citizenry know little about past battles through which the limited rights they have today were wrenched from those laying claim to the major share of the wealth produced by nature and technology. Professor Herbert Schiller explains how America's view of the world has been distorted through labor having been "sealed off" from much of their history:

> How many movies did [corporate America] make about the labor movement? After all, America is made up of people who work. Where is the history of these people? Where's the day-in day-out history of the African American population? Where's the day-in and day-out history of women? Not just one program. Where's the whole history of the people? Where's the history of protest movements in America? Can you imagine the kind of material that could come from American protest movements? The entertainment people are always saying that they don't have enough

dramatic material. Who are they kidding?[1]

Just like the windmill, steam engine, and electricity becoming so cheap that the powerful lost monopoly control, a communications superhighway has the potential of being so inexpensive that—within both the wealthy nations and developing nations—minorities, environmentalists, the peace movement, lower-paid labor, and all politically weak segments of society will be able to reach the citizenry with the histories of dispossessions, impoverishments, waste, and violence. With that knowledge, their equal share of the wealth produced by nature's resources and technologies, rightfully belonging to us all in roughly equal shares, can be reclaimed, and the waste and violence eliminated.

Powerbrokers will use all the deceits and power at their disposal to prevent or delay the loss of their niche within the economy for extraction of unearned wealth. Those powerbrokers have been buying up exclusive titles to the efficient low frequency communication spectrums with the intent of forever forcing the citizenry to pay monopoly prices:

Imagine … that you're relaxing on the white sand, with a slight breeze in the air, just steps from clear blue water. The beach is open to the public, but it's never too crowded. It's a great place to surf. But then one day you show up and there's a huge brick wall blocking your path to the shore. Without telling anyone, the government sold off this seaside spot to a private developer. … If you still want to dip your toes in the water, the new management expects you to pay through the nose. You'd be pretty angry. Right? Well that's exactly what is happening right now in Congress. Only the valuable public resource being auctioned off isn't the beach—it's a prime slice of the public airwaves. …

The airwaves being taken over by the broadcasters are the Malibu of the radio spectrum—fine beachfront property. Signals at these lower frequencies travel farther at lower powers and can go through obstacles like walls, trees and mountains. That means lower infrastructure costs for broadband providers, encouraging the development of local wireless networks and lowering prices. With more unlicensed spectrum, the "Community Internet" networks being setup across the country would be faster and even more reliable. Super-high-speed broadband connections for just $10 a month could be a reality. … We're headed for a world in which all communications—television, telephone, radio and the Web will be delivered over the Internet. … We can sell off our public resources … or we can invest in the future, bringing the benefits of broadband to all Americans. But first our lawmakers need to pull their heads out of the sand.[2]

This example of establishing exclusive title to nature's resources and technologies, and forever claiming wealth produced by others without providing equal value in return, is a beautiful example of how exclusive-title-monopolies have been structured, through unequal property rights laws, for centuries. Each of those exclusive titles, or licenses, permits massive overcharges to the public for use of what are properly social rights and human rights, their share of those social services and nature's wealth at the lowest possible price. White space (unused spectrums within current spectrums) use, approved in 2009, expanding spectrum capacity several times may lead to those lower costs.

Even as we are far overcharged, the gains we do receive are so huge, and the even greater gains possible normally totally unknown, that everybody believes what they have always been told, this is the best of all possible property rights systems. But the communication superhighways being partially operational in America, fully operational in some countries, the possibility of the entire monopoly system collapsing, and society hopefully eliminating that waste, is this book. We will confine ourselves to how a communications superhighway could be established, if planned as a maximally efficient part of **the community process.**

Through E-learning (distance learning) many professors already have their lectures and curriculum online for their students to do their studies at home.[a] The student saves lodging and travel time, but other college/university costs are still, unnecessarily, the same. Internet1 is a hodgepodge of servers and routers reminiscent of the buggy roads of 200 years ago while Internet2—utilizing Abilene, Backbone Network Service (vBNS), and Wiki software, designed specifically as a communications superhighway connecting one to sources as they write (research Google Chrome's operating system)—has downloadable and it has uploadable speeds 10,000 times greater.

Internet 2 has already proven that all we will be describing is possible. It was designed to handle the data output of the Hadron Collider in Switzerland and other research, all of which requires massive computing power.

Utilizing this latest technology, the emerging world can install communication superhighways that, relative to brick and mortar education costs, are almost free. Those satellite digital superhighways, accessed through universal wireless broadband receivers on board all new computers, can reach even the remotest rural areas at very modest costs per user. Cell phones and broadband, already operational from any place on earth, will soon relegate landlines to history. When more satellites are needed, they will be launched.

---

[a] A Google search alerts us that grade school and high school classes are also available online.

That modest investment, creating modern communication superhighways, will permit countries to educate their citizens as far as they want to go at 5-to-15% the cost of brick and mortar schools. That savings alone would, each year, more than repay the costs of establishing those information superhighways.

Communications Superhighways Eliminating Monopolization

Assuming the world breaks out from under the many forms of monopolization within unequal property rights law, specifically meaning avoiding the privatization of those efficient low frequency spectrums, a 99% reduction in consumer cost per unit of communication capacity is possible.

When those information superhighways reach each home, a population can be educated for the 5-to-15% of today's costs we keep pointing to. The emerging world has the opportunity to make an end run around those nations whose valuable communication spectrums are monopolized and their brick and mortar schools fully operational. Massachusetts Institute of Technology, NASA, and Google, combining their expertise and money to provide an indestructible, WiFi and cell phone equipped, $200, laptop computer, for developing-world governments to provide free to children might be replaced by Google's new Chrome operating system operating entirely on the web using open source software. With operating systems and software on the web for free use, the current expensive software will be discarded to the dustbin of history.

With operational costs for individual Internet service now cheaper than accounting, costs of phone calls and broadband connections can be borne by society. Already VoIP (Voice over Internet Protocol) users speak to each other for free and the reception on the other side of the world is as clear as local landlines Skype, only one of many providers, has 405 million subscribers and adding 380,000 every day. Through the community social-credit process funding worldwide communication systems—as opposed to taxes—these efficiencies can be attained.

TV and radio stations streaming their programs onto those information superhighways will eliminate the need for down-stream booster stations.[b] Consumer choices will thus expand exponentially. The shakeout within the developed world will be at the same pace as those information superhighways are installed. The brick and mortar school infrastructures of the developing world will not have to be built because they already have full access to education.

To compete, the now-out-of-work, former down-stream, booster stations must provide more interesting programming. The market for programming

---

[b] Several broadband URL connections, viewable on your TV, each with thousands of TV station choices, and adding more every day, are already available online.

without advertising will trump the advertising stations those TV and radio stations, will have to produce programming for a narrow, single-interest, audience.

News networks will face the full brunt of competition as alternative news from around the world becomes available to all. *Democracy Now, Link TV, Mosaic, BBC, AlJazeera, INN Report, Indymedia,* documentaries, and news from all countries in all languages would present their views. Major news networks will have to address those various views or become irrelevant. Perception management will be severely constrained and control of perception to protect the wealthy and powerful will quickly become impossible.

As few people can handle such an overload of viewing choices, sports will gravitate to one bloc of stations, music and sitcoms will each gravitate to their blocs, and the viewers will further subdivide into various categories, such as a bloc of channels with pay-to-play movies.

Stations forced to close will be picked up by NGOs, and political groups, for pennies on the dollar. Formerly forced to the margins, dedicated progressives, environmentalists, sustainable-living researchers, permaculturists, Greens, the peace movement, minority rights, labor rights, women's rights, children's rights, antipoverty, and a thousand more causes will be able to reach the citizenry with their views of the world over those same information superhighways.

Politicians must address questions brought up that were previously kept off the table. Alert viewers will have hard questions; those answers will be available, will be voiced, and will be understood. Propagandists will no longer be able to create justifications for war, and full and equal economic rights, with peace and prosperity for all, will be possible.

Communication Superhighways Eliminates Intermediaries and Reduces Trading Costs

The difference between manufacturing cost and the consumer price, measures the major cost of most products, distribution. Typically, manufacturing costs are under 20% of the final selling price. With mail-order shipping charges from 2-to-4% of retail price, no one would pay intermediaries three to five-times the production cost when it is feasible, in this communication superhighway age, to study the products on an Internet database, contact the producer, buy the item, and have it shipped directly at 30-50% today's cost or even less.

Large shares of the world's consumer products are imported. But, if full and equal economic rights were attained worldwide, including equally-productive labor relatively equally paid, production will be primarily regional. Shipping half way around the world what could be produced next door is economic insanity. Once the common-sense principle of equal pay for equal work worldwide is accepted, and put in place, it will be much cheaper to produce and distribute regionally; those shiploads of identical consumer products meeting and passing each other on oceans and highways —consuming enormous finance capital, industrial capital, labor, resources, and energy—will be history.

Besides doing office work at home, one can search for, and order, consumer durables. Middlemen are primarily in the information business. Over the Internet, it will be possible for producers and consumers to trade directly and cheaply again, just as face-to-face trades were finalized for thousands of years. The current army of intermediaries would disappear. As those marketing channels become operational, prices for middle-priced to expensive items will drop substantially. The savings in distribution alone will sometimes reach those savings. In short, **measured in labor time producing and distributing,** and **counting the savings from elimination of patent monopolies we discussed above**, consumer costs of small to medium size consumer durables should drop 50-to-80%.

Currently America has 10 square feet of retail floor space for each shopper while Britain has only two square feet. That surplus retail space will disappear as Internet shopping rapidly lowers costs to a fraction of current levels. A great shakeout of the retail industry is inevitable. The buildings and support infrastructure for 60%, and it could be 80%, of what the developed world today considers necessary for distribution will be available for productive uses. An efficient, productive, and sustainable economy is possible.

Bill Gates, who accumulated $60 billion because he understood communications technology better than most, said, "The information highway isn't quite right. A metaphor that comes closer to describing a lot of the activities that will take place is the ultimate market."[3] We are describing that "ultimate market."

Big-Ticket, Infrequently-Purchased Items

Autos, appliances, furniture, farm equipment, industrial equipment, and major tools are all big-ticket, infrequently-purchased items whose buying requires accurate information but not the promotional-persuasive advertising hammering at us incessantly. We trust and get information from experience and we make the most important decisions by observing products in daily use. In a communications commons, customers would make purchase decisions by dialing a database containing all manufacturers and models of a product.

That database would have information required to make an informed decision—energy efficiency, noise level, hours of useful life, price, and other features—as well as videos of the product in use. With tests by independent researchers, such as Consumer Reports, note the pressure this would put on manufacturers to produce the most efficient products and stand out in this all-important master index. Buyers would, at their leisure, study engineering specifications, styling, and actual use of the product on their television or computer. Once a decision was made, they would only need to punch in the code for the desired order—model, color, and accessories—and a databank computer would note the closest distribution point where that item was available. Or buyers could choose delivery from the factory.

The bank account number, thumbprint, eye-scan, thermogram and/or signature of an Internet shopper would be verified by a master computer and that account instantly debited. If a credit line had been established at the local credit union or bank and recorded in an integrated computer, credit would be handled simultaneously. The process, not involving advertising, sales, or banking labor, would greatly reduce transportation, storage, and sales costs. Pressures on resources and the environment are correspondingly reduced as the price of these major consumer products, again measured in employed labor hours to earn the money, fall by 50%.

Product guarantees, maintenance, and repairs would be taken care of by local private enterprise under standardized guarantees. Direct trades between manufacturer and consumer, and elimination of distribution intermediaries, will be guaranteeing high-quality products at the lowest possible price.

Both seller and buyer would save time and labor as verbal explanations and mailing of information are eliminated. The current time-consuming exchange of information would be replaced by consumers studying databases at their leisure. This would conserve millions of acres of trees and the environmental impact caused by manufacturing paper, producing brochures and distributing that information, including a large percent of the retail establishments themselves disappearing, should be of high interest to the sustainable development movement.

Every qualified producer would enjoy the right to place his or her product or service in the databank and pay a very small percent of gross sales out of cash flow. In place of millions of dollars up front to advertise through the present openly-monopolized media, there would be only a small charge for entering the product information in a database. To eliminate clogging the databanks with useless information of producers no longer in business, regular minimum payments would be required to retain the privilege of selling through this integrated communications network.

Starting up a truly productive industry would be quite simple. A new company's advertising would have full billing alongside major producers. With consumers having easy access to all choices, a few wealthy corporations would no longer decide, through promotional-persuasive advertising, what the public wants.

In the United States, once direct contact is established between producer and consumer via product databases, it would only require roughly 100,000 rail-

roaders, possibly three million truckers, and a system of organized freight termi-
nals to distribute the nation's production. It would be a freight postal system just
as with Christmas packages today. The item would be delivered, or consumers
would receive notice of the arrival of their purchases, and pick them up at the
local freight terminal.

There are normally several trucking companies in any moderate-size city,
each complete with loading docks, storage capacity, dispatching equipment, and
staff. The following shipping pattern is already operational:

1) Shippers punch into a common-use database loads to be shipped;

2) truckers with computers punch in their location, freight preferences, and
where he or she would like to deliver the next load;

3) the computer shows where the loads are, the type of freight, the required
pickup and delivery times, the rate per mile, etc;

4) the trucker chooses a load, informs the computer, and records his or her
identification number;

5) and the computer records the acceptance, removes that load from the databank, provides a contract number to the trucker, and informs the shipper.

There will be no need for duplicated dispatching services, loading docks,
storage facilities, equipment, and personnel. Competitive monopolies, created by
the minimum capital requirements for trucking companies, are eliminated, placing independent truckers on an equal footing with corporate truckers. The nation's freight will quickly settle into flow patterns, and be moved as regularly as
mail by the cheapest combination of rail, truck, ship, and plane.

It might take three days to receive small items, and up to 10 days for large
items but, at one-half the price or less while taking pressure off of resources, society is well paid. Transit time between producer and consumer will be a fraction
of that currently through jobbers, wholesalers and retailers. A barcode scanner
listing the cheapest price in the area, and on the Internet, will lead shoppers to
distribution points with prices marked down 60-to-70%.

Manufacturers' on-time delivery of parts to the factory, that greatly reduces
storage and finance capital costs, will have been expanded to on-time shipping to
consumers. Those within the retail system who, formerly bought, stored, and
sold these products, are available to share the remaining productive jobs. Society
will eventually attain an undreamed-of efficiency. Well over 50% of these intermediaries between producer and consumer will eventually be eliminated, and
assuming society was alert and restructured labor's working hours and other crucial adjustments, all would be free to share the remaining productive work with
employment outside the home of only two to three days per week.

Once those productive jobs are shared, the average workweek reduced, and
labor fully paid, the small amount of time necessary to labor for one's share of

the nation's wealth, plus resource rental costs paid into the social-credit fund, would be the proper measure of the price of products and services. That potential reduction in costs, through elimination of unnecessary labor and productive labor being fully paid, is the meaning of Adam Smith's little-noticed insightful statement, "If produce had remained the natural wages of labor, all things would have become cheaper, though in appearance many things might have become dearer."

Inexpensive, Small, Frequently-Traded Items

The markup on perishable groceries is about 100% while the markup on small consumer durables is several hundred percent. There is a competitive sales monopoly at work in the latter. Taking full advantage of modern communications would remove all purchases above an intermediate price range out of the wasteful, duplicated retail outlets. Simultaneously, the consumers' choices would multiply through access to these products in databanks.

Household supplies, cosmetics, knickknacks, and most small, inexpensive consumer items would be most efficiently distributed through the present retail outlets. The breakeven point would be in the lower range of the intermediate-priced, occasionally-purchased, items. BountifulBaskets.org is distributing within several states fresh fruits and vegetables to local pickup points at the price normally charged to the markets those truckers formerly supplied.

Wholesalers would keep the quality and price of all products posted in a databank. Once trust had been established, retailers would check those bulletin boards for the best buys. This would eliminate the need for many jobbers and other salespeople.

Shopping as a Social Event Entails a Cost

Shopping is recreation for many people and a status symbol for others. Those status shoppers would have no trouble finding merchants to accommodate the high prices associated with status shopping (Tupperware, Avon, Tiffanys, etc.). The majority would choose the most direct, least labor-intensive, cheapest, method of completing a trade. This would not impinge on coffeehouse-type trades where socializing is the primary activity.

Reserving TV Time for New Products

Innovations on a familiar product would be readily presented to the public through a databank while totally new products would require special access to the public. Complementing TV channels reserved to feature new inventions, these creations accessible in a database, would be quite popular.

Once a production-distribution infrastructure is in place, promotional-persuasive advertising becomes wasteful. Rather than titillate the consumer with thousands of toys to be played with and discarded, it would be much more socially efficient to abandon persuasive advertising and permit people to advance to a higher intellectual, social, and cultural level.

The maximum average living standard within the capabilities of the earth's resources and ecosystem can be calculated. Society could, and should, use those proven promotional-persuasive methods to educate people about the waste of the current production-distribution systems. Many in the developed world have already abandoned the "conspicuous consumption" lifestyle for rational living (see pp. 229-30 in *Economic Democracy: A Grand Strategy for World Peace and Prosperity*, 2010, by this author, also the *Anastasia* book series by Vladimir Megre).

If people are so dull that a society with a respectable living standard cannot function without promotional-persuasive advertising, which we do not believe, society could analyze advertising for essential and nonessential products for the desired standard of living. Many items—cigarettes, alcohol, and chemical-laden processed foods—lower the quality of life at a serious pace, their promotion, or promotion of food with transfats or corn syrup in them is economic insanity. The public, captivated by the enormous wealth they are unaware of as having been extracted from them, pays dearly for the debasement of their lives.

Driving a $60,000 luxury automobile while others are driving fuel-efficient $20,000 cars may draw admiration today, but that will turn to ridicule as soon as each are paid roughly equally for equally-productive labor. The resources saved and pollution prevented by that refocused social mindset would be essential to the survival of thousands of species, to humankind's quality of life, and most probably to our survival.

Music, Sports, Movies, and Game Shows

A block of channels should be reserved for sports, movies, and game shows, pay per view is already well established; however, they will be cheaper. Along with more time to enjoy TV, viewer choices would rise, and the truly talented artists would be well paid for their efforts. All would have a reasonable opportunity to prove their abilities. A formula of gradually reduced pay per million viewing hours as a show increased in popularity would compensate performers relative to their popularity, little different than now. With new performers having access to the public, monopoly control disappears.

Investment and Job Opportunities

Along with databases, a few channels should be reserved for direct communication between those offering investment opportunities and investors looking for them. As everyone with savings would have access to investment information stored in those databanks, money monopolists would be bypassed. Individual investors would put their risk capital in innovations that went unrecognized by regular loan institutions. If the investments were truly productive, investors would receive much higher than average returns. However, if their claims to insight were not valid, they would not be able to hide behind the protective shield of monopolization.

An entrepreneur who had obtained community approval, and initial investment capital from the bank, they need both now, would deposit a prospectus in a databank. Investors would study the various investment plans, buy shares in the most promising, and have their accounts automatically debited, all without intermediaries.

Talented workers would look over prospectuses, which would include labor needs and incentives, and if they saw where their talents would be used productively and profitably, and assuming they had fulfilled their contract to train a replacement, they could transfer to that new job. Labor would be mobile and free, not dispossessed as in a reserve labor force. Their right to their share of the efficiency gains of technology translates to average employed working hours of only two to three days per week.[c]

For their risk, the original innovators, investors, and worker owners would receive the initial higher profits plus the increased values of a successful company. Through sharing in the profits, workers and management who bought stock through deductions of 10-20% of their wages would be well compensated. The profit potential would increase their desire to maximize efficiency and provide incentive to look for new industries to develop.[4]

Others would quickly analyze and duplicate the innovative production or distribution process, and prices would fall to just that required to compensate the innovators, labor, and capital. Through low priced products, equal pay for equally-productive labor, and rights to a productive job, each member of society would be receiving their proper share of wealth provided by nature and the effi-

---

[c] See the work of Charles Fourier 180 years ago, and Thorstein Veblen, Bertrand Russell, Lewis Mumford, Stuart Chase, Upton Sinclair, and Ralph Borsodi in the first half of the 20th century. Late 20th century writers describing the same phenomenon are Juliet Schor, Seymour Melman, Samuel Bowles, David Gordon, and Thomas Weiskopf, Jeremy Rifkin, Andre Gorz, Hans-Peter Martin and Harold Schumann, and numerous European authors.

ciency gains of technologies; which are gifts of nature nurtured by inventors' labors and talents.

If a replacement were not immediately available, other workers at the factory could double their pay by working five days a week. Strict rules of later time off to compensate would have to be followed. Permitting doubling up on employed working hours would appropriate the labor-rights of others and subvert the economy through again creating a class with superior rights (though in a much subdued form).

With a communications reducing production and distribution costs 60%, adequate compensation to the innovators being 10%, and prices measured in hours of labor required to purchase a product, the public would benefit by a 50% reduction in the price of consumer products. Through the reduced income of a shorter workweek matching the reduction in living costs, there would be no loss in average living standards. Societies which decided to forego a throwaway society and opt for a fuel cell, hybrid car, bicycle economy, and other efficient transportation systems, would provide a quality lifestyle with even less labor.

Global warming is the world's most serious problem. A sensible world society, designed to reduce pollution, reduce greenhouse gases, and still provide a quality life for all, can be designed with each employed outside the home two to thee days per week. The human animal has tremendous energies which must then be channeled into pleasurable pursuits that do not consume precious resources or pollute the environment.

Education

Children want the approval of their parents and other members of society. They love to excel, and desire equality with their peers. They are curious and, if not discouraged, love to learn. Today's educational system creates too many barriers; "half of all gifted children float through school with average or worse grades, never realizing their potential ... almost 20 percent will drop out."[5]

There are many reasons: a child may be timid and terrified of school, an inferiority complex may prevent a student from functioning, or excessive pressure to do well may be daunting. The school district may have obsolete books and teaching aids, and students may not get the individual attention they need. Local peer groups, gangs, etc., may replace parents and teachers as role models. Parents may not be involved enough in their child's learning. Or the curriculum may be so slow it is boring. With elimination of these, and other, barriers, many with low grades will blossom right along with their peers.

Schools are a commons but they need to be modernized. With K1 through K20 downloadable or viewable from Internet2, or possibly an Internet3, every home would have every class at their fingertips, free of charge. Each subject would have several lecturers, each the best in their field. The competition would be intense for those lecture positions, and those best educators in the world would be well paid. Each recorded course would be edited for maximum clarity, simplicity, and comprehension. Everything in a book, or dozens of books, can be summarized in those recorded lectures.[d]

Reasoning is quite natural, and nothing can beat a good educator whose recorded lectures anticipate, and are carefully structured to answer, most questions. With all society having access, the fictions and omissions of history, especially omissions, would be challenged, researched, and corrected.

With their lessons recorded, these high-quality educators would be spending less time teaching than any one of the tens of thousands they replaced. They would concentrate on studying all lectures for ways to improve theirs. Role modeling is the most potent teacher of all, and these skilled teachers would be great role models.

The equipment required for each student would be a $200 computer, with the operating system and all software on the Internet, given free to every student on earth while in kindergarten, courtesy of their governments. These lessons would be in a databank, fully accessible on the communications superhighways. Classes requiring hands-on learning would be held in a classroom setting, along with supporting recorded programs.

So long as students maintain an adequate grade average, a share of the money society saved on maintaining the present school system should be paid to their family, or directly to the student. Allowing for each child's ability, it would be logical to pay this incentive for each subject, and on an average of all subjects. With spending money earned for each subject, motivated students would zip through those subjects. Developing nations do not have to deconstruct an entrenched, expensive educational system, and their citizens' motivation for education is high, so incentive pay would not be a necessity, but paying them modest sums would establish that necessary model for when their economy is developed. A small share of current classrooms would become administrative testing stations, as the citizenry educate themselves cheaply, and efficiently, at home.

With the two to three day workweek possible in a developed economy, there would be adequate time for parents to monitor their children's learning. With rapport between parent and child, the brightest would cover a current year's education in as little as four months, some in two months. The most intelligent, and motivated, would have the knowledge of PhDs at an age when they would normally be entering universities, which, incidentally, would eliminate another monopoly.

---

[d] Current access restrictions to Internet2 will disappear as other nations establish their accessible communication superhighways.

Actually those students would have a much broader education than most PhDs. Current doctoral studies are very narrow in focus. Without breadth of education, the answers to the world's problems will not be found there. Conversely, if universities emphasized graduate degrees covering a broad spectrum of disciplines instead of narrow fields, answers would be found relatively quickly. Through free studies provided on communication superhighways, students would have that broad education. This is proven by over one million American children already being successfully home schooled, doing well in universities, and their numbers are growing 15% a year, all without government support.[6]

Students would not be pressured to follow the teaching of any one professor. Others might have a different view, and students could listen to all views. Judgments would be made while still young and idealistic. All this would be gained while enjoying the irreplaceable quality time between parent and child. Talented students, lacking parental support, would find a surrogate family by immersing themselves in education.

Private or public education centers would be operated for the few who could not function under home self-education. Upon doing satisfactory work, they would still receive incentive funds. The compensations and identity received by siblings and friends for successful home schooling would be noticed by younger children, and provide motivation to avoid the formal school setting.

Most children would be proud to go shopping with their own earnings, and it is hard to visualize many children being irresponsible toward their education if it meant losing both their freedom of choice, and their spending money. They would quickly learn responsibility when it meant both financial and emotional rewards. Society would quickly become accustomed to such a system and the need for brick and mortar schools would be very minimal.

It would be logical to eliminate the senseless violence in today's children's programs. At the least, quality programming could be assigned a bloc of channels so conscientious parents could maximize their children's intellectual and moral growth.

Incentive funds, as a social right, would in no way impinge on others' rights. Those rights could only be exercised by obtaining a set grade average, and those funds go right back to the people from whom they came. Over time, such incentives would be looked upon as normal as wages.

Older students would soon learn to structure their flexible education time around a job. There need not be a sharp cutoff between school years and entering the workforce. The options for pursuing education for a career, and earning one's living, would be increased. Instead of a division between students and workers, the two would overlap until the young adults opted for a career.

Motivated children, young adults, and adults would obtain most of their education at home and at their own pace. Children with a desire to learn, which is most, would find the field wide open. Left to their own devices, they would quickly learn it was their time and labor being conserved by dedication and attention to the subjects being taught. The alert would be developing university level leaning skills while in grade school

Many talented children's potential, now lost through boredom and diversion to socially undesirable activities, would be salvaged. The brightest would attain a 12th grade education in less than eight years, the middle level in 10, and even the slower group, which currently sets the pace of a classroom, would learn more quickly. There would be adequate resources, and time, to give special support to the few who are unable to cope for various reasons. This would not only conserve society's labor, it would also economize students' energy and time. This potential was shown by an experiment with interactive videos reducing learning time while increasing comprehension by 30%.

Having watched great videos on *Free Speech TV, Link TV, The Learning Channel, The History Channel, The Discovery Channel*, public broadcasting channels, etc, we conclude the statement, "A picture is worth a thousand words," should be updated to; "One documentary is worth a million words." The best of those documentaries combines the wisdom of many researchers, which comprise many lifetimes of study. All viewers will absorb that knowledge at some level. Avid reading will seldom bring one close to the understanding gained from a well-researched documentary. The gain for the slower, and less avid, readers would still be substantial. As opposed to being bored and discouraged, students will enjoy their education.

A central testing facility would issue scholastic level certificates to adults. This would quickly equip all nations to be competitive. Since credentials are crucial for obtaining good jobs, all would have access to their scores, the right to analyze their answers, and the right to retake tests. Millions who dreamed of additional education would find it freely available in what was previously their idle time.

As no one's knowledge is complete, every curriculum would be subject to review and correction. The Great Saint-Mihiel battle of WW I that never happened, and other examples of fraudulent history addressed throughout this author's books, are not exceptions.[7] Severely distorted history is the norm, and such failures to tell the full truth seriously retards democratic development while correct, and full, knowledge is critical to understanding the world, and planning one's future.

Every day we learn something new or reinforce what we already know. To waste huge amounts of resources while continually affirming nice-sounding slogans about efficiency, justice, and compassion, while operating an inefficient economy, and violent foreign policy, seriously limits true knowledge.

It is not possible to get every student to enjoy learning for its own sake. If given a choice, most people would choose to do things that best support their need for identity and security; for many that is obtained in work, sports, and hobbies, rather than intellectual pursuits. There will be those who, though unable to compete across the board scholastically, will take great interest and do well in a field of their choice. Some, early on, will perform at a genius level, and hold that lead throughout their life.

Schools, as now structured, do perform a babysitting function. But, if that is the criterion, society should be aware that the potentials of many children are lost, and that child care is what they are paying for, not education. One must also be aware that early industrialists hoped "the elementary school could be used to break the labouring classes into those habits of work discipline now necessary for factory production....Putting little children to work at school for very long hours at very dull subjects was seen as a positive virtue, for it made them 'habituated, not to say naturalized, to labour and fatigue."[8]

Inspired Teachers for Every Student

People feel insecure at any suggestion of fundamental change in their social structure, and most are closely attached to their current institutions of education. But, in the current school structure, where is that all-important role model if the student has a poor, mediocre, or burned-out teacher? Under the system proposed here there would be all great teachers, each teaching his or her deepest beliefs, and their recorded lectures would be freely available for all.

In the soft sciences, economics, political science, finance, some social studies, and yes, history, what passes for education is, unwittingly, really perception management encasing society within beliefs protecting the monopoly system, those exclusive titles to nature's wealth we all grew up with, unaware this was the property rights structure which denied others their rightful share.

Certainly, good hands-on teachers are wonderful, but how can they hold enthusiasm with 25 or 30 children to teach? Would not the best possible teacher, backed by professional graphics, be able to put on an enthusiastic performance, and that enthusiasm be there forever in an education database, available to the world? Would not slow or timid students have a better chance of not developing an inferiority complex, and thus do better?

Parents Interacting Closely with Their Children's Education

With their increased free time, motivated parents would enjoy watching their children learn, and answering their questions. Children would ask an interested parent many more questions than they would a teacher. A motivated parent will go into deeper detail than the teacher, who has so little time to spare for individual attention. Students too timid to function freely in class would function confidently in a home setting. In the upper grades, motivated parents would share the experience, and learn with their children.

Better Institutions for Socialization

Socialization is of high importance. But the elimination of this function within education would free students for concentration on their studies, or it could remain a part of the education process if properly organized. Youth social clubs, or learning clubs, would spring up, and children would sign up voluntarily, as opposed to the requirement to attend school. When children join a social or learning club by choice, they would be bound by the rules of social courtesy, not classroom discipline, and would mix, relate, and learn social graces, at a faster pace than in a school setting. Parents would automatically seek such groups to replace the baby-sitting function of schools. With increased free time, the arts—music, dance, sculptors, singing, painting, and other skills—would expand rapidly.

Maintaining Curiosity, Creativity, and Love of Learning

Education freely available to all in their free time would bypass that greatest of all destroyers of curiosity and creativity, the straitjacketing of children into conformity. We cannot count on a great teacher in every classroom. Witness Massachusetts, a state with much higher quality schools than the average, in 1998 over half the teachers failed state qualification tests. There are over 15,000 educational experiments yearly. Some show dramatic improvements in education scores. Yet the overall average of scores does not improve. Either these better teaching methods are not spreading to other schools, or those schools do not have motivated teachers. Why not combine modern technology with the students' abilities and desires, and trade the constraints of current classroom and university systems for the opportunity of an inexpensive, high quality, and enjoyable, education?

One can point to great teachers and the gains for their lucky students. But there would be no loss to those children in this proposed educational structure. The number of children educated, to their maximum potential, would increase by a factor of two, three, or more. With easy access to classes in their spare time, many adults would broaden their education. Those who have a burning desire for another profession can gain credentials for their desired career even if finances are limited. Potentially great artists would have the opportunity to discover their talents, painters, poets, writers, singers, sculptors, ad infinitum?

There are undoubtedly many latent Einsteins, currently spending their lives in drudgery, who would educate themselves, and have their genius suddenly blossom for all the world to see, and enjoy, in the form of a book, a song, a new theory, an invention. A large percentage of society educating itself to a much higher level would develop an even more efficient and productive society, while protecting the environment and natural resources.

Once Borderline Teachable Graduating at the Top of Their Class

Inspirational teachers and programs have proven they can parent impoverished children with damaged psyches into becoming successful citizens. One such teacher is Ms. Marva Collins in Chicago. She worked among her students, rather than from her desk. Each time one did well she would put her hand under his, or her, chin, lift the child's eyes to hers, and say, "You are brilliant," or give some other sincere compliment. Minority children in her class, once deemed borderline teachable, graduated from the university at the top of their class, and went on to become professors, lawyers, and other successful professionals. Failures were nonexistent.

Charles Murray, in his infamous book, *The Bell Curve* , cited Ms. Collins, pointing out that such programs could not possibly improve academic achievement, or cognitive functioning. Having documented this teacher's successes 20 years earlier, *Sixty Minutes* went back after Murray's book came out, and checked on those 33 children.[9] Those students were the roaring successes described above, and thoroughly proved Murray's thesis was racist nonsense supported by corporate hard-right think-tank money.

While restructuring to a just society, such programs would be used to salvage such at-risk children. With equal access to a society's benefits, and opportunities, most will be good parents, and most children will be well educated.

Culture and Recreational Learning

Fine arts and recreational learning programs, such as are produced by public broadcasting documentaries, are enjoyable, and add to one's knowledge. Several channels should be reserved for these high-quality shows, and these too can be stored in databases. The social benefits of learning while relaxing are self-evident, and popular talk shows, and good recreational-educational TV commands a loyal audience.

One live commercial show can easily exceed one PBS station, or alternative view station's, yearly cost for all recorded shows. With their fair share of funds through restructured funding, as described below, the present financial struggles of those who broadcast quality programs would be eliminated, which would lead to the production of many more great documentaries.

Among the cultural and educational programs would be one, or more, channels reserved for introducing innovations, including governing, banking concepts, and inventions. Alert, imaginative minds would relate their special expertise to other machines, production processes, distribution methods, and social policies. Besides alerting consumers to new products, society would be devising simpler, cheaper, and environmentally protective methods of manufacturing, distributing, and governing.

Minority Cultures

Several channels would be reserved for ethnic minorities. Within the American culture they are inadequately represented, and their participation in national culture is, at best, restricted. With these new rights, they would quickly develop outstanding media, and political, personalities to articulate essential issues and challenge the belief systems that protect power structures, and keep others in bondage. With their own communication channels, equal access to land and jobs, and the right to retain what their labors produce; minorities would share the nation's work, its wealth, and participate in national decision making. Every citizen might, at last, attain the full rights of equal citizenship.

Foreign Cultures

When the vulnerable are not present to defend themselves, managers of state—seeking followers for aggressive intent—portray them as enemies. Programs created by cultures of other nations, correcting those views, are already streaming over communications superhighways. With the world in all living rooms, it would be difficult for managers of state to hide their aggressive intentions, as they create enemies to justify their wars.

By mutual agreement, there should be reciprocal presentations of cultural programs between countries to provide cross-cultural information. Redrawn broadcast standards would limit propaganda. Beamed to every home, programs would show people throughout the world, at work, and at play. People would begin to appreciate, and respect, both what we have in common, and what is distinctly different.

Local Television

With all TV stations able to stream over the communications superhighways, the meaning of a local station would change. Those with superior production teams could gain a national or even an international audience. As a source of community information, and culture, citizens will share ideas and experiences. Local sports, concerts, plays, and community information forums, on a broad range of issues, will be hosted. Meetings of governing bodies, normally open to the public by law, would be beamed over local TV.

Elections

With politicians having access to the public, through communications superhighways, there would be no need to spend private funds for elections. Politicians want to be just as honest as anyone else. With each of them having equal access to the voters, campaign funds could, and should, as all understand they are bribes, be made illegal. With free access to the citizenry for politicians assured by law, campaign contributions will be a liability, and disappear into history.

Those reserved TV channels would be for serious leaders to present their views. Minorities, the poor, conservationists, peace groups, and all others, will have equal standing with the, currently overrepresented, corporations and business.

With knowledgeable people invited to these forums, it would be difficult for politicians to duck the issues. Only when all have the opportunity to present their views, making perception management by a power structure counterproductive, can there be true democracy. Those who presented a consistent, and accurate, view of reality, and who promote a policy for the maximum good, would gather a loyal following. People would make value judgments on the history leading to the present problems, study the different solutions presented, and analyze the intelligence, and integrity, of the leaders.

These opinion makers would watch the information forums to inform themselves and, in turn, inform the public. To do less would leave one uninformed, and lose one's followers. With elections structured for candidates to prove their mettle, like the famous Lincoln-Douglas debates, the now-informed citizens would be enabled to make responsible voting decisions.

Monopolists will use every power at their command to prevent cheap communications between all people, and all elements, of society. However it will happen, hopefully quickly, and when it does today's monopolies will, just like aristocracy, be history.

A Socially-Owned Banking System within the Community Process Paying for Communication Superhighways

As the cost of education will drop 85%, possibly 95%, and many other aspects of communication will have even greater gains, there would be no shortage of funds for operating a communications superhighway. Access to that commons would be as cheap as highways, sidewalks, and parks. The current monopoly system stands exposed as the system of theft it was designed to be throughout the past 700-plus years, as power brokers wrote unequal property rights laws to protect, and further expand, their wealth and power. The privatizations ongoing worldwide in recent history were those same protections and expansions of wealth and power.

The above outline of efficiently educating both children and adults, only puts a framework on Nicholas Negroponte's vision of a free computer for every child in the world, so they can educate themselves. He learned this watching Cambodian school children teaching themselves on computers faster than other children were learning from books.

Expanding upon that concept, Google had the insight, and the money, to restructure computers, software, and the Internet, far beyond Nicolas's vision. Together, these two visionaries are making an end-run around the major hardware and software companies trying to undermine that threat to their monopolies.

Nigeria, South Africa, Uganda, Kenya, Tanzania, Rwanda, Burundi, Libya, and other nations are negotiating with Negroponte's group. The intention is for their governments to buy his $200 laptops and distribute them free to school children. It will take a few years to get internet access installed and those computers purchased and distributed. Within possibly one generation, an almost costless (per person) education, and communication system will be a reality across the world.

---

[1] Herbert Schiller (Interview), "The Information Highway: Paving Over the Public," *Z Magazine*, March, 1994, pp. 46-50.

[2] Craig Aaron, "Sun, Sand and Spectrum Policy," *In These Times*, September 19, 2005, p. 13.

[3] Steven Levy, "Bills New Vision," *Newsweek*, November 27, 1995, p. 68.

[4] Ibid

[5] Anne Windishar, "Expert: 20% of Gifted Kids Drop Out," *Spokane Chronicle*, January 7, 1988, p. B7.

[6] Rebecca Winters, "From Home to Harvard," *Time*, September 11, 2000, p. 55.

[7] George Seldes, *Even The Gods Can't Change History* (Secaucus, NJ: Lyle Stuart, 1976), p. 16.

[8] Juliet Schor, *The Overworked American* (New York: Basic Books, 1991), p. 61.

[9] *60 Minutes*, September 24, 1995; Herrnstein, Richard J., and Charles Murray. *The Bell Curve: Intelligence and Class Structure in American Life* (New York: Free Press, 1994), p. 399.

6. The Mighty Economic Engine of Full and Equal Economic Rights

All wealth is produced from resources provided by nature. There are no natural resources in cities, even though they are the heart of every society, and every economy. Throughout the Middle Ages the city states of Europe, also known as the walled cities of Europe, fought to control the resources of the countryside. Processing those resources into consumer products was the source of both their living and their wealth. Those city states became nations. The resources required for wealth and power still lay outside their borders. This produced more wars. Reaching for more wealth and power; seven nations of Europe rushed across the world to, with minor exceptions, claim every square mile. Those early battles between city states and the countryside, and those between individual city states, were then replayed between countries, and later by struggles between empires.

The fundamental rule, never transfer technical knowledge to other nations, was broken when Kaiser Wilhelm of Germany bought technology wholesale from his grandmother, England's Queen Victoria, and cousin, King George V.[1] The result was German technology taking over the markets of British industries leading to WW I. China, and other low-paid developing nations, taking over world markets in this century, is recognized by many as a replay of that early 20th century crisis.

But 50% of the world industrialized, armed with nuclear weapons, and battling over access to resources and markets in the 21st century, is different than 15% of the world industrialized, armed with conventional weapons, and battling over access to resources and markets in the early 20th century. There are too many nuclear weapons pointed at too many huge cities. Any nation which chooses nuclear war over sharing technology and resources will likely also be destroyed. Short of destruction by imperial nations, they committing national suicide in the process, China, India, East Asia, South Africa, Turkey, large parts of South America, Africa, and many other countries, will successfully industrialize. The monopolization of technology, the basic structure of both domestic and world economies, and a primary cause of both wars and poverty, will be history, if war can be avoided this time around.

Developing their economies and eliminating poverty were the goals of supposedly-free nations on the periphery of empires after WW II. Africa was planning on becoming a United States of Africa.[2] Think of the threat that continent, as a unified nation, would have been to the countries depending upon those resources to rebuild from that war. Knowing that is understanding the financial, economic, diplomatic, covert, and overt wars suppressing the colonial world's post WW II breaks for freedom, preventing the emergence of that super federation and—with the exception of Cuba and Asia, which were both accidents of history—preventing any nation from gaining their economic freedom.

As all these wars were waged under the flags of peace, freedom, justice, rights, and majority rule, not even the countries being destabilized realized what was happening. They knew America had become wealthy after breaking free, believed those slogans, and looked up to them as saviors, and supporters, of their freedom.

But now they understand, America had joined forces with their European cousins, to deny emerging nations their rights and freedom. The surges for equality and freedom today are identical to the hopes and dreams of the emerging world 40 to 60 years ago, and they now understand the tricks of the trade. As there are at least six centers of capital, with three being in Asia (China, India, and Japan), again each an accident of history, and more centers forming, competition for resources will be fierce. This is the **resource powers**' moment to demand freedom and equality, and they know it. After all, industries are relatively cheap to build, and the resources to build them are primarily within their borders. One of the primary purposes of this book is to document that, once a regional labor force is trained, and their own workers are used to process their resources and build and operate their industry; the finance capital cost of developing a federated region is primarily the cost of printing money; all else is a region's utilization of their labor for internal processing of resources into infrastructure, industries, and consumer products.

The entire region surrounding the three Asian centers of capital, with over half the world's population, is rapidly industrializing. It is understood that an alliance of the developed world in a war against the fast-developing world is likely to destroy both. The quagmire in Iraq proves both covert and overt destabilizations to install puppet governments are no longer options. Those acts of empire have cost America the moral high ground, and provided both the motivation, and the opening, for the world's poorest regions to start allying together. The European Union is a possible model for unification within Africa and South America or, like Europe, of each continent. Alliances between resource-wealthy developing regions, and rising centers of capital, increase the economic and political power of both. The massive resources inside the borders of those forming alliances, combined with the world's rising centers of capital, should give federating regions equal negotiating power.

Think on the various monopolies in chapters one through five exposed by applying inclusive and equal property rights laws. Currently each are laying claim to massive amounts of wealth; those unearned extracted values (mixed with honest profits) are capitalized by 10 to 30 times; and those "earnings" (thefts) are invested in treasury, water, sewer, other bonds, etc. Those from whom that wealth was extracted pay both the ongoing monopoly overcharges and payments on those bonds; and this goes on and on, into perpetuity, until it gets so out of balance the economy collapses. Considering fully 95% of America's huge blocs of accumulated capital is extracted wealth, that half its production potential is then wasted extracting more wealth, and that an equal amount is wasted destabilizing other societies, the monopoly capitalist system is a value harvesting----labor and resource wasting—machine, not an efficient producer and distributor of wealth.

The finance monopolists understand how to prevent a financial crash, just create money, pour it at those markets, and ratchet up some part of the economy, the 2002-07 housing bubble pumping up both the housing and stock market for example. The economy then rises to a higher imbalance and this one, in 2010, may unfold into a worldwide financial collapse.

This value-harvesting, resource-wasting, labor-wasting, machine has been sucking up, and wasting, the world's wealth. In contrast, the super-efficient, much-smaller, economic engine of full and equal economic rights—money created, and circulating within, a socially-owned banking system (in tandem with socially-collected resource rents) funding the real economy—eliminates the ethereal world of high finance, maximizes the utilization of increasingly-efficient technologies, shares full and equal economic rights world wide, eliminates war, expands across the earth with productive capacity and buying power in balance, has the power to eliminate world poverty in 10 years, and can provide a quality life for all world citizens in under 50 years.

That potential is not realized because the large increases in technological efficiencies are eulogized, while the even greater potentials remain unknown. To restructure to such an efficient economy within any country would be revolutionary. There is no middle ground, so we have chosen to address it as a velvet revolution. These final pages establish the framework for those peaceful revolutionary changes.

Even though many spotted the potential gains as applied to land, mainstream historians and economists did not carry their research to its logical conclusions. Peer pressure and the inability to be published by mainstream publishers within a society fiercely attacking any threatening philosophy was likely the limiting factor.

All monopolizations give superior rights to one over another. The only gains made under modern monopolies is a greater number moving from the rent paying underclass to the rent collecting upper class.

Missing in those thousands of studies, all written within the above parameters, are these four basics: 1) A measurement and study of the waste within each stage of the monopoly system, 2) A full study and measurement of the economic efficiency gains through elimination of monopolization in all its forms, 3) a study and measurement of the required full and equal economic rights of each citizen emplaced in constitutions and laws, so as to eliminate monopolization, and 4) an outline of how a socially-owned and operated banking system, along with socially collected resource rents, replaces the enormous complications, and costs, of operating a **privatized, rent-seeking, mercantile, monopoly** system.[3]

Our research attempts to stand outside those permitted parameters of debate, measure those wastes, and provide an outline of an efficient, honest, economy.

---

[1] Kurt Rudolph Mirow, Harry Maurer, *Webs of Power* (Boston: Houghton Mifflin Co., 1982), p. 16.

[2] Crucial documentary on a U.S. of *Africa Wind of Change*, order at Films for Humanity & Sciences 800.257.5126, item # BVL30750; Organizations formed to further African unity are: AU (African Union); NEPAD (New Partnership for Africa's Development) OAU (Organization of African Unity); OAAU (Organization for African American Unity (founded by Frantz Fanon); OCAM (Organization Commune Africaine et Malagache); OERS (Organization of States Bordering the Senegal River); UDEAC (Customs Union of Central African States); OERM (Economic Organization of North Africa); EACM (East African Community and Common Market); CEAO (West African Economic Community); CEDEAO (The Economic Community of West African States). Follow Democracy Now, Free Speech TV, Link TV, .informationclearinghouse.info, commondreams.org, globalnet news, globalresearch.ca/, and europac.net/ to stay up with world developments.

[3] Robert B. Eklund, Robert D. Tollison, Mercantilism as a Rent-Seeking Society (Texas A&M U Press, 1981). Too many pages supporting this analysis to cite.

7. Summary

Power brokers have spread the unequal property rights system, **aristocratic exclusive title to nature's resources and technologies, denying others their rightful share, of what nature offers to all for free,** far and wide. Recognizing the power and wealth this system accrues to them, regional puppets worldwide, owning the greater share of their nation's wealth, will be hard to displace, and the imperial centers' mighty militaries are in place to protect it all. So the odds are greatest the world will continue battling over the world's resources rather than choose the path of peace and prosperity. But this short reality list demonstrates that, this time, the ongoing populist revolution may be successful:

1 Full fledged ballot-box revolutions, after both WW I and WW II, threatening to eliminate unequal Western property rights put in place the past 700-plus years, were far closer than our history books acknowledge. Each time all of Europe was almost lost.[1] With the loss of its core, the Western monopoly system (there are other methods of monopolization), the primary causes of both poverty and wars worldwide, would have been weakened.

2 Above and beyond the supporting rationales, the primary purpose of those two world wars were, as addressed above, to prevent Germany from taking over England's markets. If that were to happen, Britain's empire would have quickly collapsed and that would have either collapsed the monopoly system, or placed Germany at the helm.

3 A further hidden reason, and the real purpose of WW II, was to take out the Soviet Union whose economic successes, starting from one of the poorest and most inhospitable regions on earth, also spelled doom for the Western monopoly system. Forget the massive perception management, imposed belief systems, propaganda, keeping their successes from the consciousness of the world. The world could not be kept under control so long as that ongoing successful example was there for the world to see.

A secret agreement had been reached with Germany to take out that threat. Knowing France and England would enter the fray, and dictate the peace, as they were busy defeating the Soviet Union, Germany, through conquering all nations between her and the Atlantic Ocean, took care of her back door first. Germany then flew their second in command, Rudolf Hess, to Britain, in what turned out to be a one-way mission, to get the original agreement back on track, only this time it would be on their terms.[a] She then attacked the Soviet Union.

Britain could not shift the beliefs of her people from Germany as an enemy, to an ally, in so short a time, and the historic three-way struggle for control of Europe by competing capital (German, British, and the emerging Soviet federation [which represented labor worldwide]) became intense. The struggles between centers of capital are well understood, while the struggles of labor for freedom and full and equal economic rights, is buried history. Specifically, labor had the vote and they could not be controlled anywhere in the world, once the Soviet system provided a better living standard to workers.

America's embargo of Japan's oil and steel, planned to shut that economy down in 60 days, led to Pearl Harbor. America joined the battle on both fronts and the rest is history. A part of that scenario is not what is recorded in history but, realistically, that is what happened. Hess finished his life out in Spandau prison permitted only to see his family and, under guard; only family matters could be discussed.

4 Though few realize it, the 45 years of the Cold War were specifically to suppress both post WW II ballot box revolutions within Europe, and full fledged revolutions for freedom around the world. The struggles to prevent labor from taking over governments of Europe (totally unreported in the corporate media), were only continuations of the, almost successful, post WW I ballot box revolutions throughout Europe addressed above; which is a part of the struggles of labor worldwide, in which the real reasons were conveniently left out of history books.[2]

5 Power brokers have spread the unequal property rights system**, aristocratic exclusive title to nature's resources and technologies, denying others their rightful share of what nature offers to all for free,** far and wide. Recognizing the power and wealth this system accrues to them, regional puppets worldwide, owning the greater share of their nation's wealth, will be hard to displace, and the imperial centers' mighty militaries have been, until recently, in place to protect it all. The imperial world will still try to control the world's resources rather than choose the path of peace and prosperity. But this short reality list demonstrates that, this time, the ongoing populist revolution may be successful:

The emerging world also understands that the slogans of peace, freedom, justice, rights, and majority rule, have also been covers for suppressing their freedom and rights. So the option of developing a few nations under the above slogans as

---

[a] Undoubtedly the terms would have been that England, France, other nations in Europe, and Germany would all be free. But Germany's control of the enormous resources of the former Soviet Union would mean that Germany would be far the stronger nation and may even have equaled America in productive capacity.

allies against the remaining periphery nations is no longer viable. The cover story, bringing democracy to the world, is believed by no one. That true democracies have been subverted, and overthrown, for the past 60 years, and violent, dictatorial, puppet governments installed, is well understood. Imperialists are trapped as certified-free elections replace those puppet governments with more honest ones. Imperialist control is so well understood that, even countries where external control of elections were once blatant—Brazil, Venezuela, Bolivia, Nicaragua, Ecuador, and Chile for example—have thrown aside those puppets by the ballot. As the War on Terror worldwide is against them, and they are fully aware of the above deceptions,[b] the Muslim world interprets the "war on terror" as being against their religion. Thus, for each Muslim killed in this war, several more take their place. As all this unfolded, more of the citizenry, both within the imperial nations and the periphery nations, understood that America and their allies were an allied empire.

6 Fully 60% of the industrial capacity of the world is now outside the borders of Europe and America. This is the same trade and political structure which led to WWs I and II, and this current crisis for the imperial centers is many times greater.

All rapidly developing nations are busy developing brand names for consumer products. With hollowed out industrial economies, the profit structure within wealthy nations will collapse as those brands, one by one, hit Western markets, and the wealth is retained by their traders, not those of America, Europe, and Japan. The current, 2008-10, crisis in world markets, the bankruptcies of leading brand name cars, and China's gain in technology if she purchases brand names intact, quickens the arrival of that crisis moment.

Through brand names, China, and other lower-paid nations, will be banking the profits of capital, the wages of labor, and those huge trader profits. The current account deficits of the historic imperial nations will increase in step with foreign traders replacing domestic traders.

7 Fast developing Asia may settle for equality but, whether America and Europe like it or not, and even though they do not want a confrontation with the developed world, nor do they want the imperial economies to collapse (such social crises cause wars), they will not settle for second place.

8 As their enormous wealth, and military might, is based upon theft of the wealth of weak nations, and assuming America does not use its nuclear weapons to maintain its current control of resources throughout the world, long before

---

[b] The alert throughout the world will be aware of General Wesley Clark's interview on *Democracy Now*. There he explained that, while America was attacking Afghanistan immediately after the 9/11/2001 terrorist attack on the World Trade Center, the order came down through the Pentagon that they were going to take out the governments of Iraq, Syria, Lebanon, Libya, Somalia, Sudan, and Iran. Taking out governments, of course, means replacing them with puppets. Read Naomi Klein's *The Shock Doctrine: The Rise of Disaster Capitalism* to understand those plans.

Asia and other emerging nations reach 50% equality, the economies of America and Europe, dependent upon inequalities in trade, will collapse.

9   All the world's major banking systems know that day of reckoning will come. Various countries will be getting out of the dollar, and into other currencies. Girding to fight that battle, America's Federal Reserve quietly noted they would no longer release statistics on how much money they are printing.[3] The citizenry are not to be made aware of the massive sums of money being created to buy their own treasuries, and that the battle of the titans has begun. Seeing the writing on the wall, half the presidents of America's Federal Reserve banks resigned. Markets are in chaos as we speak. A Google search for "Eric deCarbonne 15-Fold Increase in US Monetary Base" will alert us to the massive sums expected to be created to buy America's own treasuries. That expected 15-fold increase would be roughly $12 trillion newly created dollars.

10   The imperial rulers are totally out of sync with their peripheries, who are demanding their reasonable share of the world's wealth. The populist uprising is picking up momentum, the communication superhighways to sustain that revolt are being put in place, and sooner or later, if the world's leaders do not wake up and run this world responsibly, the imperial nations will not be able to contain this worldwide populist revolution. Under the tutelage of President Hugo Chavez of Venezuela, South America is tying their nations, and economies, closer together, and moving towards a regional currency, the sucre.

There is a difference between aristocracy denying the common people rights for centuries leading to the French Revolution (taken back by aristocracy only 26 years later), and financial aristocracy today denying the citizenry worldwide their reasonable share of the world's wealth. Modern communications, outside the control of the imperial centers, will permit a large share of the world to revolt simultaneously.

11   And, as there is enough on this earth for all if it were shared equally, instead of fought over, wasting over 50% of the resources and labor in the process; these battles over control of the wealth producing process are unnecessary. So, although the struggle may go on for many years, there are only two choices:

1   Powerful nations giving up their selfish ways, governing responsibly, and sharing the wealth of the world relatively equally.

2   Or this world is shattered, and made largely uninhabitable, by a 3rd World War using nuclear weapons.

Another two possibilities may avoid a world war, but both they, and option 2, are so morally repugnant, we will not even consider them:

3   The current fast developing nations will come to an agreement, with the old imperial nations, that together they will militarily control the world, and share the wealth. Africa, South America, parts of Asia, and the Muslim world—targeted to be outside that circle of wealthy nations—will never accept that. Laying down

their tools, sabotaging resource extraction, roadside bombs, and suicide bombers, will grind the world economy to a halt. Already there are signs China, and others, are starting to decouple from the American and European imperial economies, and, in trade for access to resources, couple with Africa and South America.

4 Fascist-control of periphery nations, and their resources, by imperial nations, through puppet governments, is how periphery nations have been controlled ever since WW II. That colonial system, hiding under false cover, is falling apart as we speak, and though habituated powerbrokers will surely try to perpetuate it; we do not believe these last three possibilities are worth considering.

If the current alliance of America, Europe and Israel use nuclear weapons on re-calcitrant nations, that could be a preview of WW III. Other nations are being asked to agree to a far lower share of the wealth than that consumed by Europe and America. That would also mean Africa, South America, and the Muslim world, will have to accept their resources providing a large share of that wealth as they receive the smaller share. We do not believe any of those nations will accept that.

The world's corrupt and selfish rulers must be replaced by others with vi-sion and responsibility. As the crisis in Iraq winds down, and that in Afghani-stan rises (2010); President Barack Obama will be studying his choices closely.[c] His meeting with Muslim leaders and President Hamid Karzai meeting with the Taliban is highly encouraging.

The list and comments above are optimistic. In *Nemesis: The Last Days of the American Republic* Chalmers Johnson says Americans are so dependent upon the military as a Keynesian infusion into the economy that they can never reduce it, let alone get rid of it. For all the reasons laid out above, and more, he sees no way America can survive. There we disagree. Once the collapse occurs, and since half the world's potential is currently wasted, America, and all other nations, can restructure to full and equal economic rights for all, and survive superbly well, with a quality life for all world citizens.

If we are in error; we feel it will only be one of timing. There is the possibil-ity fascist control of resource wealthy nations, and the wealthy imperial centers, could go on for another generation. There is the possibility that battles over the world's resources will go on forever. We think both those scenarios are unlikely. It will be either peace with sharing of the world's resources or it will be nuclear

---

[c] Many governments stay in power only at the behest of those imperial leaders. Under threat of not having access to American banks or markets (sales or purchase), banks all over the world cannot do business with any nation America decides to embargo. Those who turn to the Euro will discover those nations have not given up the prerogatives of empire. Corporations of any nation who break that embargo can do no business in the United States. If all that fails covert specialists are called out.

WW III and we choose to assume the first of those possibilities, the world restructuring to permanent peace with a quality life for all.

If peace does come to this world, it will be because historic powerbrokers are faced by equal power, the current leaders are pushed aside by democratic forces, and new leaders agree to equitably share the wealth. Ever since WW II, only the alliance of developed nations, the ones imposing those unequal trades, has had choices. If the "**resource powers**" are ever to rise out of poverty, they must ally together, and force the imperial nations, and fast developing nations, to include them equally in the wealth-producing, wealth-sharing, process. Once allied, their power—most the world's resources being within their borders—will equal that of the imperial world. No combination of military power can offset half the world laying down their tools, and fighting back with industrial sabotage, suicide bombs, car bombs, and roadside bombs.

Having been extracting the wealth of periphery nations, under various cover stories, for centuries—they are not really people, they have no souls, they are not capable, and new rationales keep being created—the West refuses to bite the bullet, and restructure to honest, truly productive, societies. But there are signs that the **resource powers** are allying for their protection. All the ASEAN countries, Indonesia, Thailand, Malaysia, Singapore, Philippines, Brunei, Vietnam, Laos, Myanmar and Cambodia, plus Japan, China, India, South Korea, Australia, and New Zealand, representing half (three billion) of the world's people, met in Malaysia, December 2005, for the inaugural of the East Asian Summit (EAS). That America was not invited is significant. Interest quickened at the April 10, 2006 meeting of the South Asian Association for Regional Cooperation (SAARC), and Russia, China, and the Central Asian nations, forming the Shanghai Cooperation Organization (SCO), whose primary purpose is to offset US-NATO moves to control the oil of Central Asia, further weakened imperial nations. Look for these groupings to decouple to a safe distance from the imperial economies.

Eighty percent of South America has governments fully aware that American foreign policies are designed to maintain access to their resources below fair value, and that this, and a refusal to share technology and markets, is the cause of their poverty. Rumors are flying that America is backing the one country still in their camp, Columbia, to overthrow those populist revolutions. Honduras is, so far, the only Latin American country reclaimed by the empire.

Venezuela is now fully literate, and forming alliances promise to free more countries, in a shorter span of time, than Simon Bolivar almost freed in his lifetime. President Chavez has nationalized Venezuela's banks, is working on a single currency for South America, and is suggesting a new world reserve currency. All are prerequisites for the former colonial world to attain their freedom. Venezuela's offer of cheaper oil to South America's Mercosur alliance—Brazil, Argentina, Uruguay, Paraguay and Associate Members Chile, Ecuador, Columbia, and Peru—their funding of satellite TV, radio, phone, and broadband coverage for Latin America—plus the elections of more populist governments, is turning that long-standing free trade alliance into an affiliation for economic freedom, comparable to the East Asian Summit.

Those alliances have the tools to thwart imperialist ambitions. South America's Telesur satellite is operational. Named after Simon Bolivar, and engineered by China, it has brought the Arabic station, Al Jazeera, and others, on board to expand to the entire world in various languages.

That breathtaking advance towards full freedom is as catching as a cold. Communications will be beamed out of these countries, as well as into them. The three billion people represented in that East Asian Summit, those in Central and Western Asia, and others in Africa, will broadcast their views of current and past history to the world. Russia will also be heard. With the views of the world's dispossessed broadly disseminated, corporate media, within the West, must address the world more broadly, and accurately, or be irrelevant. That relevancy is already highly visible on CNN, and occasionally on NBC, CBS, and ABC.

What can greater relevance to reality accomplish? President Chavez is so popular that the opposition, backed by America, dropped so low in the polls they withdrew from the 2005 elections, and all South America and beyond is poised for, or has already had, a Bolivarian Revolution overthrowing unequal trade agreements. Africa will notice, and this gives insight into how fast a movement for freedom and rights can spread, when unique world events, and communication superhighways, provide that opening. The international havoc of America's disastrous foreign policies, an extension of European colonialism, totally discrediting the U.S. in the eyes of the world, and costing them the moral high ground, is just such an opening; the emerging world now has the communication facilities to inform their citizenry of the wealthy world's many methods of denying emerging nations their share of the world's wealth. All people want to be free. Understanding how their impoverishment has been imposed by imperial nations is a crucial step towards gaining their full freedom.

Only by coming together in firm alliances, and federations, and educating their citizenry on the importance of coalition and cooperation, can freedom, with full and equal economic rights, be attained. Japan, China, and India are already signing mutually-protective, trade deals with forming alliances across the developing world. That, and Russia, China, and several other nations requesting a totally new world trading currency, just as we have suggested for years, has imperial managers of state in a panic. Still trying to maintain control, the imperial powers are thinking in terms of three world currencies, the dollar, the Euro, and china's Yuan each, being the trading currency for their 1/3 of the world. Establishing that, if it happens, may only be temporary. Hugo Chavez says "China is not intent on establishing an empire." Hopefully their goal is equality of development and full and equal rights, and that they intend to do this by offering development to the **resource powers** in trade for resources

Imperialists are undoubtedly concerned: President Chavez has moved Venezuela's reserves to Europe, and is establishing a "Bank of the South." A new currency, called the "sucre" (Unitary System of Regional Compensation [also the name for Ecuador's currency]), is being planned. Iran and Syria have shifted their reserves to safer havens, and all Muslim countries are considering that move. China announced it is diversifying its reserves of $2 trillion. Iran's oil bourse (bypassing traders whose pure-gambles, derivative trading, currently accounts for 1/3 the cost of oil) by selling directly to the final buyers, was delayed in becoming operational by the cutting of five undersea cables.[d] With the Chinese signing trade agreements with the East African Community (Kenya, Tanzania, and Uganda, [CEDEAO]), the Economic Community of West African States, and the African Union, that continent is stirring.

Europe, North America, Australia, Japan, China, India, Russia, Taiwan, South Korea, Indonesia, Malaysia, Brazil, Argentina, Venezuela, Turkey, etc, over half the population on earth, will soon be modernized and the remaining developing world, those with the resources necessary to keep the world's industries running, will be catching up fast.

Let's face that reality: Under what strategy will a technologically developed China, India, Japan, Russia, or any other rapidly developing country, be the most prosperous—with America and Europe as their primary trading partners, or by sharing technology with Africa, South America, and Central Eurasia in trade for resources? Obviously, measured in consumer products and services provided their citizenry, they would be much wealthier under the second option than the first. Massive accumulations of dollar reserves would become valueless in an inflationary spiral, an economic crash, or war. America would cite security needs to prevent those reserves from buying up their properties, or they would create massive sums of new dollars. Using the same creation of currency option— China, India, Brazil, and Rus-

---

[d] In the price rise of oil from $44 a barrel to $70 a barrel in early 2009, each barrel of oil changed hands 25 times. That oil bourse trading directly between oil producing nations and the final processors of that oil would have increased the net returns of oil exporting nations, or saved the final consumers of the importing nations, roughly 50%. The disappearance of the 33% now claimed by oil traders would wipe trillions of dollars in value off the world's stock markets, and collapse imperial economies. Watch for Iranian banks to be embargoed, and Iran fighting back by coalitions trading in other currencies. With their weak dollar, America could lose that war. This is really what the embargoes and potential war with Iraq is all about.

sia, plus Malaysia, Indonesia, and the substantial industry already in Brazil, Argentina, etc.— have enough technology to rapidly develop the remaining poor nations, even as they increase the products and services provided their citizens. We must remember that the world being relatively developed by 2050 has been updated to 2035, only 25 years away. Later developing nations can industrialize quickly with the support of earlier developing regions.

Japan's success in the late 19th and early 20th centuries, based on empire, ended with their defeat by more powerful empires. The struggle between the British and German empires over control of world trade led to WW I, and the fear of the Soviet Union, and ballot box revolutions in Europe, was the direct cause of WW II. Those holocausts taught Western empires that they had nothing to gain by fighting each other; NATO and the European Union evolved out of that realization. Occasional surface disagreements notwithstanding, the historic empires of Europe and America have been an allied empire ever since.

One hundred and twelve years ago, we had an example for what may happen. Propaganda notwithstanding, the Soviet Union was not an empire. Those fifteen individual nations quickly, and peacefully, federated after WW I. Openly declaring they would live off their own resources, they released title to all natural wealth outside their federation, and took title to all within their borders.

Another legal structure prohibiting the extraction of the wealth of either internal labor, or that of other nations, was a serious threat to empires whose unequal property rights were designed to appropriate the wealth of both internal labor, and the periphery of empire. The expenditure of 85% of Germany's firepower against the Soviets, and they still winning, was the primary reason for post WW II Cold War alliances such as NATO and the European Union. Not only was it crucial to contain Soviet cooperative and sharing, philosophies, the colonial world's breaks for freedom also had to be suppressed. Though the cost in lives and treasure—both within the imperial centers and on that periphery— were enormous, those suppressions were, until these latest worldwide populist revolutions, successful.

The periphery's breaks for freedom again threaten imperial unequal property rights. As already addressed, financial, economic, covert, and overt warfare will have continual diminishing returns. Though the full transformation may take many years, our analysis will proceed on the assumption that the world will break free, and the imperial-centers-of-capital will negotiate a sharing of technology in trade for resources.

Those unequal agreements imposed upon periphery nations by financial, economic, diplomatic, covert, and overt warfare can be quickly set aside; various countries around the world are renegotiating their resource extraction contracts as we speak.

That stirring will turn into a biblical flood once the **resource powers** start reclaiming control of their resources through collecting the rental values on nature's resources, and using that huge flow of money to build infrastructure and industry.

International law prevents reclaiming title to resources without compensation. However, applying the foundation principle of collecting the rental values on nature's resources and technologies reclaims that stolen wealth without the need to compensate the thieves. Corporations can retain title to that natural wealth, but all they can earn is fair compensation for their labor and capital. The rental income from nature's resources and technologies goes to the proper owners of the land; the citizenry of those resource wealthy nations.

The latest WTO Doha round has totally collapsed. Recognizing that the 30 OECD (Organization for Economic Cooperation & Development) nations' $350 billion per year agriculture subsidies permitted imports to undersell India's farmers, Trade Minister Kamal Nath—before leaving for the December 2005 WTO negotiations—said, "importing food is as good as importing unemployment," and he could sign a trade agreement on the terms offered, only if the U.S. is "willing to provide a visa to every farmer displaced as a consequence of the import of cheaper and highly subsidized food." Minister Nath kept that promise.

When first developing, periphery nations need both money and industry. Assuming those alliances included any two, or all of the three Asian centers of capital, Brazil and Russia, they would have adequate technology and capital to eventually develop the 50% of the world that has little industry. Normally it would take many years for a fully allied, federated, South America and a federation of Africa to form. But these are not normal times. Industrialized nations need the resources of the "**resource powers**" just as badly as those emerging nations need technology and an efficient economic infrastructure. The only way those developing nations will be fully paid for their resources, and gain access to technology, is by allying together and demanding that price.

The flow of money is a super efficient accounting system and that flow is a mirror image of an economy. We just looked into that mirror and saw that over 50% of the current flows of money were wasted efforts, both within internal economies and in world trade.

Proof that this is monopoly capitalism rather than honest capitalism is provided by economic efficiency doubling when those exclusive titles are restructured to conditional titles, as we do theoretically in the above chapters and the conclusion.

All are morally entitled to their share of nature's wealth, and that can be attained only through eliminating those monopolies we are taught do not exist. Once eliminated, the costs of government (national, state, and local) are paid from resource rents, and profits from a socially-owned banking system. Any necessary increase in the money supply is covered by building infrastructure with socially-created money (up to the point of monetary balance). Once that monetary balance is reached, additional essential services—education, water systems, sewers, roads, railroads, communications superhighways, health care, and retirement, will all be covered by socially-collected resource rents and banking profits.

Monopolies claim a large share of the wealth produced—waste enormous amounts of resources, capital, and labor—restrict the efficiencies of an economy, and claim unearned wealth. All this more than doubles the cost of production. The social efficiency gains reclaimed (over 50%) are so enormous that we will be challenged. But the truth is, if technology had been shared—both internally and in world trade—rather than monopolized, the entire world would have developed in step with those efficiency gains, and there would have been little poverty and few wars. With all societies utilizing the latest technologies, the pace of inventions would have quickened. War and poverty would have been the exception, rather than the rule, over the past 300 years.

Exclusive titles to nature's resources and technologies are little more than aristocratic property rights. Aristocracy fought for centuries to protect those exclusive rights and today's battles, both worldwide and within internal economies, are a continuation of those struggles. Full and equal economic rights for any great numbers have never been attained, and we outline herein how—through utilizing the mighty economic and financial engines of inclusive property rights applied across the full economic spectrum—they can be attained for all.

Add up the waste within America's internal economy as herein addressed, add in that wasted and destroyed worldwide by both covert and overt war the past 60 years, add in the GDP for a respected living standard for roughly five billion impoverished people who could be enjoying a quality life today except for monopoly capitalism's last fifty years of warfare—a struggle led by America for the purpose of controlling resources and the wealth producing process, and the imposition of their system of property rights (aristocratic exclusive title to nature's resources and technologies) on the world (preventing their economies from developing)—and you arrive at how much more wealth has been effectively destroyed or production forgone, as opposed to how much wealth America produces. That honest look highlights America as a negative producer, consuming, wasting, and destroying far more wealth than she produces.

Full and equal economic rights, through restructuring exclusive titles to nature's resources and technologies to conditional titles, are applicable across the full economic spectrum. That simple change in property rights eliminates both the unacknowledged primary monopolies—land, technology, money, and communication—and the secondary monopolies that are so proliferate in the American economy. Through conditional titles, monopoly values are transposed into relatively equally-shared use-values.

All trained in classical and neoliberal economics will say, "Those appropriated blocs of capital owned by individuals were, and are, necessary to finance an economy." They will claim that "governments are inefficient allocators of financial and industrial capital." Both claims are unequivocally untrue. Financing is not needed to build land, nature built it. A large amount of financing is not needed to start up a bank. The only labor-created value there, beyond a small amount of brick, mortar, and computers is its license. Yes a private bank requires a minimum level of startup funds but a socially-owned banking system simply creates that money. Private banks essentially own nothing but ideas that are thousands of years old, and use their exclusive titles to extract more wealth from others. This has to be the greatest fraud ever imposed upon mankind.

Inventions are produced by labor. But currently the greatest shares of technologies values are pieces of paper—monopoly patents and stock market values based on the capitalized value of those unearned "profits." Communications need financing, but that finance capital need is primarily buying and selling the enormous capitalized values of monopolized spectrums and patents; both are a part of nature offered to us all for free. Financing is needed for roads, railroads, water systems, sewer systems, post offices, electric systems, and communication superhighways. But, in the early stages of federated regional development, those can be built with socially-created money. Up to the balance point of an adequate money supply, even first industries can be built with created money. In a crisis, as demonstrated in the Conclusion, such money can be pointed directly to any distressed sector of the economy, natural or manmade. Socially-created money can be pointed towards alleviating any natural disaster. Nothing could be fairer then created money quickly replacing values destroyed in natural disasters such as Hurricane Katrina which destroyed New Orleans.

Instead, current capitalism **monopolizes all resources and technologies, denies others their rightful share of what nature offers to all for free, and loans those extracted values back to those from whom it was unjustly taken, over and over, on into perpetuity**. Those annual, privately-collected rents, improperly called earnings, are extracted values which are then capitalized 10 to 30 times by the markets.

The reason finance capital is so hard to obtain under the errors of monopoly capitalism is that those monopoly values, and the 95% of America's finance capital that funds those unearned values, reverses the proper order of money and wealth creation. Inclusive and equal property rights correct that. During early development, stage one: Money is socially created to fund infrastructure (debt free) and first industries, the savings within that circulation of money builds more private businesses. Stage two: As development progresses, money is socially-created to fund (debt free) only that infrastructure not fundable by incoming resource rents. Savings within the circulation of money funds all private industrial development; as well as housing and other consumer needs. The developed stage: 3) Infrastructure is now funded through socially-collected rental values of nature's resources and by banking profits. Money is now created only when it is needed to expand the economy or rebuild from a natural disaster. This eliminates the need for disaster insurance for hurricanes, earthquakes, floods, and large fires.

In an efficient economy, with full and equal economic rights for all, there are no unearned values. Instead of financing unearned, monopoly-created, values, touchable and useable use-values are financed, created, and bought and sold. Both planning and financing are regional and local.

Private industries and serving consumer needs are properly financed out of savings. We are proposing a constitutional right to finance capital for federated regions of the world, countries, regions within countries, states, local communities, and entrepreneurs. Individual financing is much simpler under full and equal economic rights than under loans backed by monopoly capitalism's unearned values. Needs can be calculated and allotted relatively easily and loans would be more on merit and less on equity.[e]

The infrastructure operating monopoly systems, and collecting those rental values, are today's pyramids. They waste resources, capital, and labor, lowering economic efficiency by over 50%. The efficiency gains of technology are so enormous that, even though massive wealth is produced, much more is wasted while an even greater amount of wealth that would have been produced under an efficient economic structure is not even realized. This waste is unknown due to the centuries of justifications by the economic classics claiming these systems of theft were efficient economies.

Walk into the heart of any city, look up at those huge skyscrapers, walk in, look at the plaques on the doors, and—when one understands monopolies intercepting, as opposed to producing, wealth—one realizes this is the superstructure of a wealth extraction system. The entire building, and the next ones, are unnecessary, as are a share of the companies which built them, those that built the furnishings, and those who service and clean them. (Google Annie Leonard, *The Story of Stuff* . Also see http://www .naturalnews.com/021872.html and http://www.ied.info/articles/nuggets to realize this statement is conservative.)

The unnecessary offices and staff (the superstructures) extracting wealth through banking, technology, and other monopolies (except land, wasted labor within that monopoly structure is minimal), waste enormous amounts of wealth.

---

[e] As we addressed in Chapter five, "Investment and Job Opportunities."

Those labors and resources are no longer wasted under the full and equal economic rights of a modern commons guaranteeing all their share of what nature offers to all for free. Necessities of life such as universal health care and retirement are addressed in law as a human right; other necessities, such as insurance, are addressed in law as a social right.

The quality of life rises rapidly even as the hours of employed labor are reduced over half. The precipitous drop in GDP measures the previously wasted labor, capital, and resources of a monopolized economy. Quality of life rises as people utilize their new free time to develop their many artistic talents, and socialize with friends and family.

By analyzing the forthcoming struggle of those employed in the educational system to retain their current highly respected—but now obsolete—positions and identities, one can understand why, and how, as the efficiencies of technology advanced, full and equal economic rights were historically withheld from the masses. The efficiencies of technology continually eliminate jobs through which identity, respect, power, wealth, and the needs for every day living, are distributed. Those in positions of respect and power destined for elimination quite naturally used, and still use, their power and wealth to protect their power and wealth. With their living tied to those wasteful arteries of commerce, the citizenry unwittingly defend a system which is denying many their right to a quality life.

When discussing this thesis of the enormous wasted labor, capital, and resources with others, they easily understood the waste in all segments of the economy except theirs: "Oh no! Not my job! My work is necessary;" and a litany of reasons why pour forth.

What takes place is the instinctive protection of territory within the economy from which one obtains respect, identity, and their living. I have watched teachers and professors bristle at the thought of their replacement by video lectures and documentaries presented by the world's best teachers. Unless, and until, the current system totally collapses, which it will, monopolies always do—and just as those whose identities and livings are tied to the arteries of commerce in other sectors of the economy destined for shrinkage to a fraction of current capital, labor, and resource needs—neither politicians nor the educational industry will make any serious effort to fully modernize their economic sector.

If you have a slave society, banks must finance buying and selling the capitalized value of slaves, but they would never finance a slave for any personally conceived endeavor. If you have a monopolized economy, banks will finance the buying and selling of the capitalized values of monopoly profits. In both cases they are financing the theft of wealth produced by others.

When primary and secondary monopolies are eliminated, use-value (a total of labor costs, resource rent costs, and finance capital costs) will determine market value. Under full and equal economic rights, all are reasonably well paid, none receive compensation beyond the value of their mental and physical labors, capitalized values disappear as use-values match market values, there would be no inflations or deflations, there is no space for an ethereal world of high finance, and thus, there would be no economic collapses. The price of gold will remain forever stable as a commodity for manufacturing jewelry.

An individualized society with 80% of their waking hours free and each searching for identity would become chaos. A cooperative, communitarian society utilizing the efficiencies of honest precepts of capitalism—providing camaraderie, a sense of belonging, and an active life interacting with family and friends as home production and education expanded, yet retaining the efficiencies of money and competition (honest capitalism)—would thrive. Those who study gangs filling those primal emotional needs in an individualized society, and those experienced in communitarian societies, understand this well; we will leave that to be sorted out by the alert within these newly-free societies.

As different societies sort this out within the dynamics of their own culture, there are four basics to full and equal economic rights: 1) Society must collect the rental values of nature's resources and technologies, and use those social-credits to build and maintain economic infrastructure and essential social services. 2) The banking system must be socially-owned and operated, and those funds also used to fund essential social services. 3) Productive jobs must be shared, reducing employed labor time to two to three days per week, leaving four to five days per week for family care, socializing, and pursuing personal goals. 4) And each must be paid equally for equally-productive labor with possibly no greater than a two times wage differential (key management a somewhat greater spread).

There will always be talented people who earn far above that wage differential. But it will be earned compensation (Oprah Winfrey, artists, presidents, etc.), not monopoly extractions of what is properly others' wealth. Highly talented people would have several days a week to produce with their talents. There would be so many of them that the price of their art or talents would be only modestly above normal labor costs. Talented carpenters, repairpersons of all kinds, etc, free lancing would earn money to purchase other's free lancing talents and art, which further reduces what is thought of as "one's job."

The many customs that identify cultures beyond those four basics would flourish, and retain cultural identity. However, domination of one by another will quickly be identified and abandoned. With full and equal economic rights, those once dominated would quickly see to that.

With efficient and moral centers of capital supporting them, a federated region, even entire continents, can develop and provide a quality life to all its citizens within two generations. Compare that with the monopolized economies of

America and Europe, which have been industrialized for 150 years, and they still have large impoverished populations.

If the principles of full and equal economic rights had been in use the past few hundred years, instead of the current monopoly system, production would have immediately doubled, doubled again in a few years, doubled again the next few years, etc, on up to the level of a fully sustainably developed world, and all without poverty or war.

Instead of the simplicity of a cooperative system, the original designers of unequal property rights (the monopoly system) did not even consider the possibility that a large share of their citizenry could one day be well off, let alone should be, or would be.

The substantial development of wealth in Asia was an accident of history, a need for allies to stop fast expanding socialism. Not only did monopolists need allies to maintain control of the world, they also needed the allegiance of their own citizenry. That, and the enormous efficiency gains of technology, provided a quality life to many more people than ever anticipated. Those enormous gains were under exclusive, and unequal, property rights designed for the elite to have the greater share of that wealth.

Shared technology cannot be taken back, and the rapid industrialization of the world is destroying the world monopoly structure. Those who keep track calculate the larger share of the world will be relatively well developed by 2035, and that is only 25 years away.[f]

That plunder by trade is the cause of poverty in the emerging world is now understood, and alliances within the developing world are forming to take control of their destiny. Venezuela and Bolivia are leading the way through taking control of their carbon fuels. Russia renegotiated their contracts and oil companies now retain only six cents of every dollar above $27 a barrel.[4] Through a modern communications superhighway being put in place—the many national

---

[f] With care in planning and elimination of the over 50% of today's economic and military activity that is wasted, the ecosystem can be well protected. Tiny Tikopia Island, addressed above, has successfully practiced three-dimensional orchard farming for 3,000 years. That permaculture mixing of annual and perennial tubers, berries, vegetables, fruits and nuts is enormously productive and, due to that closely-planted mixture building its own defenses, essentially free of disease and destructive insects. If the world replaced monoculture farming and shipping from hundreds or thousands of miles away with three dimensional orchard permacultures in back yards and surrounding communities, society could be living in a Garden of Eden continually improving soils as opposed to its rapid depletion under monoculture farming.

and international news programs on Free *Speech TV, Link TV* , Al Jazeera and other emerging TV networks, controlled by the world's previously dispossessed, are spanning the world—the emerging world will be watching these dramas unfold, and strengthening their alliances to attain more negotiating power.

We assume the imperial centers' mighty military and financial power will eventually be checkmated, and a substantial reduction in their extraction of wealth from the periphery of empire will be reflected in a further collapse of their stock and financial markets. Since the alternative news and new world-wide communications systems will be telling that story, corporate owned media within those imperial centers will have to address the reality that past imperial foreign policies have created a disaster.

Once allied, and hopefully federated, each unified economic region should, and we assume will, establish a regional central bank, create a regional currency, and sign contracts with developed centers of capital to trade resources for access to technology and training for industrial development. The developing world's need for trade with Europe and America will continually shrink. As the waste within Europe and America shrinks, only increasingly efficient economies will keep their citizenry cared for.

That explains why America embarked on regime change in Iraq. A success there would assure worldwide control of other resources far into the future. If that colonial adventure had successfully installed a puppet government, or if Iraq had been split into two or three isolated political units, with the oil regions controlled by historic imperial-centers-of-capital. If that control had expanded to the oil wealth of Central Asia, and if control was retained in Saudi Arabia, the old empires could offset the power of those forming alliances, and retain access to resources worldwide on the same unequal terms. Other nations, and alliances, will have to abide by trade rules laid down by the imperial nations, or they would get no oil. But the Iraq occupation became a quagmire. The world understands America's plan; every abuse of power engenders a countervailing power, and the opposing alliances described above are forming.

The developing world understands well that the United Nations is not democratic. Planned and established by the winners of WW II, with other nations essentially voiceless, that body, as an extension of colonialism, is a fait-accompli.

That intended "irreversible accomplishment" is centered in the Security Council. Each member has one vote and decisions are made by an affirmative vote of at least nine of the 15 members, five permanent and the other 10 slots rotating every two years among the remaining 182 UN members. A 'yes vote' of all five permanent members—the United States, Britain, France, Russia, and China—is required before any action can be taken. A 'no vote' by any one of the five is a veto. Thus nothing of importance happens without the unanimous approval of those five permanent members.

While other departments of the UN can make recommendations, and many good things are proposed and accomplished, the Security Council alone has the power to make decisions on all matters of major importance, and the UN charter obligates all member nations to carry out those decisions. In short, on important issues, there is no United Nations; there is only a Security Council comprised of five of the seven most powerful nations in the world. The two other major powers, Germany and Japan, lost WW II and were never given a voice in the UN commensurate with their economic power.

As the UN, fronting as a quasi world government, has been used as cover for control of nations worldwide, most the 10 rotating members of the Security Council, and likely two of those permanent members, Russia and China, want a truly democratic institution.

The other three permanent UNSC members—the U.S., Britain and France—are allies.[g] Russia knows well how the former Soviet Union was destabilized by that alliance, and China knows just as well that there are powerful financial interests behind political factions within both American political parties, and throughout Europe, who want to do the same to her.

Those same movers and shakers in the former administration, that of President George W. Bush, openly stated they are not going to tolerate any nation, or group of nations, to militarily challenge America. Translated that means maintaining worldwide control of resources and the wealth producing process through military force.

As addressed above, a major move towards assured control of resources by the historic imperial centers was the occupation of Iraq which turned into a disaster. Not only does America have most Iraqis against them, the entire Muslim world is also aware that, with possibly 70% of the world's known reserves of easily-accessible oil within their borders, they are the primary target.

The world is aghast at the destruction, torture, and oppression of American foreign policy.[5] Once the moral high ground is lost, a nation's power is greatly diminished, and this has America's mighty military essentially immobilized. Cover stories will be ignored, attempts at regime change anywhere in the world would be recognized for the imperialism it is, and at some level, sanctions against aggressor nations, posing as moral societies, would be invoked worldwide.

The Iraqi suppression alerted the former provinces of the old Soviet Union, oil and mineral rich Central Asia, to further protect themselves by trade and de-

---

[g] With centuries of colonial experience, France would not agree with U.S. President George W Bush on attacking Iraq. The 2003-10 quagmire in Iraq proved them right.

velopment agreements with Russia, China, and India. The immobilization of America's mighty military, due to loss of the moral high ground creates an opening for the formerly voiceless to insist that their votes will count.

The key factors are the immense resources within the yet undeveloped world, the roughly 60% of the world's industrial capacity, the many trillions of dollars in reserves outside the imperial nation's borders, and the current immobilization of imperialism's mighty military due to America's loss of the moral high ground. Understanding those realities provides the opportunity for developing nations to take control of their destiny, through insisting on an equal voice in the UN, and they are attempting to do so as we speak.

Attempting to retain control by the imperial centers, former U.S. Ambassador to the UN, John Bolton, threatened to defund the United Nations if they do not accept U.S. dictates on world trade. Instead of capitulating, the Doha round of world trade talks collapsed, with China, India, and other countries refusing to open their borders to cheap imports, because it would destroy their economies.

Those same movers and shakers in the former administration, that of President George W. Bush, openly stated they are not going to tolerate any nation, or group of nations, to militarily challenge America. Translated that means maintaining worldwide control of resources and the wealth producing process through military force.

As addressed above, a major move towards assured control of resources by the historic imperial centers was the occupation of Iraq, which turned into a disaster. Not only does America have most Iraqis against them, the entire Muslim world is also aware that, with possibly 70% of the world's known reserves of easily-accessible oil within their borders, they are the primary target.

The world is aghast at the destruction, torture, and oppression of American foreign policy.[6] Once the moral high ground is lost, a nation's power is greatly diminished, and this has America's mighty military essentially immobilized. Cover stories will be ignored, attempts at regime change anywhere in the world would be recognized for the imperialism it is and, at some level, sanctions against aggressor nations, posing as moral societies, would be invoked worldwide.

The Iraqi suppression alerted the former provinces of the old Soviet Union, oil and mineral rich Central Asia, to further protect themselves by trade and development agreements with Russia, China, and India. The immobilization of America's mighty military, due to loss of the moral high ground creates an opening for the formerly voiceless within the UN to insist that their votes will count.

The key factors are the immense resources, and the roughly 60% of the world's industrial capacity within the yet undeveloped world, the many trillions of dollars in reserves also outside the imperial nation's borders, and the current immobilization of imperialism's mighty military due to America's loss of the moral high ground. Understanding those realities provides the opportunity for developing nations to take control of their destiny, through insisting on an equal voice in the UN, and they are attempting to do so as we speak.

Attempting to retain control, former U.S. Ambassador to the UN, John Bolton, threatened to defund the United Nations if they do not accept U.S. dictates on world trade. Instead of capitulating, the Doha round of world trade talks collapsed; with China, India, and other countries, refusing to open their borders to cheap imports, because it would destroy their economies.

The once powerless are getting stronger and they recognize that the imperial centers are getting weaker. Alliances and federations of the **resource powers** will be difficult to challenge. Once they are strong enough, they can serve notice to the historic imperial nations that the UN be restructured into a democratic and moral forum, or they will form their own world governing body, which effectively would be a federation of 70% of the world.

That ultimatum would be rejected by imperial powers. On the chance that the previous creators of history—those major imperial powers—will change their minds, the new world governing body, should retain ambassadors and skeleton staff at the UN, and reconvene under a new name in a major city within those alliances. The world will have moved closer to being, openly and officially, what it has been ever since the end of WW II, a wealthy and heavily armed imperial world, in open struggle with the emerging, previously unarmed, world over control of resources, and the wealth producing process. All nations should be invited to that new world-governing body.

World federalist organizations have been working to have a constitution ready for that momentous day. The World Constitution and Parliament Association (WCPA), as does others, have one ready for revision and acceptance by just such an alliance of nations.

This forming federation can choose the best features of each constitution, add what they feel is necessary, and accept it as their foundation law. The inequalities, and injustices, within the United Nations Charter, compared against the equality and justice within the new world-governing body, will highlight the efforts of the old power structure to dictate, and the new power structure to rule cooperatively and democratically.

With a name picked and a constitution for that governing body in place, the first order of business should be how best to move forward on world development, alleviation of poverty, and global warming. Even though they would retain their staff at the UN, the relatively well developed China and India, will surely join. Japan and Russia will just as surely see the advantage in developing the poorer parts of the world in trade for access to resources. The presence of those four in that new governing body would be counter-weights to the well-armed nations that had historically denied freedom to the periphery of their empires. Russia's and China's veto power in the UN Security Council eliminates the option of a military assault under cover of the United Nations. The loss of the moral high ground, and the insanity of attacking the, now-allied, 70% of the world's population seeking the same freedoms America attained in their revolution, should keep the imperial nations' mighty militaries immobilized.

The first discussions between the fast-developing nations, and the "**resource powers**," should be on access to resources for these rising centers of capital, in trade for industrial technology, and training, for the emerging world. As they are busy signing such agreements as we write, we believe China, India, and Japan, would see the greater security to each of a fully developed world and agree. With their technology, arms, and resources, Russia would join. The ironclad rule to never share technology, except when allies were needed, will then be replaced by equal access to (a sharing of) technology, and equal access to (again a sharing of) resources. An economy requires modern industrial capital, resources, skilled labor, finance capital, markets, and—up to this point in history—a military to protect it all. Though nothing can protect against madmen, those powerful fast-developing nations—China, Russia, India, Brazil, Turkey, etc.—give these forming alliances substantial security. Both developed, and fast developing, nations know they must join or their access to resources and markets will be at risk. At that point, financial and military monopolization would be checkmated.

Once the Iranian oil bourse has been activated, and contracts are directly between oil exporting nations and refiners, either profits of oil exporting nations will increase 50% or the costs to buyers will drop 30%. Those oil trader profits (33% of the price of oil [derivative trading by traders who never use oil]) will disappear, and stock markets will shrink in step with that wealth extraction collapse.[h]

Economic alliances of a large share of the world's population, with the greater share of the world's resources within their borders, would spread shock through the markets of the imperial-centers-of-capital. As every democratic government must do, every nation or region must maximize their capital, labor, and resources for their own people. That principle, applied to all nations, requires equality of access to resources, technology and trade.

That is the trap the imperial nations find themselves in after centuries of appropriating the wealth of others, and becoming enormously wealthy, with no concern of others' rights, or that it may all have to end some day. As they want

---

[h] Which is why five undersea cables were cut just days before that bourse was to open. Not even a telephone call could get through to the island on which that bourse was located.

to avoid war, current rapidly developing nations will want to help those crumbling empires restructure; but they will not want to do so at the expense of their own development. Such a seismic shift in relationships between societies takes more time than allotted in this theoretical analysis, which condensed the time frame to make the process understandable.

In a reasonable time frame, the unequal aspects of property rights monopolists have created over the past 700-plus years, must be replaced by a fully federated world with **honest property rights, providing each citizen of the world their share of nature's wealth that she offers to all for free.** We will be using a theoretical restructuring of the American economy as an example. Such restructuring, needs to be applied to monopoly laws throughout the world. The emerging world understands this and—as addressed in *Economic Democracy: A Grand Strategy for World Peace and Prosperity* by this author—they also understand that the imperial-centers-of-capital's financial, economic, and military power, have suppressed every such attempt the past 65 years.

We assume the certainty of the aggressor, and aggressed, both being destroyed, will eliminate nuclear war as an option. The power of monopolized capital, and their mighty military, will be checkmated. At this historic moment, an equal share of the levers of power will be in the hands of the "**resource powers,**" and their allied centers of capital decoupling from the collapsing imperial centers. This new balance of power will permit the now-allied "**resource powers**" to bargain with the former imperial powers for continued access to their resources. We also assume America's loss of the moral high ground will advance that natural flow of events, towards a fully federated earth, by many years.

Capital fleeing to cheap labor has de-industrialized the United States. Just as early America ignored Britain's patent laws and copied British industry, China, and other countries, are ignoring monopoly patent laws and producing copies of every manufactured product in world trade. Those knock-offs, and the graduation of over 100,000 PhDs per year in the hard sciences, and that number increasing 30% a year, will soon bring Chinese technology abreast that of the wealthy world. The de-industrialized American economy will be in grave danger. The monopoly system will be collapsing due to the allied "**resource powers**" ignoring patent monopolization laws, just as America and other nations did when they were developing.

To replace the complexity of theft through plunder by trade, with the simplicity of sharing and cooperating, will require deep soul searching. As the only other choice is nuclear war, we will assume leveler heads—backed by a now-conscious population—will be humbled, and negotiate as equals, not as the powerful centers of empire they once were.

Key to those agreements between the federating, fast developing, world, will be placing patents into the public domain. The first such steps have been taken. In the contract to launch satellites for emerging nations' communications superhighways, China has agreed "there are to be no technological secrets kept from those South American nations." Establishing industries to build machinery for construction of both communications and transportation superhighways, throughout the forming alliances, with no royalties charged, would be a big move towards breaking patent monopolies. President Chavez understands this, and has vowed to "shake up the rules governing intellectual property rights on medicines and other products."

Communication highways keeping all citizens abreast of plans to provide a quality life for all citizens of the world, is becoming a reality. With many times the population of the wealthy world, with an equal per capita percent—but a far greater total—of geniuses, educating many times the engineers and scientists, with those four centers of capital sharing their technological knowledge with the emerging world, and if WW III is avoided through the world allying under the new world governing body; within two generations the citizenry of current fast developing **resource powers** could be living a quality life.

As opposed to ad-hoc development, the alert and moral will recognize that security for all requires poorer nations reaching a planned, sustainable, development level. The developed portions of this federated world, and the collapsing highly developed imperial world, should provide technology, training, and first industries, in trade for access to their reasonable share of resources. If that sharing is honest, the labor, capital, and resources of the emerging world will be producing most the necessities for their citizenry within one generation, and they should attain engineering, infrastructure, and production equality within two generations.

Towards that goal, all resources should be mapped and banks, roads, railroads, alternative energy power systems, industries, water and sewer systems, and all other infrastructure for an efficient, sustainable, regional economy should be planned. This takes care. Large industrial capacities for tractors, construction equipment, etc, are required to industrialize a developing region, but once developed, only small production capacities are adequate to produce parts for that machinery.

Japan has far more industry than necessary to produce for her 120 million citizens. Under monopoly rules, those exports are necessary to pay for imports, but they are not necessary within a properly-planned, sustainably-developed, economically balanced, region. In that peaceful world, Japan's defense needs disappear, three dimensional orchard farming (permaculture) on its own land can provide their food,[i] and they can provide technology, development, and manufactured products to Africa and South America in trade for resources.

Cultures within these emerging federations are not locked into **the aristocratic system of exclusive titles to nature's resources and technologies,**

---

[i] See Tikopia Island in Jared Diamond's *Collapse: How Societies Choose to Fail or Succeed,* 2005.

denying others their rightful share of what nature offers to all for free (the monopolization, wealth extraction, process). They were forced into that system of unequal property rights, and when the opportunity arises, they will replace it with an efficient economic structure.

The choices are only three: 1) retain the Western system of exclusive title to nature's resources and technologies, denying others their share; 2) revert to some form of command economy, communal socialist, or 3) turn to an honest economic and financial engine of full and equal economic rights for all through conditional title to nature's bounty, tempered by communitarian principles.[j] Those who chose options one or two would soon change their mind as the higher productivity, and lower labor and resource costs of those who chose the inclusive, efficient, intensely competitive, principles of full and equal property rights were proven.[k]

---

[j] This is a synthesis of capitalist, socialist, and communitarian *property rights*.. The dynamism of capitalism and the justice and equality within other philosophies are each retained.

[k] Many see a fully developed world as destructive to the environment. Tiny Tikopia Island, addressed above, has successfully practiced three-dimensional orchard farming for 3,000 years. That permaculture mixing of annual and perennial tubers, berries, vegetables, fruits and nuts is enormously productive and, due to that closely-planted mixture building its own defenses, essentially free of disease and destructive insects. Under such advanced permaculture, one's yard could produce a large share of a family's food needs and sharing between neighbors will provide variety. If the world replaced monoculture farming and shipping from hundreds or thousands of miles away with three dimensional orchard permacultures in back yards and farming communities, society could be living in a Garden of Eden continually improving soils as opposed to its rapid depletion under monoculture farming.

---

[1] Edmond Taylor, *The Fall of the Dynasties: The Collapse of the Old Order, 1905-1922* (New York: Dorset Press, 1989), chapters 17-19. This author's *Economic Democracy: A Grand Strategy for World Peace and Prosperity*, 2nd edition , 2010 (235 Dabney Lane, Pamplin VA, The Institute for Economic Democracy)

[2] Ibid

[3] Robert McHugh, "Money Supply versus Interest Rate Policy," *Comer*, January 2006, pp 18-19.

[4] Ian Bremmer, "Who's in Charge in the Kremlin" World Policy Journal (Winter 2005/06), p.3.

[5] Alfred W. McCoy, *A Question of Torture: CIA Interrogation from the Cold War to the War on Terror* (NY: Henry Holt and Company, 2006). Steven Hiatt, Editor, *A Game As Old Empire: The Secret World of Economic Hit Men and the Web of Global Corruption* As (San Francisco, Barrett-Koehler, 2007), Chalmers Johnson, *Nemesis The Last Days of the American Republic* (Metropolitan Books, New York, 2006), run keyword searches.

[6] Alfred W. McCoy, *A Question of Torture: CIA Interrogation from the Cold War to the War on Terror* (NY: Henry Holt and Company, 2006). Steven Hiatt, Editor, *A Game As Old Empire: The Secret World of Economic Hit Men and the Web of Global Corruption* As (San Francisco, Barrett-Koehler, 2007), Chalmers Johnson, *Nemesis The Last Days of the American Republic* (Metropolitan Books, New York, 2006), run keyword searches.

8. President Barack Obama's Economic Transition Team's Stabilization policies

It was not unexpected that President George W. Bush's Emergency Economic Stabilization Act of 2008 was designed to bail out the major banks and financial institutions which caused the current financial and economic crisis.

Those financial institutions receiving trillions of dollars in bailout money had copied Enron's off the books accounting, leveraged their investments 30:1 or higher, produced nothing, pocketed massive sums of money, and it was those policies of investment banks which brought on the current financial crash.

As values collapsed, those 30:1 leverages (debt to equity ratios) doubled, tripled, and kept on climbing. Citibank's leverage rose to 280:1 and required massive infusions of government money to prevent the nation's collapse. Others, Goldman Sachs, JP Morgan, Wells Fargo, Bank of America, HSBC, and banks across the world are caught in the same sand trap.

The rescue of those major banks, the American International Group (AIG) and other financial institutions, required trillions of dollars in bailout funds. The trillions spent, and the trillions more pledged, as the U.S. and world economy worsens, measures the huge vacuum building beneath the massive sums of unearned wealth which is currently called "our finance capital." Fully 95% of that finance capital is doing nothing more than extracting ever-more unearned wealth out of the economy. Key members of those non-productive bankers became President Obama's advisors, and they have convinced him that the best way to protect the nation is by continued protection of their massive sums of unearned wealth.

President Obama spotted the error of pouring money at Chrysler and General Motors. He fired the CEO of GM, and told them, and Chrysler, to produce viable plans for profitable companies before they received any more bailout funds. He needs to realize that the many trillions of dollars in finance capital he is currently protecting is even less productive, and point those trillions of dollars of your and my money at the real economy, you and me.

Most of the nation was upset over those many trillions of dollars going to the very people who had dropped the value of their 401K pensions by 45%, and destroyed millions of jobs.

The economy may yet calm down. Massive funds are parked in treasuries, other safe havens, and they will pour into the markets if the economy stabilizes. However, a deeper look tells us it may not. Much of the rest of the world's economies are dropping faster than the U.S., not all their central banks have the strength to bail them out, and some parts of the world have no way to protect themselves.

Added to that ongoing worldwide collapse are the **resource power's** breaks for freedom picking up speed. If they succeed in decoupling from the imperial world, that will deny the empires massive sums of extracted wealth. As they will be retaining the wealth once extracted from them, the **resource powers**, and the emerging centers of capital, can actually develop more rapidly as the empires collapse. Others will, formally or informally, quickly join those successful federations.

If those bailouts fail and/or if the world starts decoupling from the American and European economies, the president's only choice is call in the loans to those banks, nationalize them, and turn the money creation powers of those now nonbankruptable banks towards restructuring the real economy.

We now turn to the Conclusion where we demonstrate the simplicity of stopping this financial and economic collapse in its tracks, supporting the world's struggle for freedom, restructuring to full and equal economic rights for every citizen of this earth, reducing employed hours of the industrialized world by half even as poverty disappears, all citizens enjoying a quality secure life, and all this while taking pressure off resources and alleviating global warming.

President Barack Obama's ultimatum to the automobile industry, his start towards normalizing relations with Cuba, his sincere move for massive reduction in nuclear weapons, his not pushing for NAFTA and other unequal trade agreements at the Organization of American States Summit, and his alert to Israel that America will be backing a viable Palestinian state, hints he may have the intention to living up to his pledge for honest change.

The world may yet go peaceful, with full and equal economic rights, and a quality life for every citizen of this earth. If it does, this president will be recorded in history as the greatest leader of all time.

9. Conclusion: An Open Message to President Barack Obama's Economic Recovery Team

In every extreme crisis, such as the aftermaths of WW I and WW II, or the Great Depression of the 1930s with its 89% collapse in values, the imperial-aristocratic system of property rights came close to being overthrown by ballot box revolutions.[1] It is not reasonable to think that the citizenry of America and Europe will patiently watch the developing centers of capital—China, India, and Russia, along with Japan, successfully ally with the emerging world while the West's economies, historically dependent upon those cheap resources and labor, become moribund and their children cold and hungry. As war against 70% of the world will be unacceptable to the developed world's own citizenry, we trust that President Barack Obama will live up to his announced dedication to change.

Only a powerful president with exceptional vision and integrity, such as Franklin Roosevelt in the Great Depression of the 1930s enacting revolutionary legislation within 100 days, can guide this nation and the world to its salvation through applying these simple principles for efficient economies.

In this crisis, like all others in history, families will be cold and hungry as values collapse all around them. All know that monopolists (those with the un-earned money to loan) firmly enforce the rule that the final mortgage holder will own all property backing defaulted loans. This president and his advisors will know those collapsed values are pledged to loan institutions. Those privately-owned loan institutions going broke right along with their customers will be, by the same custom and law, owned by the Federal Reserve, the socially-owned lender of last resort that has been loaning, possibly giving, trillions of dollars to the very people who caused the current financial crash.

Three times—after WW I, in the depth of the Great Depression of the 1930s, and after WW II—the monopoly system avoided its overthrow by ballot box revolutions only by the major share of those countries turning to fascism. This time, with half the world industrialized, but divided into various centers of capital, and the yet-unindustrialized fully aware, there should be no way to save the centuries-old property rights system designed to protect wealth and power, at the expense of the powerless. This president will realize that America's socially-owned Federal Reserve, with its money creation powers, taking over management of those bankrupt banks is the only option.

The president's advisors understand the process very well. They were using these principles to prevent financial collapses and protecting the ethereal world of high finance for 30 years. The 1982 Savings and Loan scandal, the one-day stock market collapse of 22.6% in 1987, the 1990 Citibank bailout, the 1994 Mexico financial crisis, the Asian currency crisis in 1997-98, Long-Term Capital Management's bankruptcy crisis in 1998, and the dotcom crash of 2000-01 were only different in that the U.S. economy was not collapsing, and the money necessary to turn the economy back up was modest.

If the citizenry remain passive, an economy can balance anywhere for periods of time, and there is the possibility that the American economy can be stabilized at its current poverty level. However, massive productive capacity throughout the world going idle, and that which is humming is building the emerging world, tells us Western economies may not rebalance. Their economies have yet to face the hurricane of the emerging world retaining the "earnings of their natural wealth," and the imperial centers losing those massive sums which previously went to their side of the accounting ledger.

If it does not stabilize, President Obama should organize a new recovery team with no ties to the ethereal world of high finance, call in those "loans" to distressed banks, nationalize them just as the law requires, start pouring created money at the real economy, rather than to those financial monopolists who created this crisis, and guide this world to a quality life for every citizen of this earth. If the goal is equality and honesty, bankrupt private banks converted to socially-owned banks can stop any financial crash in its tracks, and quickly rebuild an economy.

With higher interest to depositors and lower interest to borrowers, due to lower operating costs, and backed by the Fed's money creation powers, both depositors and borrowers will flock to those secure, socially-owned banks. Already in trouble, the rest of the private banks will turn in their keys as fast as their customers start transferring to those secure banks. The entire banking system will quickly be, as it should be, socially-owned, socially-operated, and more powerful than an army.

The goals must be the greatest good for the greatest numbers—food, fiber and shelter for everybody, and protecting the savings, equities, and livelihood, of the maximum number of people. This requires financing both consumers and the real economy as opposed to the current financing of the ethereal world of high finance, the ones who created this crisis.[a]

The president and his new advisors already understand this socially-owned banking system's creation of money powers for stopping the financial collapse in its tracks, quickly restructure the economy, and reestablish prosperity. A decree is issued for every head of household—husbands, wives, or singles—without a job and without other income or resources, to apply to their bank/credit union for a monthly subsistence based on single households receiving 75% that of married couples and an allowance for each dependent.

The loan institutions will put the applicant's electronic transfer number on that application. That form will include testimony, under oath, that they have no income or resources. Upon signing, and on the 1st of each month thereafter until receiving their first full paycheck, subsistence funds will be computer-deposited into those accounts.

Heads of families will walk out with funds in that secure bank to cover food, fiber, and shelter for that month, and each month thereafter until employed. Those who would be against a non-bankruptable bank and subsistence funds for those with no equity and no income would be so out of sync with events they will be few and irrelevant. Though only modest amounts of cash can be withdrawn, all trades will be quickly consummated through checks, credit cards, or debit cards, which is the real money in a modern economy.

With this latest break from unequal property rights, as applied to nature's resources and technologies, all Americans are now fed, clothed, and housed, and the worst aspect of the crisis, a cold and hungry citizenry, is under control. Spending of those subsistence funds will increase demand and, since every citizen has a livable income, quickly stabilize the economy. With money flows across national borders controlled through countries and regions issuing new currencies spendable only within their borders, any shortage of circulating money for subsistence payments, and construction and repairing of economic infrastructure can, up to the level of a balanced money supply, be created.

These are the **dual currency** systems handling world trade within a cooperative, federated, world system we addressed periodically. World currency systems are under discussion, but they do not have the simplicity and power of a

---

[a] A banking system can be balanced anywhere from highly efficient to its current, extremely corrupt, monopolized inefficiency. The world economy is just as unbalanced as national economies. Debts between, and within, all nations will have to be renegotiated along the lines of renegotiating debts within America as we are addressing. This will be a huge effort but, as demonstrated by this simplified example, it can be done. Each nation or region will have to operate their economies with a new currency as they renegotiate contracts and debts with all other nations and regions denominated in a world currency (a **dual currency** structure). Sacrifices will be required by all.

currency for all nations, and useable only in trades between nations and regions. Inflation threats due to too much circulating money are easily handled when a currency is spendable only within a nation's borders. Mandated reserves may at first be necessary but a socially owned bank automatically has 100% reserves, and fractional reserve banking is not necessary once an economy of full and equal economic rights is established and in balance. Once the currencies of resource-rich developing world regions and nations are protected, trading access to resources for technology will boost the circulation of those "values" (money).

An efficient economy with full and equal economic rights, balances through resource rents and banking charges maintained at levels that cover the costs of infrastructure construction and maintenance, operations of government, education, universal health care, retirements, etc.

Keeping intermediately developed, and developing, regions of the world going requires currencies that cannot be spent outside economically viable borders, and a world currency handling trades between those viable regions, or nations, as they rebalance their trades with the imperial economies. Under a **dual currency** system, each viable region can create base money to build infrastructure or, early on, even loaned to build industries. With the understanding that a slowing of the velocity of circulating money permits base money creation at an appropriate level, it is possible to operate an economy at very high levels of created money spent on essential needs in a crisis, or for initial development of emerging economies. Once a nation is developed, money creation will be only when natural disasters, such as hurricanes, tornadoes, floods, and earthquakes, destroy value, or when an economy is expanding. Note the savings when major natural disasters are insured through created money replacing destroyed wealth, instead of through insurance policies. Owners having to shoulder some loss will protect against fraud. Blocks of homes burning would be, of course, a natural disaster.

Forced to start decoupling from the American economy before that full federation, other nations, and the emerging world, will be restructuring their banking systems with their own regional currencies spendable only within their borders. With banking systems protected against cross-border flows of money, and with development planning carried on through regional alliances, each region can develop sensibly, and steadily, at the maximum pace allowed by construction equipment, trained labor, and resources available.

With the dollar the world's current reserve currency, the U.S. has had the power to create money (value) that properly belongs to other nations. While costing nothing to create, that money has a firm claim against real wealth. Though they do not put it in these words, China, Russia, and other countries are demanding a world currency that protects their right to their share of created money, and that protects their money's value. America and Europe responded by offering IMF Special Drawing rights, backed by a basket of four currencies, as that world currency. The struggle for equal rights to the protective power, and efficiency, of an inter-country trading currency has just begun.

This president initiating negotiations for **dual currency** systems protecting each currency from rapid money flows across borders (full and equal currency rights placed on the table for the first time in history) could lead to a true international currency for a peaceful federated earth. A world currency is, of course, what we have always had, except America was in charge the past 60 years, there were no cross border controls, and leaving an imperial power in control of the world's trading currency, is an open invitation for financial destabilizations, within the alliances we are addressing as crucial for the world's final break for freedom.

America's counter offer, IMF Special Drawing Rights backed by four currencies (the dollar, pound, Euro, and Yen), can only be that world currency if all other currencies have equality and protection. The structure should be a democratic "Bank for International Settlements;" **an honest World Central Bank (the one in Basel Switzerland only if totally reformed) overseeing that dual currency system**. That honest world currency would handle trades between economically viable nations and regions. As the money of a properly-structured world bank will be only numeric values stored within computers, there will be no world paper currency. This will eliminate counterfeiting, money laundering, most black market exchanges, etc. The "flickering beginnings" of a world federation with a world central bank will have become a steady glow.

Having addressed control of the flow of money across borders so economically viable federated regions can create money and rapidly develop, we return to the collapsing American economy which has just been theoretically stabilized by creating money for subsistence payments to the unemployed, for restarting the economy, and for economic restructuring we have yet to address. Once monopolization is eliminated, only 5% the former level of finance capital will operate the American economy efficiently. Ownership of that capital will be very broadly diffused, and it will be democratically, and equally, shared with all transactions visible, touchable, and understandable. The ethereal world of high finance, which is nothing more than massive sums extracted through unequal property rights, will be history.

With the old powerbrokers keeping a low profile and an appreciative citizenry paying close attention, this alert president realizes lobbyists can no longer block universal health care being legislated as a human right. Faced with the logic of single-payer health care at half the price, with over 500 physicians petitioning President Barack Obama to put it into law, with almost 50 nations having already established it, and with Britain a stark example of 100% coverage at 43%

America's per capita cost,[2] with 90% approval of their system by the British and 70% disapproval of their system by Americans, and with British doctors better paid than America's, universal health care will quickly be legislated into law.[b] The once cold and hungry citizenry are now warm, well fed, and their health care costs are covered by the social-credits (profits and society's savings) of the socially-owned banking system. With food, fiber, shelter, health care, and retirement for each citizen secure, addressed just below, crime will drop rapidly and the prison population and legal system will eventually shrink to a shadow of its current self.

The genie will be out of the bottle and it cannot be put back. The advantages and efficiencies of a socially-owned banking system, universal health care, and retirement as social and human right, would be so obvious that the citizenry will be looking forward to a continued restructuring to full and equal economic rights. A dialog on abandoning the monopoly system, structured within property rights laws for the past 700-plus years, will be on-going world-wide, as the world awakens to the efficiencies of a federated world with full and equal rights economies. Once the insurance industry is analyzed and that segment of the economy restructured along the lines of Social Security, the now empty insurance offices would be turned to productive use, even as all citizens are fully insured at half the cost. The subsistence-pay-protected displaced insurance workers will be assured of a respectable job when this economic restructuring is finalized.

By this time monopolists will know their secret was out, and they will not be investing in monopolies they know will soon no longer exist. Citizenry world-wide will be watching closely the on-going drama, and by now will understand the key concepts for an efficient economy: Human labor did not produce land (resources), nature offers it to all for free, and a rightful share for each can be had through socially-collected resource rents funding essential services. The citizenry will watch taxes disappear as those funds (bank profits, created money, and resource rents) are returned to them as social-credits running governments, building and maintaining economic infrastructure (water and sewer systems, roads, railroads, electricity, communications superhighways, and all other natural monopolies), universal health care, retirement, and in an emergency, any social need.

In short, all money once paid to monopolists (that unearned 95% of current finance capital) now provides a community with social-credits, eliminates taxes,

---

[b] This will take a full restudy of nutrition and drugs without input or interference by food or drug companies, and providing the citizenry with the knowledge to take control of their own health. Remember deaths go down when doctors go on strike. Both deaths and food costs will drop rapidly when the processed food craze is understood as a primary cause of diabetes (processed carbohydrates) and heart disease (transfats), and avoided.

and that double savings is realized by employed working hours dropping by half or more and still providing a quality life for all.

With that explained, the citizenry will understand those quintuple plus gains when society collects all resource rents, and expends it as social-credits funding infrastructure and social services; that law will pass by legislation or referendum. The mother of all monopolies (land [resources]) will have been eliminated,[c] all would be receiving their share of the wealth produced by nature, and for the first time in history, an honest capitalist society will have been established. This funding of the real economy, stopping the financial collapse in its tracks, is many times cheaper than the current pouring of tens of trillions of dollars at the ethereal world of high finance which caused this crisis in the first place. In fact this social-credit plan will cost nothing when it is fully in place. A restructured, federated, world economy, that provides a quality life for all its citizens, provides far more use-value with far less resources and labor than a monopolized economy.

As opposed to the excluding social structures designed by monopolists the past 700-plus years, under the principles of full and equal economic rights, taxes will be quaint history. The equal sharing of jobs, a reasonable pay ratio between higher skilled and lower skilled labor, and an ongoing analysis of an economy requires an accounting system.

Each person is responsible for most the amenities of their lives and these are paid for from wages and profits. Universal health care and other social and human rights are efficiently funded through socially-collected profits from society's banking system and resource rents. As proven by the savings possible under an economy of full and equal economic rights, investment funds from socially-collected resource rents and bank profits replacing extracted values capitalized into huge blocs of privately owned capital, are so enormous that money to fund this peaceful society will be in plentiful supply. A shortage of investment capital is fiction. Currently only 5% of finance capital, at best, is operating the real economy in America. The rest is only extracting wealth.

While all the above is taking place, accountants experienced in real estate will be assessing the value of all property both before and after the financial collapse. The price mechanisms of capitalism had measured those values, but those monopoly-created values, and the 95% of the current blocs of capital created to buy and sell them, were not legitimate then, and are not legitimate now. Protection of honestly-earned savings mixed with those monopoly values, requires reduction

---

[c] Land as the mother of all monopolies is obsolete. This treatise proves that monopolization of both banking and technologies are equally as powerful and damaging to an economy. We have addressed above the elimination of the monopolization of technology as the key to developing the impoverished world. Thus patent monopolies have adverse effects equal to either land or banking monopolies.

in debts, at the same ratio as the rationalization of property values. Capitalized (monopoly) values will have disappeared, and only labor-created values (use-values) remain.

With reassessment ongoing, this alert president proceeds to clear up titles to all property and, with the greatest good for the greatest number in mind, restore the financial health of the citizenry, and the nation. The land under all homes, all farms, all mines, and all industries, will remain under the name of the current owners (previous owners if property has been foreclosed upon) but they now must **pay monthly resource rents to society (themselves)**. Considering all taxes disappear, and those funds come right back as social-credits operating governments, building infrastructure, education, universal health care, retirement, etc, paying resource rents to the social-fund is the most profitable investment a society can make.

The property owners have all rights to that land as before, except the right to collect a private tax, the land rent. Wages should be recalculated to be adequate and low-paid retirements must be recalculated upward, to that necessary for a quality life.

As land now has no capitalized value, loans against it must be erased from the records, and that against structures built upon it reappraised to current, labor-created, use-values. If 50% of loan values were backed by the land before the crisis, that 50% loan value is erased. The remaining 50% will be discounted to 50% those structures' current value. Autos, boats, and other loans would be similarly restructured. Paid-for real-estate would not be affected, except there will be no taxes on structures, and land rents will be paid into the social fund.

Those with more than one home, or if they have other resources, will not be receiving subsistence payments until those residuals of massive unearned wealth have been consumed. That rule would not apply to an owned, productive, business in which that person is directly employed, and which is temporarily idle due to the crisis. Such productive resources would be entitled to protection, and support, from the socially-owned banking system in the same manner as these suggestions for protection of titles to homes.

Under the financial crisis, most second homes or investment properties carrying debt will have been repossessed. Those renting would be first in line to purchase; financing would be available. The socially-owned banking system, being not-for-profit and not bankruptable, will have replaced trillions of dollars in uncollectable debts on homes with collectable debts, at the same debt-equity level as before the collapse.

A private bank can write off only a modest amount of loans before they are bankrupt; a socially-owned bank can erase all debt that is necessary. The process is simple, and the rights of all can be protected while stabilization of a severe crisis is not viable under private banking; restructuring an economy is impossible without the cornerstone of a **community social-credit process, the banking system**, under public ownership. Such protection for borrowers would be in direct conflict with current unequal property rights, and private banks' maximization of profits.

With the citizenry now understanding **the monopoly, wealth extraction, process** they previously were unaware existed, and with property rights of all secure; this is the time to eliminate the doubling of consumer costs due to patent monopolies. Explanations to the now alert citizenry on how consumer product prices are at least twice that necessary will make those legal changes imperative. By Congressional action, or by referendum, those patent laws will change to paying inventors well, and placing patents in the public domain. When that law is fully in place, 85% of the activity of casinos known as stock markets, where those unearned profits are collected, will disappear. The resources, and talented labor previously battling within equity markets over who shall claim the enormous wealth produced by technology, will be available for truly productive use.

Current patents will be in force for up to 20 years. Transferring technology to **"resource powers"** in trade for access to resources while letting those monopoly rights run out within the developed world, will give corporations those 20 years to unwind from their monopoly positions. When unwound, their production-distribution capacities will be intact. But they will no longer be extracting wealth through monopolization. As the gains and protections of society as a whole are obvious, developing countries will adopt that patent structure as fast as they can negotiate use of the latest technologies in trade for access to resources.

The wealthiest nations have greater dependence upon emerging world resources. Rising centers of capital are transferring technology and building infrastructure in trade for access to resources as we speak. This federating world will recognize those imperial unequal property rights (monopolization patterned after aristocratic property rights) had effectively collapsed, and they will adjust their laws accordingly.

Monopoly values of corporations are primarily capitalized values of wealth extracted through **exclusive title to nature's resources and technologies, denying others their rightful share of what nature offers to all for free (the monopolization, wealth extraction, process)**. These are all big boys fully believing in the system they had created, and which has now crashed. As most those values had been extracted from productive labor over the years, and those unequal property rights— now proven as a system of theft—have been abandoned, nothing is owed there.[d] The economic collapse, plus the loss of monopoly values, will drop the value

---

[d] The simplicity of inflation and deflation control proves that inflations are conscious decisions. An example is the 2002-06, housing bubble. Money had to be created to buy and

of most corporations below their debt values (values collapsed 89% in the Great Depression). As the original private banks will have been holders of 1st mortgages, the now socially-owned banks will own most of those corporations, and the looming elimination of patent monopolization, along with the economic crisis, will, as in all great crashes, collapse stock values to that of wallpaper. As private property, and free enterprise, should be maintained, shares should be distributed to labor and management within those corporations as loans at market-value. Those loans repaid along the principles of the subchapter "Investment and Job Opportunities" (p. 115, a percent of wages deducted each month) would resolve that equitably. With its own workers the new owners, those industries would be operated efficiently.

By the same debt revaluation formulas; the modest market values acknowledged in those payments would be distributed to the few creditors still standing. As in all economic collapses, those values will be low to nonexistent. It will be the responsibility of the new manager-owners to operate a productive-profitable company, and rebuild values. For that purpose and for new entrepreneurs, a department within the socially-owned banking system would fund major industries and businesses. That financing of worker-owned businesses and cooperatives would be the economic ideal of labor employing capital. Since this banking system has the power to direct both primary created money (base money) and savings to areas in need while simultaneously holding required reserves high enough to destroy surplus buying power, and maintain a steady money supply, funding would not be a problem. Loans to cover expansions and new enterprises would be available at interest rates high enough to cover risk. And we reaffirm that, once this efficient economy is in balance and the banks socially-owned, there will be little need, likely no need, for mandated reserves.

The many subdivisions of financial empires within the ethereal world above the real economy will have collapsed when the economy crashed. The socially-owned banking system will keep the real economy operating; those many methods of intercepting wealth within the vapory ethereal world of high finance, that are reducing economic efficiency by fully 50%, can wither on the vine. As most are financial empires built capitalizing extracted values, 95% of America's current huge blocs of finance capital are both unearned and unneeded. That ethereal world of high finance is only laying claim to wealth produced by others. Except for bonds not revalued through bankruptcy, most those intangible ethereal val-

---

sell those doubled values. So that housing bubble was a planned event, utilizing created money to rescue the stock market, which only creates another imbalance that has to be weathered. All such maneuvers, protecting power and wealth, disappear when an honest banking system fully funds the real economy, and the many games in the ethereal world of high finance, extracting massive wealth, are history.

ues will have disappeared in the economic collapse. With their total disappearance, GDP will measure only economic activity in the real economy.

A great hue and cry will go up that these blocks of capital are necessary to operate an efficient economy. That warning will be muffled as the mighty economic and financial engine of full and equal economic rights doubles the efficiency of the economy. Once established, a slim, trim, "real" economy will replace the inefficient ethereal economy which had evolved into a crazy quilt of methods to extract wealth produced by productive labor. Each of those best and brightest, who once owned and operated those niches within a monopolized economy, will be guaranteed a "productive" job. There will be no need to carve out an inefficient financial empire. Those who see new opportunities will have access to investment capital through loan officers trained, and experienced, in financing promising new endeavors. Socially-owned risk capital, charging higher than normal interest, would be paid from cash flow and those entrepreneurs, no longer monopolists, would retain the honestly earned values of their successes.

Due to a socially-owned banking system being more powerful than armies, what we have addressed philosophically can be done. That power is denied a private banking system because their unequal property rights are designed for maximum rights to monopolists, and minimum rights for all others. In each financial crisis, the relative wealth of deeply entrenched monopolists increase as the entire nation goes broke. If your property is half paid for, the creditor owns half and you own half. But, when a financial crisis hits, values drop, the creditor owns it all, and you own nothing. Instead of monopolists claiming what is properly your equity, a socially-owned banking system can rebalance debts to match value collapses, and protect everyone's honestly-earned equity. However, it has no responsibility for protecting unearned wealth extracted under unequal property rights laws. A large share of the unearned wealth will have disappeared in the above collapse and revaluations. Once all monopolies are eliminated through the restructured economy we lay out, there will be no deflations. Inflations from shortages caused by the weather will be regional and temporary.

The goal is to restructure the unequal property rights laws established by imperial power brokers over the past 700-plus years—which caused this, and all past, economic crises—to inclusive property rights with a quality life for all while employed only two to three days a week, and all with no risk of poverty or economic collapses. This philosophy eliminates monopolies while retaining an honest capitalist economy which accomplishes both socialist and communitarian goals.[e]

---

[e] In either case it is possible to create money for both infrastructure and industry, and control the money supply through higher mandated reserves.

Recognizing the security of titles to land with an initial purchase price of zero due to paying all resource rents to society; noting the efficiencies and equality of a socially-owned banking system providing equality in social-credits; with the properties, and equities, of the maximum number protected; with insurance priced at half the old norm; with universal health care and retirement as social and human rights, and all this now part of the social dialog; a mandated reduction of the workweek to create a highly-efficient economy with a quality life for all will not only be an imperative, it will be an easy sell.

Among the large numbers of unemployed will be people well qualified to calculate the number of productive jobs in a fully rationalized, efficient, economy. We will assume their calculations match ours, two to three days work per week outside the home for each employable citizen. From that calculation, Congress would pass, and the President would sign, or a voter referendum would mandate, a reduction of the work week to that level. A productive, well-paid, job for each citizen is now guaranteed.

Subsistence payments, continuing as wages during the first one to two months, or more, of an employment-learning period, will readjust the workforce smoothly. Highly skilled jobs, pilots, railroad engineers, etc, will take substantially longer. A few skills, such as scientists, are unique. They are on intense searches that leave little free time; their pay is primarily emotional. Society, and those scientists, both gain by a doubling in manpower with little reduction in each one's search for those secrets of nature.

All that, and a stable money supply, can be seamlessly accomplished. As the workweek is lowered, and respectable, well-paid jobs become available, subsistence payments will be withdrawn. All this can be done much faster, much cheaper, and create a far more efficient economy than pouring those massive sums of created money at the same ethereal world of high finance that extracted their wealth from others, and created this crisis (2008-10).

Some people are much more productive than others but not so productive as to justify the current wide disparity in pay. There will be exceptions—an Einstein, an Oprah Winfrey, a president, and a few others—but serious researchers have concluded that most should be paid equally with a differential in pay no greater than two to one is reasonable, and that great a differential only in exceptional cases. As these adjustments are made, the wages of the underpaid must be increased. Once those adjustments are made, both poverty and subsistence payments are history. Cost of products and services, measured in hours employed to purchase them, will drop 50%, or more.

The crisis will quickly subside as all checks, credit and debit card charges against adequate bank balances, within the socially-owned banking system, are honored. With debts restructured, property titles secure, and all adequate bank balances honored, proving a socially-owned banking system automatically has 100% reserves, and with money in consumer's pockets, an economy, America's or any region of the world that puts this together, has nowhere to go but forward.

There will be other problems to resolve but, once the banking system is under social ownership, monopolies are eliminated, and the goal of planners is full and equal rights for all, those are all solvable. Most will have lost everything as the economy collapsed and everyone comes out of the economic crisis with secure title to homes and businesses, secure jobs, and equal and adequate pay. Those full and equal economic rights create an economy that, so long as monopolies and ethereal worlds of high finance are avoided, will maintain stable and secure values for millenniums. After historic past economic collapses, citizenry distrusted banks and were afraid to go into debt. In contrast, this, potentially the worst of all collapses in history, would be so short, and security restored worldwide so quick, the citizenry will soon spend and save normally.

Communication superhighways are so efficient that they have the potential, possibly the certainty, of destabilizing the entire world monopoly system. It was studying that possibility that led to this analysis of the least traumatic way to restructure to a peaceful and prosperous world. So we allow the communications industry as quickly restructuring to those superhighways along the lines of chapter five. Monopolization of phone, cable, TV, and radio, as well as 85% of the brick, mortar, and labor of the developed world's education system and possibly 60%, or more, of the infrastructure of retail industry, are replaced by those communication superhighways.

With the old power structure totally discredited and thus without a political voice, alert and moral managers of state, and an equally moral, but more likely frightened, American Congress,[f] or voter referendums, would pass the necessary restructure laws as described above. With a citizenry enjoying the security and higher quality of life of these restructurings, constitutional and other legal challenges can be quickly set aside by national referendums.[g]

Only under a socially-owned banking system can you quickly provide subsistence payments to a cold and hungry citizenry and simultaneously restructure

---

[f] In the crisis of the 1930s, the legislators were just that frightened, which is what permitted the passage of many laws giving Americans rights taken for granted today (Social Security, Unemployment Insurance).

[g] The powerful have established many blocks to changes, constitutional and legal, into their property rights laws. But with an alert leader quickly providing security to a cold, hungry, and panicky citizenry, and with promises of total security for the foreseeable future, few legislators or judges would dare stand against it; national referendums would override those hold outs.

debts and an entire economy. It is that quick alleviation of the crisis, and rapid restructuring, which alerts a citizenry to the full, and equal economic rights possible by abandoning the monopoly system, so carefully structured the past 700-plus years; which economic classics have told us is the best of all possible systems in which monopolization does not exist.

Until an example of an efficient economy, with full and equal rights for all, has been put in place, most will be unaware they had been living under a monopoly structure. Besides the classics, that misguided belief system is due to monopolists funding justifying philosophers, primarily through the spin of philosophically hard-right think tanks, in step with establishing, and as a part of main taining, the monopoly system. That also explains suppression of the developing world's breaks for freedom the past 65 years. If any example of full and equal economic rights for all ever successfully established itself, the now-exposed monopoly system would have collapsed.

An efficient, federated, world economy requires each region producing most of their consumer needs. Part of restructuring the American economy to keep everything local will be rebuilding regional industries that were sent overseas in the race for the unearned profits that created this crisis. A nation or economic region can only be secure when they are producing the essentials of a quality life for their citizens. Bananas, coconuts, minerals, and many other commodities have to be paid for either by surplus commodities or manufactures. Such resource and production balances require planning and cooperation, not winner take all laissez-faire.

Developing nations require a regional currency acceptable only within the borders of an economically viable region. With that regional currency, money to build both industry, and infrastructure, can be created, and that, plus resources and skilled labor, are the fundamentals of wealth production. That foundation of an industrial economy, plus the wealth produced, backs the socially-created money. Each time a unit of money (base money) circulates, it equals the use-value being bought or sold, and its circulation now operates only the "real economy." An ethereal, unproductive, wasteful, economy no longer exists.

Necessary adjustments will be made after an analysis of how these monopoly laws evolved over the centuries. The conclusion can only be that they were unequal property rights put in place undemocratically to lay claim to wealth properly owned by others, and those huge blocs of capital invested in bonds are, beyond that which is part of the roughly 5% which were honest earnings and savings. Those representations of value are invalid because their owners were paid those massive sums while producing nothing.[h]

Government and infrastructure bonds are the final sanctuary for that appropriated wealth. While all other values are collapsing, interest rates fall and the values of earlier-issued bonds with higher interest rates rise. A doubling of bond values as real property values crash can be a quadrupling in relative values. By moving into bonds as interest rates peak, and into stocks as interest rates bottom, a managed rhythm, massive more wealth is extracted from its proper owners.

Just as aristocracy's titles to land was for centuries the proverbial elephant in the living room denying all others the right to enjoy their full and equal economic rights, that elephant's children, the share of those huge blocs of capital (the 95%) once buying and selling capitalized appropriated values (misnamed profits) within the ethereal world of high finance, that have moved to other investments, primarily government and infrastructure bonds, would still be preventing full realization of rights.

For centuries the money realized from selling capitalized appropriated values have been moving into other investments, some into productive industries—addressed above in which those extracted values had now disappeared through bankruptcy—and some were invested in government and infrastructure bonds in which those values, both honestly earned and extracted, have, assuming bankruptcy had not lowered their value, possibly doubled or tripled in value as industry values collapsed.

Both the profits and the interest on that unearned wealth have to be paid for by the very people from whom that original unearned finance capital was first extracted. And, until the economy is fully restructured, it will be paid for again and again, on into perpetuity.

Current titles to nature's resources, and technologies, derived directly from aristocratic property rights law, and fine-tuned for the past 700-plus years as monopoly property rights law, are unequal, inefficient, and unethical. That marks a substantial share of properly-invested funds as unearned wealth including all "earnings" such as those who rode up the value of land or bonds as addressed above. So we have moral investors with unearned savings functioning within an unethical system. Those unethically earned, yet morally invested in bonds, are both perpetuating the cycle of unearned wealth, and blocking honest investment of honest savings, and socially-created money.

---

[h] Bonds and treasuries held by financial institutions of other countries will require negotiation. A just settlement will require sacrifices from all parties.

We addressed above how the need for safe investments for these blocs of extracted wealth led bankers to ignore the efficiencies of resource rents and bank profits providing social-credits for education, highways, railroads, water systems, sewers, communication superhighways, libraries, parks, universal health care, retirement, running governments, etc. Such simple financial efficiency was ignored to provide a safe place (government and infrastructure bonds) to invest the massive sums extracted through unequal property rights.

Unearned money invested in government and infrastructure bonds would both deny society the right to create debt free money to build infrastructure, and penalize honestly earned savings. After all, resource rents and bank profits now funding all social needs, exposes where these massive sums came from, resource rents and bank profits (Most other profits are winnings [derivatives] gambling with those unearned profits). If one traces those blocs of savings back to where they were supposedly "earned," one will find most originated as unearned wealth.

It is impossible to restructure to an efficient economy without directly addressing those huge blocs of wealth which were unethically earned but ethically invested. Like the proverbial elephant in the living room, others cannot exercise their rights so long as that beast, extracted wealth invested in government and infrastructure bonds or which weathered the crisis in another safe niche, is still there.

The conundrum of honest investing of unearned wealth, within the rules of a corrupt system, can be resolved through negotiation. Either those bondholders accept rational payments for their bonds that acknowledge those original unearned values or they will be revalued through bankruptcy of the pledged properties. After all one cannot rob a bank, invest it honestly, and claim the earnings are honest when they are finally caught.

There will be derivatives and hedge funds that will, after the shakeout and like bonds, place title to much of the nation's wealth into the hands of very few people. Along the same lines as **changing the rules** when the Hunt brothers had the silver market cornered, which saved the market and came close to bankrupting the Hunts, these unearned wealth accumulations can be, and must be, set aside.

Once the principles of full and equal property rights—as related to nature's resources and technologies—are in place, operation of an economy will be simplicity itself. There need be no taxes unless society decided to fund retirements through payroll deductions so as to have an accounting system measuring the economy, and those would be insurance premiums, not taxes.

Keeping the value of one's currency in line with the currency of other nations of these forming federations requires an honest World Bank for International Settlements that is mandated to protect honestly earned values of all nations, and regions (the one in Basel Switzerland needs restructured). Blips on computers, at this honest World Bank, will replace current international trading currencies. While exports and imports are sold and purchased in this international currency, each nation or federated, economically viable, region will have full control of money within their economies. With their currencies having no value outside their borders, their banking systems can create money to build infrastructure and industries, rapidly develop their economies and those are the values that the new World Bank must protect.

We have structured our theoretical economies, with full and equal economic rights, which will stay in balance forever. Once regional economies are developed and efficient, currency values between regions will balance. Until that time, trade between regions must be managed; that is what trading resources for technology and establishing regional and international currencies were, in this example, all about.

Once each region of this fully formed federation is sustainably developed, its labor equally as productive, and equally paid, those relatively equal currencies could be made interchangeable. But controlling cross-border flows of drugs, illegal harvesting of resources, criminal activities, keeping a finger on the pulse of the world, resolving problems before they get out of hand, elimination of currency speculations distorting and sabotaging an economy, and the right to experiment with a potentially more efficient social structures require **dual currency** world trading systems.

As economies develop, infrastructure costs will be covered by resource rents, and banking profits, transposed into social-credits. To stay within the earth's capacity, a fully developed world economy, with a quality life for all, as opposed to an ever-expanding economy, will create only the money destroyed through natural disasters; effectively it is insurance, paid to those who took the loss. Base money that has been destroyed is replaced by paying directly to those who had those catastrophic losses.

For the world to become peaceful, for poverty to be eliminated, and for protection of resources and the environment, something similar to what we lay out has to happen in a relatively seamless web worldwide. With modern communications informing the world, as it breaks out from under its centuries of monopolization, that can happen.

As the resource rich, but financially poorer, world is developing, surplus labor within the wealthy world will have been released by the rationalization of their former inefficient monopolized economies. A part of those surplus labors should be turned to installing communication superhighways throughout the emerging world, and providing those first industries and training.

There are simple and cheap ways to train human capital. Labor for intermediate technologies can be trained, work as apprentices, and when fully trained, join the expanding labor force. They, in turn, will train more apprentices. Under such policies, practiced by guilds for centuries, but that too was under a monopoly structure to avoid training oneself out of a job. By avoiding those monopoly structures, which form naturally as each protects their access to a share of society's wealth production, a skilled labor force can rapidly expand.

If the world community is serious, communications superhighway, recordings in databases on all subjects for all classes, and local scholastic testing stations, will be operational within a developing region within five years of a decision to install an efficient education system. Education would be available as fast as communication superhighways are installed, and free laptop computers distributed.

As motivated students breeze through these classes at two to three times the speed of brick and mortar schools, first beneficiaries will be ready for college courses before communications superhighways are fully in place across a federated region. Within 15 years all will be literate, within 20 years a population will be fully educated, and within 40 years their education level will be relatively equal to the rest of the world. With tests showing the world's highest scholastic levels, Cuba has already proven this even with brick and mortar schools. Venezuela and Bolivia will prove it shortly, and other nations will follow.

Simultaneous with establishing a modern educational system, resources will be mapped and power systems, industries, railroads, ports, airports, roads, etc, planned. As energy is the resource in shortest supply, special attention must be given to solar and other non-polluting renewable energies. Permaculture and three dimensional orchard farming will create a secure food base while protecting, actually rebuilding, the soil and the environment.

A federated world will have no wars and such wasted monies can be turned to fulfilling the agreement to trade technology, and training, for equal access to resources. Appendix II outlines how master home builders and permaculturists can be quickly trained; quality homes cheaply built from local soils, rock, timber, etc; production of a region's own food; and industries built to provide windows, trim, furnishings, etc.

Those factories, homes, and industries that emerge to provide services, consumer products, and wages will be the productive wealth that backs the newly-created money.

Care must be exercised to create high use-values. Comfortable rammed earth homes with ceramic interiors that will last for centuries can be built for little more than, and in some regions cheaper than, the cost of mobile homes that have a lifespan of 30 years. Three wheeled, 300 miles per gallon, gas-electric runabouts, about 20% the weight of today's automobiles, will be for sale by the time this book is in print. A Google search for "Bloomberg electricity" alerts one that the cost of producing electricity will eventually drop by half or more. Commuting without environmental damage can be at a reasonable price.

The entire process will require management and oversight by a fully democratized United Nations or its replacement. That world legislative body will eventually replace negotiations overseeing the equal sharing of the world's resources. As opposed to the federation of the United States, the European Union, and China centuries ago, all of which became powerful but internally unequal, a federation of the earth, with full and equal economic rights, will maintain peace, tranquility, equality, and a quality life for all the world's citizens for millenniums.[i]

This is not a prediction of what will happen or even of what can be easily established. We even acknowledge the high possibility that President Barack Obama's massive throwing of money at the ethereal world of high finance, the people who caused this crash, may rebalance this highly unequal and unjust economy. If he does, it will still be inefficient, unequal, and it will eventually crash again.

The cheapest and quickest route to full and equal economic rights, elimination of poverty, and restructuring to a quality life for all is the current, ongoing, collapse being total. Only then will the monopoly structure be rejected, and hopefully replaced by an **efficient, easily understood, fully federated, community social-credit process**.

Computer modeling will prove this utopian living is possible; let's do it.[j]

---

[i] The elimination of monopolization of technology permits the rapid and low-cost development of poor regions of the world even as the environment and resources are protected. It is time to eliminate all forms of monopolization and share this world in peace.

[j] Professor Michael Hudson's *Super Imperialism: The Origins and Fundamentals of U.S. World Domination* has been on the best seller list in China, is going into its 5th printing, all his many books are being translated by the Chinese Government Printing Office, and he lectured at the new Marxist School in Beijing in the fall of 2009. As shown by the popularity of Hudson's books, the Chinese are studying on how to defend against financial and economic warfare. That nation has the social cohesion to put this efficient economy into practice. Starting from further back, and with their massive resources, South America and Africa could put this philosophy to work quickly and lead the world within two generations

---

[1] Taylor, *Fall of the Dynasties*, chapters 17—19.

[2] Thomas K Grose, "Free Health Care for All," U.S. News (March 24-April 2, 2007), p. 65.

Appendix I: Myths in Monetary Theory

The error of paying off debts destroys money: Logic proves that paying off debts does not destroy money as stated by both MMM and some monetary theorists. If you take in cash to pay off a $10,000 loan, the bank is not going to burn that money. They are going to put it in their vault right alongside their other cash. If you pay by check, those digital funds are debited from one reserve account and credited to that bank's reserves. Digital money is destroyed when debts are unpayable and then only to the extent not recoverable through bankruptcy sales of pledged assets. What is currently called a destruction of money is only a slowing of the circulation of base money.

By keeping her banks running, even when they were technically bankrupt, Japan demonstrated how to avoid the destruction of base money as just described. Simply do not enforce bankruptcy laws. Their economy slowed, the circulation of money slowed to the same pace, which did effectively reduce the money available and thus reduced the money supply, but base money was only destroyed by bankruptcies.

The misunderstandings of 100% reserves: Early 100% reserve theorists suggested that the government print currency and use it to buy up treasuries and other debt instruments of banks. That money was to be stored in their vaults and each dollar on deposit was then guaranteed by a matching dollar in those vaults. Later variations had the banks borrowing enough currency from the Treasury to match all deposits.

These are severe contradictions. 1st variation) A government earning interest on those debt instruments instead of the banks would be a massive loss to banks which would have to be replaced by higher interest rates, effectively a tax paid by every citizen. 2nd variation) Paying interest on sterile money, no matter at how low a rate, would be economic nonsense.

The myth of debt money: Note the massive wealth extracted via unequal property rights law, as applied to resources and technologies, denying others their rightful share of what nature offers to all for free. Because that wealth was essentially taken from us, it has to be loaned back to us so we can live and that form of debt money is what these theorists are really looking at. Those appropriated blocks of capital are so massive they are beyond the capacity of monopolists (who are unaware that most their wealth is unearned) to consume or invest it all. Those blocks of unearned wealth, mixed in with earned wealth, keep getting larger and larger, the ethereal world of high finances must expand to provide a place to invest (actually to gamble with) it, the percent claimed by the top few percent rose from 2% of corporate earnings to 40% and it all came crashing down in 2008-10.

Though we have outlined an efficient economy that would operate on roughly 95% less borrowed money; debt at a much lower level is a feature of an efficient economy. Mandated reserves, managed by a Federal Reserve to maintain the right monetary balance between honest savings and the necessary borrowing we all incur, known as the money supply, is pure gold to a monopolized economy and unnecessary in a full and equal rights economy.

Unless it is a gift or inheritance, nobody starts life with adequate finance capital; it must either be earned or borrowed. Earning takes a long time whereas borrowing takes minutes. With borrowed finance capital, gifted people can put their talents to work producing with the efficiency addressed throughout this book. This is why rights to finance capital—for federated regions of the world, for countries, for regions within countries, for states, for communities, and for individual entrepreneurs—are so important. Yes, an efficient economy requires debts to keep products and services flowing but those debts are not money per se (meaning it is not debt money). They are just what we think they are, loaned money. That loaned honest money can be either created money or savings (stored labor) but none will have been appropriated.

Let's assume private banks-create-money monetary reformists carry the day. The Federal Reserve calls in those rotating loans, takes over the banking system, and Congress legislates that created money will be spent into existence through building infrastructure (a fundamental of our thesis) and through paying for health care, retirement, and other social necessities—all of which are advocated by these monetary theorists who are (theoretically) now in charge. Also, by their theory, exclusive titles to nature's resources and technologies, all monopolies, remain.

But what will that hybrid banking system, creating money for all essential services and a still monopolized economy, be in practice? The economy will be rolling once again, those unearned huge blocs of capital will stay in place or rebuild, but they will have nowhere to invest 95% of their appropriated wealth. As this is many times more money than can possibly be spent on high living and all avenues of safe investment are blocked, those appropriated funds can only be turned to buying up property in the rest of the world. If it ever got off the ground, which it couldn't; the finest plunder machine imaginable will have been established (which is what existed until the periphery of empire understood it).

This very structure is, in part, being put in place in Eastern Europe. With their living standards well below that before their socialist governments were voted out and, in part, East Europeans realize their error. But Western capital has bought up all their valuable productive property, there is no way to get it back, and they do not have the money to build new industry or the markets in which to sell what they would produce. Eastern Europe has become a cash cow for Western Europe but their leadership will not admit it because doing so would be in direct conflict with their loyalty to Western Christianity.

Western capital pays East Europeans $2 an hour to work in modern factories. The managed economies they are returning to can provide enough food, fiber, and shelter for basic necessities but no luxuries. Capitalist blood is flowing through socialist arteries, sucking all surpluses out of East Europe, and banking those profits in the West. We said above this couldn't get off the ground. It has for a while but those massive sums extracted from East European economies will be destroyed when their debts prove unpayable.

This again measures the enormous waste of the monopoly system the past centuries as we have been exposing. It is that waste we spoke of when we kept repeating that "If sharing property rights had been established instead of unequal property rights, economic efficiency would have doubled. Assuming technologies were continually shared with others, production would have doubled again in a few years, and again, and again, up to the level of a sustainably developed world; all without war or poverty"

That is the efficient and peaceful world we have philosophically laid out. It cannot happen until the current corrupt economies collapses. When it does, let's be ready.

Appendix II: A Practical Approach for Developing Nations & Regions

Trying to provide an answer to capitalism, socialism, and communism the past 50 years, the Progressive Utilization Theory (Prout, www.prout.org) integrating economic democracy and spiritual values, is, speaking to full and equal economic rights for each and every person, very similar to our approach. Those reading both philosophies may want to add a spiritual approach to our strictly economic approach and perhaps add a full understanding of conditional titles to nature's resources and technologies applied across the full economic spectrum and a so-cially-owned and operated banking system to Prout's cooperative philosophy.

While waiting for the world to throw off the current beliefs which maintain their poverty, let's design an emerging-nation development plan utilizing cheap, broadly-available resources that can be accomplished within the current monopoly structure. Many countries have traditional, fireproof, rammed earth homes hundreds of years old. Most developing nations have large numbers of unemployed labor who can build high-quality earthen homes cheaply. Firing the inside of earth homes creating ceramic walls and floors opens an unlimited potential of beautiful, clean, easily maintained, yet cheap, housing. Some regions traditionally use other building materials such as stone, straw-bale, timber, bamboo, etc.

Local master-craftsmen can train the apprentice home builders, and these newly-trained practitioners can teach others on the job. The teachers would be paid but the workers' pay would be their training as master home builders. Assuming five workers to a crew on an adobe or rammed earth home, every three or four houses built will result in five more master builders who can return to their home regions, sign up apprentice home builders, and rapidly expand the home building project. Different building materials will require differing periods of training to produce master craftsmen, but the principle is the same. (See Hassan Fathy's book, Architecture for the Poor, for an inspiring account of the method that was used to create a total-process system of adobe construction in Egypt.) Having designed and built sustainable housing and major architectural projects in many countries, Phil Hawes (phil-hawes@amaonline.com) is an internationally known expert as is Richard Register, ecocitybuilders.org.

Additional industries are necessary to produce doors, windows, plumbing and electrical systems, flooring, roofs, and furniture. These industries will expand in step with the expansion of home building.

Though these homes will be built cheaply, they have full, actually superior, use-value. As some projects mature, labor will be paid, while in others the master-builder will train volunteer workers to build more homes for themselves, family, and friends, and are thus paid indirectly, but paid well.

Since real value is being produced utilizing local and regional resources, base money can be created by any nation, or region, up to the value of those homes, businesses and inventory. That created money is the proper financial source to utilize a nation's own resources to build infrastructure, industries, businesses, and inventory necessary to service a developing community. The circulation of that base money will build and operate distribution systems and repair systems and provide wages which becomes the buying power to purchase the production of those industries. As most this will be volunteer labor and high value is created, creating money to pay the master builder and other costs will not be inflationary.

Simultaneous with building homes, a country or region must develop a prosperous agriculture. Permaculture fruits, nuts, berries, tubers, and vegetables work well with eco-village housing. Master permaculturists can be trained and returned to their regions to train more just as described above with master builders. Farms, equipment, and the food produced have value and, as it is locally produced, money can be created for that development as well. All resources should be processed locally into high value-added products both for regional consumption and export. As economic activity and production increases, buying power increases to purchase the new production, and community values rise.

So long as countries or regions are utilizing local resources and labor, money can be created to build those industries and infrastructures. This includes high-tech industries wind generators, small hydro generation units, and photovoltaic cells. These can convert the naturally occurring, non-fossil fuel forces of wind, waterpower, and sunlight into electrical energy. It is possible to train ambitious local inhabitants to assemble electronic equipment, such as TVs and computers, which can provide a free education via information superhighways. At all times wealth (use-value) is being produced. The circulation of that created money purchases the produce of other workers, and further develops an economy.

However, a developing country or region will soon need technology and industries that, unless the revolution we addressed throughout this book has taken place, that is firmly under the control of the imperial centers. It is at this point, the local production of wealth, that regions must federate (ally together) to negotiate with the imperial centers to trade access to resources for access to technology. To not ally together would result in the locally created wealth being eventually transferred to those imperial centers via unequal pay for equally-productive labor. Local resources will be purchased far below their full value, resulting in the familiar inevitable debt traps for the developing regions sucking up any money that has been created and taking title to that locally produced wealth in the process.

The key is cheap, quality, local production of social infrastructure. But the money created must be protected against claims by international creditors. Collecting the rental values of nature's wealth as per the inclusive property rights laws, chapters 20 through 25, eliminates capitalized monopoly values of what nature offers to all for free, provides development funds, and protects the entire nation from having those values attached to repay debts. The principle of society collecting socially-created rental values is essential both for economic efficiency and protection against creditor nations laying claim to a weak nation's wealth. The use-value is still there but society collecting resource rents and profits of banking prevents those nature-produced values from being capitalized, and keeps them out of the hands of creditors; thus the earnings of nature's wealth can be utilized to fund essential infrastructure and social programs.

By classes being available via information superhighways and studied on home computers, it is possible for the emerging world to educate their citizens for 5-15% the cost of conventional brick and mortar schools. Not only would the youth become well educated, so also would many older citizens. Apprentice labor working side by side with skilled labor will soon build a highly skilled labor force.

Currency values can only remain stable if a country's productive capacity is efficient and stable. So a country needs to develop infrastructure cheaply and efficiently and the above building of quality homes and support industries cheaply is an example but only a start.

With technology and markets monopolized, high technology industrializing is more problematic. The key is maximum production of high-value-added products rather than selling raw resources. Example: an oil producing nation has the option of refining its oil, producing plastics, etc. The monopolies of wealthy nations are so powerful that such industries will require trading alliances or full federations between weak nations, a step toward the full federation of all nations.

Stevia is 30 times sweeter than sugar, is cheap to produce, cheap to process, and it does not have the health damaging effects of sugar. William Hayward, haywardwj@execs.com, has containers filled with Stevia plants, processing equipment, and instructions ready to ship anywhere in the world. Africa also has a couple indigenous sweet plants that may replace sugar. The gains to a society both financially and in health care substituting any one of these sweeteners for sugar is huge. As this simple development plan is put together, other areas of utilization of local labor and resources will become visible.

Bibliography

101 Famous Thinkers on Owning Earth (New York: Schalkenbach Foundation);

Aaron, Craig. "Sun, Sand and Spectrum Policy." *In These Times*, September 19, 2005

Aptheker, Herbert. *The American Revolution*. NY: International Publishers, 1985.

_____. *The Colonial Era*. 2nd ed. New York: International Publishers, 1966.

_____. *Early Years of the Republic*. New York: International Publishers, 1976.

Bandler, Richard, and John Grinder. *Frogs Into Princes*. Moab, UT: Real People Press, 1979.

Banco, Anthony. "Playing With Fire." *Business Week* (September 16, 1987).

Beard, Charles A. *An Economic Interpretation of the Constitution*. New York: Macmillan Publishing Co, 1941.

Berlan, Jean-Pierre. "The Commodification of Life." *Monthly Review* (December 1989).

Bernstein, Merton C., Joan Brodshaug Bernstein. *Social: The System That Works*. New York: Basic Books, 1988.

Bhagirath Lal Das, *WTO: The Doha Agenda: The New Negotiations on World Trade*. London:: Zed Books, 2003.

Bishop, Abraham. *Georgia Speculation Unveiled*. Readex Microprint Corporation, 1966.

Blaug, Mark. *Great American Economists Before Keynes*. Atlantic Highlands, NJ: Humanities Press International, 1986.

Breckinridge, S. P. *Legal Tender*. New York: Greenwood Press, 1969.

Budiansky, Stephen. "An Act of Vision for the Third World." *U.S. News & World Report* (November 2, 1987).

Chase, Stuart. *The Economy of Abundance*. New York: The Macmillan Company, 1934.

_____. *Men and Machines*. New York: The Macmillan Company, 1929.

_____. *The Tragedy of Waste*. New York: The Macmillan Company, 1925.

Cohen, Carl, ed. *Communism, Fascism, Democracy*. New York: Random House, 1962.

Conine, Ernest. "U.S. Should Take a Tip from Canada." *Missoulian* (Apr. 2, 1990).

_____. John B. Cobb Jr. *For the Common Good*. Boston: Beacon Press, 1989.

Diamond, Jared. *Collapse: How Societies Choose to Fail or Succeed*. New York: Penguin, 2005.

_____. *Guns, Germs, and Steel: The Fates of Human Societies*. NY: W.W. Norton, 1999.

_____. *The Third Chimpanzee: The Evolution and Future of the Human Animal*. New York: HarperCollins, 1992.

Dine, Janet and Andrew Fagan, Editors. *Human Rights and Capitalism*, NorthHampton, MA, 2006.

Dorgan, Byron, Senator. *The North Dakota REC* (May 1984).

Earth Rights Institute, earthrights.net

Echeverria, Durand. *The Maupeou Revolution*. Baton Rouge: Louisiana U Press, 1985.

Eklund, Robert, Robert D. Tollison, *Mercantilism as a Rent-Seeking Society*. Texas A&M U Press, 1981.

Fathy, Hassan. "Architecture for the Poor. Google search.

Fawthrop, Tom. "Havana, Operation Miracle" *The Scotsman*, Google search.

Feagin, Joe E. *The Urban Real Estate Game*. Engelewood Cliffs, NJ: Prentice-Hall, 1983.

Gaffney, Mason, Fred Harrison. *The Corruption of Economics: With The Development of Democracy, Mind Control Became the Urgent Need: Neo-Classical Economics Was the Tool.* London: Shepheard-Walwyn, 1994.

Galbraith, John Kenneth. *Economics in Perspective.* NY: Houghton Mifflin, 1987.

_____. Money: *Whence it Came, Where it Went. New York: Houghton Mifflin, 1995.*

_____. *Money.* New York: Houghton Mifflin, 1976.

Goldhaber, Michael. *Reinventing Technology.* New York: Routledge & Kegan Paul, 1986.

Grant, Phil. *The Wonderful Wealth Machine.* New York: Devon-Adair, 1953.

Greider, William. *One World Ready or Not.* New York: Simon and Schuster, 1997.

_____."Annals of Finance." *The New Yorker,* (November 9, 1987; Nov. 16, 1987; November 23, 1987).

_____. *The Education of David Stockman and Other Americans.* New York: New American Library, 1986.

_____. *Secrets of the Temple.* New York: Simon and Schuster, 1987.

_____. *Who Will Tell the People?* New York: Simon and Schuster, 1992.

Grose, Thomas K "Free Health Care for All" (U.S. News, March 24-April 2, 2007).

Hahn, James S., A.B. "How Does Canada Do It." *The New England Journal of Medicine* (Sept. 27, 1990

Hartzok, Alanna. *The Earth Belongs to Everyone.* www.ied.info/. The Institute for Economic Democracy, 2008.

Herman, Edward S, "The Assault on Social Security." *Z Magazine* (Nov. 1995).

Henwood, Doug. *Wall Street.* New York: Verso, 1997.

Hiatt, Editor, Steven, *A Game As Old As Empire: The Secret World of Economic Hit Men and the Web of Global Corruption,* San Francisco, Barrett-Koehler, 2007.

Himmelstein, David Steffie Woolhandler, Dr. Ida Hellander, *Bleeding the Patient: The Consequences of corporate Health Care.* Common Courage Press, 2001.

Hixson, William F. *It's Your Money.* Toronto, Canada, COMER, 1997.

_____. *Triumph of the Bankers: Money and Banking in the Eighteenth and Nineteenth Centuries.* Westport, Conn.: Praeger, 1993.

Hufton, Olwen. *Europe: Privilege and Protest.* Ithaca, NY: Cornell U Press, 1980.

Hudson, Michael, Baruch A. Levine. *Privatization in the Near East - The Story of Power.* Cambridge: Harvard University, 1996.

Hudson, Michael,. *Super Imperialism: The Origins and Fundamentals of U.S. Imperialism,* London Pluto Press, 2003.

Hunt, E. K., Howard J. Sherman. *Economics.* New York: Harper & Row, 1990.

Hurwit, Cathy. "A Canadian Style Cure." *Dollars and Sense* (May 1993).

Iglehart, John K. "Health Policy Report: Germany's Health Care System." *The New England Journal of Medicine.* (Feb. 14, 1991.)

Johnson, Chalmers. *Blowback: The Costs and Consequences of the American Empire.* New York: Henry Holt & Company, 2000.

_____. *The Sorrows of Empire: Militarism, Secrecy, and the End of the Republic.* New York:

_____. *Nemesis The Last Days of the American Republic* (Metropolitan Books, New York, 2006.

Josephson, Matthew. *Robber Barons.* New York: Harcourt Brace Jovanovich, 1962.

Kelly, Marjorie. *The Divine Right of Capital: Dethroning the Corporate Aristocracy.* Berrett-Koehler, San Francisco, 2001/2003.

Kennedy, Paul. *The Rise and Fall of the Great Powers.* New York: Random House, 1987.

"Kids in the Cuckoo's Nest." *Utne Reader* (Mar./Apr. 1992).

Kilmer, Jeanie, "Public Power Costs Less." *Public Power Magazine* (May/June 1985).

Kindleberger, Charles P. *Manias, Panics, and Crashes.* New York: Basic Books, Inc., 1978.

Klein, Naomi.. The Shock Doctrine: The Rise of Disaster Capitalism (New York: Metropolitan Books, 2007).

Korten, David. *When Corporations Rule the World.* West Hartford, CT: Kumarian Press and San Francisco: Berret-Koehler, 1995.

Kropotkin, Petr. *Mutual Aid.* Boston: Porter Sargent Publishers Inc., 1914.

_____. *The Great French Revolution.* New York: Black Rose Books, 1989.

Krugman, Paul. *The return of Depression Economics and the Crisis of 2008*. New York, W.W. Norton, 2009
Kurtzman, Joel. *The Death of Money*. New York: Simon and Schuster, 1993.
Lacey, Robert. *Ford*. New York: Ballantine Books, 1986.
Lambert, Angela. *Unquiet Souls*. New York: Harper & Row, 1984.
Lee, Katherine J. "Justice Has Broken Down." *Americans For Legal Reform* 4:2 (1985).
Levy, Steven. "Bills New Vision," *Newsweek*, November 27, 1995.
Livingston, James. *Origins of the Federal Reserve System: Money, Class, and Corporate Capitalism, 1890 to 1913* (Cornell University Press, 1986.
Lyon, Peter. *To Hell in a Day Coach*. New York: J. B. Lippincott Company, 1968.
Mackay, Charles. *Extraordinary Delusions and Madness of Crowds*. 2nd. ed. New York: Farrar Straus and Giroux, 1932.
Makin, John H.. *The Global Debt Crisis*.New York: Basic Books, 1984.
Marshall, Alfred. *Principles of Economics*, Amherst, NY, Prometheus Books, reprint of Macmillaan, 1920
Martin, Edward Winslow. *History of the Grange Movement*. New York: Burt Franklin, 1967.
Marx, Karl. *Capital*, 3 vols. edited by Frederick Douglas. New York: International Publishers, 1967.
McCoy, Alfred W. *A Question of Torture: CIA Interrogation from the Cold War to the War on Terror*. New York: Henry Holt and Company, 2006.
McHugh, Robert. "Money Supply versus Interest Rate Policy," *Comer*, January 2006.
Metcalf, Lee, Vic Reinemer. *Overcharge*. New York: David McKay, 1967.
Mill, John Stuart. *Principles of Political Economy*. New York, Oxford University Press, 1998
Miller, Christian, "Wall Street's Fondest Dream: The Insanity of Privatizing Social Security," *Dollars and Sense* (November/December 1998).
Mirow, Kurt Rudolf, *Webs of Power* (Boston: Houghton Mifflin, 1982)
Modern Money Mechanics (MMM, http://landru.i-link-2.net/monques/ mmm2.html),
Moffitt, Michael. "Shocks, Deadlocks, and Scorched Earth: Reaganomics and the Decline of U.S. Hegemony." *World Policy Journal* (Fall 1987).
_____. *The World's Money*. New York: Simon and Schuster, 1983.
Mumford, Lewis. *The City in History*. New York: Harcourt Brace Jovanovich, 1961.
_____. *Pentagon of Power*. New York: Harcourt Brace Jovanovich, 1964, 1970.
_____. *Technics and Civilization*. New York: Harcourt Brace Jovanovich, 1963.
_____. *Technics and Human Development*. New York: Harcourt Brace Jovanovich, 1967.
Murray, Charles, Herrnstein, Richard J. *The Bell Curve: Intelligence and Class Structure in American Life*. New York: Free Press, 1994.
_____. *Losing Ground*. New York: Basic Books, 1984.
Nadudere, Dan. *The Political Economy of Imperialism*. London: Zed Books, 1977.
101 Famous Thinkers on Owning Earth, New York: Robert Schalkenbach Foundation, no date.
Owen, Wilfred. *Strategy for Mobility*. Westport, CT: Greenwood Press, 1978.
Parenti, Michael, *Power and the Powerless*. New York: St. Martin's Press, 1978.
Pilzer, Paul Zane. *Unlimited Wealth*. New York: Crown Publishing, 1990.
Polanyi, Karl. *The Great Transformation*. Boston: Beacon Press, 1957.
Prados, John. *The Presidents' Secret Wars*. New York: William Morrow, 1986.
_____. *The Presidents Secret Wars*, revised. Warwick: Elephant Paperbacks, 1996.
Public Power Directory and Statistics for 1983. Washington, DC: American Public Power Association, 1983.
Rasell, Edie. "A Bad Bargain." *Dollars and Sense* (May 1993).
Renard, George, *Guilds in the Middle Ages*. New York: Augustus M. Kelley, 1968.
Robinson, Donald. "The Great Pacemaker Scandal." *Readers Digest* (Oct. 1983).
Rodell, Fred. *Woe Unto You Lawyers*. Littleton, CO: Fred B. Rothman & Co., 1987.

Rousseau, Jean Jacques. "A Discourse on the Origins of Inequality." *The Social Contract and Discourses*. New York: Dutton, 1950.

Routh, Guy. *The Origin of Economic Ideas*. Dobbs Ferry, NY: Sheridan House, 1989.

Sale, Kirkpatrick. *Human Scale*. First Peregree printing. New York: G. P. Putnam and Sons, 1982.

Sally Jesse Raphael Show (May 30, 1988). Patient Advocates Bill Johnson and Tom Wilson.

Schor, Juliet B. *The Overworked American*. Basic Books, 1991.

Seldes, George. *Even the Gods Can't Change History*. Secaucus, NJ: Lyle Stuart, 1976.

———. *In Fact*. New York: Lyle Stuart, Inc., 1968.

Shealy, Tom. "The United States vs. the World: How We Score in Health." *Prevention* (May 1986).

Shiva, Vandana. *Stolen Harvest: The Hijacking of the Global Food Supply*. Cambridge: South End Press, 2000.

Smith, Adam. The Wealth of Nations. New York: Random House, 1965.

Smith, J.W. *Economic Democracy: A Grand Strategy for World Peace and Prosperity, updated 2ⁿᵈ editon.* www.ied.info/. the Institute for Economic Democracy, 2009.

Spencer, Herbert. *Social Statics*. Schalkenbach Foundation, 1850 unabridged ed.

Swann, Robert. *The Need for Local Currencies*. Great Barrington, MA: E.F. Schumacher Society, 1990.

Taylor, Edmond. *The Fall of the Dynasties:: The Collapse of the Old Order, 1905-1922,* New York: Dorset Press, 1989.

Thoren, Theodore R., Richard F. Warner. *The Truth in Money*. Chagrin Falls, Ohio: Truth in Money Publishers, 1994.

Thurow, Lester C. *Head to Head: The Coming Economic Battle Among Japan, Europe, and America*. New York: William Morrow, 1992.

_____. *Generating Inequality*. New York: Basic Books, 1975.

_____. *The Future of Capitalism: How Today's Economic Forces Shape Tomorrow's World*. England, Penguin Books, 1996.

_____. Thurow, Lester, *Building Wealth: The New Rules for Individuals, Companies and Nations in a knowledge Based Economy*. New York: HarperCollins, 2000.

Train, John. *Famous Financial Fiascoes*. New York: Clarkson N. Potter,1985.

Tokar, Brian. *Redesigning Life? The Worldwide Challenge to Genetic Engineering*. London: Zed Books, 2001.

Tucker, George. *The Theory of Money and Banks Investigated*. New York: Greenwood Press, 1968.

UnderKufler, Laura, *The Idea of Property: Its Meaning and Power*. New York, Oxford University Press, 2003.

Vidal, Gore. "The National Security State: How To Take Back Our Country." *The Nation* (June 4, 1988).

Waldron, Jeremy. *The Right to Private Property*. NY, Oxford U Press, 1988.

Weisman, Alan. "Columbia's Modern City." *In Context* 42 (1995).

Wessel, James, Mort Hartman. *Trading the Future*. San Francisco: Institute for Food and Policy Development, 1983.

Weil, Robert. "Somalia in Perspective: When the Saints Go Marching In." *Monthly Review* (Mar. 1993).

Wild, Rolf H. *Management by Compulsion*. Boston: Houghton Mifflin Company, 1978.

Windishar, Anne. "Expert: 20% of Gifted Kids Drop Out," *Spokane Chronicle*, January 7, 1988, p. B7.

Winters, Rebecca. "From Home to Harvard," *Time*, September 11, 2000, p. 55.

Wolf, Eric R. *Europe and the People Without History*. Berkeley: University of California Press, 1982.

Zinn, Howard. *A People's History of the United States*. New York: Harper Colophon, 1980.

_____. *The Politics of History*. Chicago: University of Illinois Press, 1990.

Index

About the Author

With a PhD. in political economics from Union Institute and University, J.W. Smith has presented these concepts in nine countries. This is his 7ᵗʰ book on the causes and cures of world poverty and elimination of wars.

The Indonesian University System appears to have named their "Centre for Economic Democracy Studies" after his *Economic Democracy: The Political Struggle of the Twenty-First Century*. That book has been translated, and is in use in Indonesian classrooms.

A contact on official business has been passing out copies of *Economic Democracy: A Grand Strategy for Global Peace and Prosperity* to officials in various countries of Africa. One thought enough of it we have a picture of him presenting a copy to an official of the Nigerian government.

Three of this author's books are in print in India: WHY? A deeper History of the September 11ᵗʰ Terrorist Attack on America was accepted by a Book of the Month Club there.

University research libraries have been a primary market for this author's work and all have seen use in the university classroom.

Until he wrote this book, Smith felt his moving Henry George's philosophy across the full economic spectrum was almost certainly his most important contribution to economic theory.

He now thinks his melding of Henry George philosophy with the exposure of Western economic classics as justifications for unjust and **unequal property rights laws, as applied to nature's resources and technologies, denying others their rightful share, of what nature offers to all for free,** rather than philosophies for economic efficiencies is even more important.

We think many will agree: The restructuring of aristocratic exclusive title to nature's wealth to conditional titles eliminating those huge blocs of monopolized capital, the reforming of those appropriated values into relatively equally-shared use-values, and the doubling of economic efficiency is quite persuasive.

His 170 word full economic treatise for full and equal economic rights can be visualized by all who read it, testifies to an even greater contribution to economic theory.

Smith not only takes a different view from most economists on how economies are currently structured and how they should be structured, his views on money also firmly challenges some theories on monetary theory.

Go to www.ied.info/ for further updates. Please join us:

The Institute for Economic Democracy

Global peace and sustainable development equals peace and prosperity for all
To join, email ied@ied.info
www.paypal.com/, account: ied@ied.info www.ied.info/

World Prout Assembly

Economy of the People, For the People and By the People!
To join, email gardaghista@gmail.com
www.worldproutassembly.org/

International Philosophers for Peace

Developing a just social, economic, & political basis for peace and human well-being
www.ippno.org/

Institute on World Problems

Creating a world order of peace, justice, and freedom
To join, email gmartin@radford.edu
www.worldproblems.net

Earth Rights Institute

Dedicated to securing a culture of peace and justice by establishing dynamic worldwide networks of persons of goodwill and special skill, promoting policies and programs which further democratic rights to common heritage resources, and building ecological communities.

www..earthrights.net

The Hour Money Institute for Global Harmony

Dedicated to establishing an hour of work as the money unit worldwide
www.hourmoney.org/

Global Issues (www.globalissues.org)

Rights are available for publishing in your region, in English or translations, www.ied.info/. We are available to present these concepts to your class or group. www.ied.info/.ied@ied.info

WHY: The Deeper History of the September 11th Terrorist Attack on America, 3rd edition, 2005, J.W. Smith

Cooperative Capitalism: A Blueprint for Global Peace and Prosperity, 2nd edition, 2005, J.W. Smith

The Institute for Economic Democracy is dedicated to producing a philosophy for elimination of waste within the economy, that ends poverty, and that provides a quality life for each citizen of earth. Towards that end we have published the books listed below. For later books go to www.ied.info.

A Constitution for the Federation of Earth, 2010, Glen T. Martin

Triumph of C ivilization: De mocracy, N onviolence, and Pilotin g Spacesh ip Earth , 2010, Glen T. Martin

Weaving Golden Threads of Sociological Theory, 2009, Bob Blain

Dawn Dancing – A Collection of Poetry, 2010, Elaine F. Webster

Economic De mocracy: A Gra nd Strategy for World Peace and Prosperity , 2nd edition, updated, 2010, J.W. Smith

Emerging World Law, 2009, Editors Eugenia Almand and Glen T. Martin

Travesty in Ha iti: A True Ac count of Christian Missions, Orp hanages, Fraud, Food Aid, and Drug Trafficking, 2009, Timothy Swartz

An Unknown God: Essays in Pursuit of the Sacred, 2009, Tony Equale

The Emperors God: Important Misunderstandings of Christianity, 2008, Michael Rivage-Seul

The Earth Belongs to Everyone, 2008, Alanna Hartzok

Ascent to Freedom: The Philosophica l Foundations of Dem ocratic World Law, 2008, Glen T. Martin

Twenty-First Century De mocratic Rena issance: Fr om Pla to to Ne oliberalism t o Planeta ry Democracy, 2008, Errol E. Harris

World Revolution Through World Law: Basic Documents of t he Emerging Earth Federation, 2005, Glen T. Martin

Millennium Dawn: The Philosophy of Planetary Crisis and Human Liberation, 2005, Glen T. Martin

A Constitution for the Federation of Earth, 2008, Editor Glen T. Martin

Earth Federation Now! Tomorrow is Too Late, 2005. Errol E. Harris

Economic Democracy: The Political Struggle of the Twenty-First Century, 4th edition, 2005, J.W. Smith